JON BON JOVI

JON BON JOVI

LAURA JACKSON

CITADEL PRESS
Kensington Publishing Corp.
http://www.kensingtonbooks.com

CITADEL PRESS BOOKS are published by

Kensington Publishing Corp.
850 Third Avenue
New York, NY 10022

Copyright © 2003 by Laura Jackson

Previously published by Portrait, an imprint of Judy Piatkus (Publishers) Limited, 2003

All Kensington titles, imprints, and distributed lines are available at special quantity discounts for bulk purchases for sales promotions, premiums, fund-raising, educational, or institutional use. Special book excerpts or customized printings can also be created to fit specific needs. For details, write or phone the office of the Kensington special sales manager: Kensington Publishing Corp., 850 Third Avenue, New York, NY 10022, attn: Special Sales Department, phone 1-800-221-2647.

CITADEL PRESS and the Citadel logo are Reg. U.S. Pat. & TM Off.

First Citadel printing: March 2004
First Citadel paperback printing: March 2005

10 9 8 7 6 5 4 3 2 1

Printed in the United States of America

Cataloging data may be obtained from the Library of Congress

ISBN 0-8065-2600-9

Dedicated to my husband David
– an extraordinary and unique man

Contents

Acknowledgements

Thanks to everyone who helped with this book, including: David Warner; Clive Whichelow; Tower Records, London (Kazia); International Talent Booking, London (Francesca); Elgin Library staff; MTV; *Time Out*; Spotlight, London (Sue Atkinson); VH1; Vic Flett and Gary, Sound and Vision, Elgin; *Daily Mail*; *Select*; *Halliwell's Film & Video Guide*; *Q*; *Classic Rock*; *People*; *Rolling Stone*; *Kerrang*; *Record Collector*; *Raw*; *No. 1*.

Special thanks to: David for his essential support in so many ways. And to Alice Davis and all staff at Piatkus Books, London.

CHAPTER 1

Not Just a Face in the Crowd

2003 MARKS THE TWENTIETH ANNIVERSARY of the creation of the multi-platinum American supergroup Bon Jovi. In support of *Bounce*, their eighth studio album, and having notched up global album sales in excess of 100 million, the band launched their latest hugely successful world tour, which has already blazed a trail through Australia, Japan, the US, UK and Europe.

For two decades, the linchpin and relentless driving force of this phenomenally popular rock outfit has been the charismatic frontman Jon Bon Jovi, whose magnetic stage presence and star quality have always been matched by boundless energy and fierce commitment.

With his abundant fair hair, remarkable blue eyes and strongly determined jawline, Jon's flawless features have been a decided asset in his inexorable rise to the top. But those same handsome looks, coupled with a million-watt smile and potent sex appeal, have too often overshadowed his talent as an inspirational songwriter. For years, the music press wasted column inches on the length and style of the singer's hair, rather than examining the essence of his song lyrics, which speak uncompromisingly to the common man, urging him to get out from under in life and to never give in to adversity.

Rock and roll is said to be the great revenge, but New Jersey-born Jon Bon Jovi was never an angry young man carrying a giant chip on his shoulder, and he never pretended to be one. Yet there is a dynamic defiance stamped all the way through him which reveals itself in the rousing lyrics of songs like 'Bounce', 'Everyday', 'It's My Life' and, of course, the early classic, 'Livin' On A Prayer'. It also shows in the sheer passion of his live delivery of such numbers.

Very much his own man, Jon Bon Jovi is strong-willed, tenacious and disconcertingly frank at times. As a second-generation Italian-American, the basic human values of loyalty, faith and the sanctity of friendship are deeply ingrained in him. Though married since 1989 to his high school sweetheart, and with an expanding young family, he has sampled his share of rock and roll excess and debauchery. Some of this has been displayed nakedly, other elements have been hidden behind a tantalising veil of secrecy and innuendo.

Such secrets he seems to have shared only with the members of the famously close-knit band he single-handedly pulled together in 1983. These were four hand-picked, dedicated musicians who would surround his talent as a singer/songwriter: drummer Tico Torres; keyboard player David Bryan; bassist Alec John Such; and lead guitarist Richie Sambora. Since the mid-1990s, with the departure of Alec John Such, Bon Jovi has officially been a four-piece band, although bass player Hugh McDonald performs on record and on stage with the rest of the original line-up. As the hirer and firer in Bon Jovi, it was Jon's task to cut professional ties with Alec John Such. It was one of those occasions when being the standard-bearer for the band proved to be an unhappy responsibility, but it was the kind of tough business decision from which he will not shy away.

A confessed workaholic, his tireless individual vision for

the band has at times strained internal relationships to the nth degree. But the underlying brotherhood of Bon Jovi has ultimately held together, although the killing pace of touring throughout most of the 1980s left Jon so burned-out and dangerously claustrophobic that his wife once had to stop him jumping from a speeding car.

Creatively curious, in recent years Jon has released a successful solo album, *Destination Anywhere*. His score for the soundtrack to the Hollywood movie *Young Guns II* earned him a Golden Globe award as well as an Oscar nomination. He has also turned actor, appearing in a series of roles with varying degrees of exposure and success. He calls acting 'a serious passion', and he is indeed a natural before the camera, but while acting holds interesting possibilities, it is unlikely to overtake his day job. For he spent too many of his formative years throughout the 1970s avidly soaking up the sounds of the home-grown talent flourishing in the hotbed of the famous New Jersey shore clubs, yearning to make it in music. And now he is established as one of the top four front men in rock music alongside Bono, the late Freddie Mercury and Mick Jagger.

Jon Bon Jovi is not the first working-class guy to become a celebrated rock god, but in today's depressing climate of manufactured lightweight pop stars, whose individual shelf life will be lucky to stretch to 12 months, he may very well rank among the last of a dying breed. Entitled to feel himself the embodiment of the American Dream, he never fails to stoke self-belief in others, a legacy of the sturdy belief imbued in him from a young age by his supportive blue-collar parents that he need not be just another face in the crowd

Jon Bon Jovi's real name is John Francis Bongiovi. Born on 2 March 1962 in Perth Amboy, New Jersey, he was the pride and joy of John and Carol Bongiovi, their first child. The Bongiovi family came originally from Sicily. A slim-built, attractive man of medium height, John Bongiovi senior, a former marine, then plumber, became a hairdresser by trade in the 1960s. His easy-going nature was the perfect foil for the tireless vivacity of his wife, whom he had met when she too was serving in the marines. Carol's natural poise and beauty had, in her late teens, secured her the title of Miss Erie, Pennsylvania, and she was also, for a brief spell, a Playboy bunny. As Jon grew up, his mother held down a variety of jobs; both his parents had a strong work ethic which they instilled firmly into their children.

In due course, two more sons would arrive – Anthony, almost five years later, and Matthew, much later, in 1975. In 1962, however, Jon was the adored single focus of attention at home. As an adult, Jon remarked that his mother had found the US Marines' boot camp a piece of cake, compared to life growing up in Erie. Perhaps that sheds light on Carol's high hopes for, and unstinting devotion towards, her children. She once explained that during her first pregnancy she used to regularly tell her unborn child that she could not wait for his arrival, vowing him 200 per cent of her support for all of his life. At first, the trio lived with Jon's grandparents. Then in 1966 the family moved from Perth Amboy to settle in nearby Sayreville. This small working-class town, embedded in the industrial east coast area of New Jersey, lies some 30 miles south of New York City. The smoke belching from the tall chimney stacks of the local factories hung over the wooden houses with front porches, some built cheek-by-jowl. The ethnic mix was predominantly Italian and Irish, and there was a strong sense of community binding the townsfolk together. This had its good and bad points. Jon later reflected, 'We all came from the kind of same family background.' His youngest brother Matt ruefully recalled that in such a close-knit environment tales of the Bongiovi boys' pranks would soon get back to their parents' ears. 'You couldn't get away with much in that town.'

As a child, Jon was vibrant and alert, and he quickly became very much his own person, developing a fundamentally determined streak that would grow stronger throughout his life. His was a stable home environment. His parents worked ceaselessly to provide for their family, and although they had no money to spare for anything but essentials, no one ever went hungry. There was no sense of individual disadvantage – everyone was in the same boat. And family was paramount, though the age gaps between the three brothers meant that it was only when they were older that they had the chance to become really close.

One of the other traditional influences in Jon's development might have been the church, considering that he was born into the Catholic faith. But religion was not, overall, destined to have a particularly prominent place in his life. Indeed, with characteristic bluntness, he has openly questioned the general premise of organised religion. In terms of Catholicism specifically, he has queried the kind of Christianity which sets out that if a baby dies prior to being baptised, then that infant will not go to heaven since he or she is deemed to have original sin. Not halting there, he highlighted the hypocrisy of those priests who are exposed for being busy pontificating in church while behind the scenes they are on the take or, worse still, interfering with young altar boys. Queried Jon, 'You go to mass, sing a song, put money in the plate and that's supposed to absolve you of your sins?' He, frankly, has a hard time blindly accepting the validity of a whole raft of elements in religion. But, by and large, Jon invites no discussion about his religious beliefs. He considers that they have no bearing on what he does in music and that on a personal level it is no one's business but his own.

Scholastically, Jon was never going to shine. It was not a lack of intelligence; he simply had no interest in applying himself to academic studies. And, while fervent participation in sports is part of the very fabric of US school life, that too left the growing boy completely cold. Like any other youngster, though, he would play ball games in the street, and Jon is an ardent fan of the American football team, the New York Giants.

Growing up in an era energised both socially and politically, he would become totally absorbed in music. Through the 1960s, however, the future rock star was too young to appreciate the seismic shifts taking place in the music scene, particularly in the second half of the decade. In that period the biggest threat to the British domination of the popular music world was the incredible west coast sound that began to swamp all in its wake in America. The acceptable, clean-cut surf sound had been overtaken by the infectiously mellow sound of electric folk-rock. Rising exponents of this skilfully produced style included Bob Dylan, the Byrds and New Jersey-born Paul Simon. Simon's song 'The Sound of Silence' leapt to number one in the US singles chart, launched Simon & Garfunkel on to the music map and became an instant folk-rock classic.

By 1967 LSD-powered psychedelia had arrived with the so-called Summer of Love, stylising music and sending multitudes of long-haired hippies to mass flower power sit-ins for peace and tolerance. But within two short years, dark days had arrived when LSD consumption was overtaken by speed and heroin, and the powerful youth movement had become progressively politicised, meshing itself with the thorny issue of the Vietnam war.

Although the most important decade in popular music had ended, what it stood for had sown the seeds for generations of music makers to come. And Jon's home state of New Jersey would continue its heritage of producing notable stars. Before Paul Simon, there had been the legendary 1950s crooner Frank Sinatra, whom Jon came later to hold up as a kind of professional yardstick. In the early 1970s, rocker Bruce Springsteen emerged, and, much later, Whitney Houston, the Newark-born cousin of Dionne Warwick.

In 1969, Jon's mum brought home an acoustic guitar from a trade fair, and encouraged the seven-year-old to take an interest in it. Music already featured in the Bongiovi household, for Carol would line up with her elder son before a full-length mirror and together they had fun watching themselves performing songs. Guitar lessons were organised for Jon with a man who ran the local music shop. It turned out to be a short-lived arrangement. Jon started off essentially unmoved by the guitar at this early age, and he was well and truly put off by these sessions, which were conducted in a poky little back room with a man who smoked a smelly pipe and was prone to nodding off while his reluctant pupil struggled with basic scales. Quickly bored out of his skull, Jon returned home one day, tossed the guitar down the basement stairs and left it there.

Over the next few years he was more interested in being a typically boisterous kid. His favourite pastime was dirt biking. He and a group of friends would head across town to the clay pits, where they rode their bikes at breakneck speed for endless hours. The cross-town journeys to and from the clay pits frequently pitched the boys into trouble for, as Jon has confessed, he and his mates rode their bikes on stretches of the railway lines and other prohibited places. The local cops would regularly curb this youthful enthusiasm by temporarily confiscating their wheels.

Despite enjoying the rough-and-tumble of growing up, Jon needed something more. And music began to impinge on his consciousness after all, with his first serious focus settling on Elton John. It's not surprising that the flamboyant English singer/songwriter, who in the early 1970s was as famed for his absurd stage outfits as for his songs, should have attracted Jon's attention. Elton John was in everyone's face right then in America. His double album, *Goodbye Yellow Brick Road*, released in late 1973, was a dual number one on both sides of the Atlantic. So was its follow-up, *Caribou*, which Jon rushed out to buy. At that point, Elton John had signed the most lucrative music contract in the world and was front cover material in the US. Jon became a huge fan.

Treading the time-honoured path of so many youngsters, he began spending hours flopped out on his bed, wearing the headphones to his sound system and, with the volume up full blast, losing himself in a world he began to realise held a strong lure for him.

In fairly short order, the nucleus of Jon's burgeoning fascination with music shifted away from the Elton John pop song towards heavier, grittier material. One of the first groups he related to was the J. Geils Band, in those days a rhythm and blues outfit.

Newly a teenager, in 1975 Jon seriously set about trying to teach himself the guitar. It was never his ambition to become the next Eric Clapton. Playing the guitar would be more of a tool; he already envisaged himself as a singer/songwriter. Right then, though, he was just thrilled when he managed to master the E chord. His proud party piece quickly became the easy, repetitive but satisfyingly raucous 1955 hit 'Bo Diddley', by blues giant Bo Diddley, who, more than a decade earlier, had inspired the likes of Rolling Stones' founder Brian Jones to go into rock music. Recognising the limited achievement in playing that song, Jon fondly reminisced, 'The only thing was, you couldn't move, because E was the only chord you knew. But you've got it down, man!' That said, it was obvious that he could not do this alone. So, for a second time Jon took up guitar lessons. This time, it was a very different setup.

Living across the street from the Bongiovis was Al Parinello, a musician who played in a local band and was a trendy child of the sixties. One night Jon grabbed his previously discarded guitar, went over and brassed his case. Would he help him? Al Parinello did not profess to be a guitar teacher, but he agreed to put his keen young neighbour through his paces – as long as he was genuine in his desire to learn. He would brook no time wasters, as Jon soon discovered. When Al set Jon the task of mastering the chords to the Animals' 1964 hit, 'House of the Rising Sun', and Jon hadn't worked at it, he warned his pupil that if he didn't come up to scratch by the next lesson he would 'kick his ass'. These unorthodox tactics worked for Jon. Indeed he became so absorbed with the instrument that there were nights at home when he fell asleep with it in his arms. At times the steel strings bled his fingertips raw, but after six months Jon had overcome the pain barrier and secured the breakthrough he yearned for. By this time he knew in his bones that he was irresistibly drawn towards becoming a rock star. His self-belief that he would achieve his goal was astoundingly complete; this ruling passion would propel Jon through the rest of his adolesence.

Looking around, though, he found little to inspire him in terms of what was happening in the singles chart. Summer 1975 was peppered with sugar-coated romantic numbers by Frankie Valli, Tammy Wynette and wholesome brother/sister duos the Carpenters and Donny and Marie Osmond. The crowded tour circuit, however, was a different matter. There, bands ranged from Kiss, the New York City-formed four-piece who, with their outrageous stage clothes and elaborate comic-book style painted faces, emphasised highly visual rock theatrics, at one end of the spectrum, to the no-nonsense hard-rocking formula of the Robert Plant/Jimmy Page-led giants Led Zeppelin at the other. Within less than ten years, Bon Jovi would be opening around Europe for Kiss. But it was after seeing the progressive rock band Rush perform live in New York City that Jon dashed home to Sayreville particularly fired up. Watching their eldest son immerse himself ever more deeply in music, John and Carol Bongiovi recognised the extent of his commitment and were prepared to help him pursue his dream.

Over the next couple of years Jon added Thin Lizzy to his growing list of influences, when the Irish rockers' album, *Jailbreak*, finally broke into the US Top 20. And he couldn't help but be aware of the fast rising Aerosmith, whose striking frontman Steve Tyler, with his generous mouth and skeletal build looked to be a second-generation Mick Jagger. But Jon's intrinsic interest in music went far deeper than the obvious. He was heavily into the British band the Animals at a time when, in terms of chart positioning, they had never repeated their number one success in America with 'House of the Rising Sun'. Lead singer Eric Burdon had subsequently gone solo; as Eric Burdon & War he had notched up a Top Five single in the States with 'Spill The Wine' in summer 1970. But really, Jon's friends looked blankly at him when he would bang on about this great foreign band from another era.

The knockout event, however, for the music-mad 13-year-old undoubtedly occurred in autumn 1975 with the arrival of Bruce Springsteen. The 26-year-old New Jersey-born singer/songwriter had already been recording for two years. Springsteen was a product of the club, pub and coffee house scene in Red Bank, Long Branch and Asbury Park, all dotted along Jersey's east coast. His 1973 debut album, *Greetings From Asbury Park*, had sold disappointingly, despite the artiste being pushed by the record company as the new Bob Dylan. Undaunted, Springsteen and his backing group, the E Street Band, garnered strength through live performance, and although his second album also failed to excite record buyers in vast numbers, influential music critics were sitting up and taking notice. Famously, *Rolling Stone*'s Jon Landau went so far as to declare after watching Springsteen play a club date in Cambridge, Massachusetts, 'I saw rock and roll's future – and its name is Bruce Springsteen'. With that kind of endorsement, it was hardly surprising that Springsteen's third album, *Born To Run*, should land with a gigantic splash.

Swept up with the euphoric buzz surrounding Springsteen's very name, Jon instantly added *Born To Run* to his record collection, and played the album until the grooves on the vinyl practically disappeared. Springsteen indisputably made a big impression on Jon, although over the years, the music press tended to inflate that influence disproportionately. Bruce Springsteen's spiralling success certainly focused Jon's attention now on the hotbed that was Asbury Park and satellite towns. Metaphorically, it was in the Bongiovis' back yard. Over the next few years Jon was drawn like a magnet to the music, energy and ambition which was awash in the area, and became a devotee of Southside Johnny and the Asbury Jukes, as well as of musician Steve Van Zandt.

By 1977, Jon was a hyped-up 15-year-old, thinking, living and breathing music 24 hours a day. His bedroom walls had vanished behind a mass of posters and pictures cut from rock magazines. His guitar playing was improving, and he had occasionally indulged in some singing lessons too. Sometimes he could afford to travel into New York City to catch a gig at, say, Madison Square Garden where he would be mesmerised by the sight of the star names in performance. Yet, as ambitious as Jon would become, at this age his aspirations were something less than to headline at such prestigious venues. He has said, 'In my mind, I felt I was going to be a musician. I believed it.' But years later he put his teenage dreams in context when he explained, 'All I ever wanted to be then was an Asbury Juke. They weren't a big band. They played regional gigs and that, to me, was being a rock star!'

Needless to say, such single-mindedness had a knock-on effect in all other areas of the teenager's life. By now Jon attended Sayreville War Memorial High School. 'Attended' was the most you could say, for, while he showed up physically at the school each day, mentally and emotionally he was miles away. He must have been something of an enigma to those around him, for his personality appeared to have two co-existing sides. On the one hand, he was driven by an infectious verve for music. He looked different, too; his hair was much longer than the other boys' and he continually wore sunglasses to school. Yet he was a loner who rarely spoke, and was given to deep introspection. Because he'd never had any interest in academic subjects or school life, he had no connection with anything everyone else around him was involved with, and this must have produced a sense of isolation. None of that mattered to Jon; he was too self-contained an individual.

Outside school, when not indulging his obsession with music, he hung out with his friends, enjoying the traditional teenage pursuits of underage drinking or riding around in cars. Jon Bon Jovi would never be a drug user but he has admitted to a very brief and mild flirtation with cannabis in his mid-teens. He reflected that at 15, 'I was smoking dope and drinking Black Label beer down in friends' basements.' Camaraderie was, and has always remained, very important to Jon, and he valued these years as part of a close-knit network of local friends. Among them was Dave Sabo, later guitarist with Skid Row, who lived very close to the Bongiovis. Endlessly discussing music, Jon and Dave one day made a solemn pact that whichever one of them achieved success first, he would help the other on to the ladder. It was a promise that Jon would not forget.

In addition to his hometown buddies and beer drinking, Jon's other extramural pursuit was now girls. He is not the first guy to allude to a sexual initiation at the hands of a much older and experienced woman, but that apart, Jon's sights were firmly set on the nubile beauties of his own age, and as a rascally romancer must have broken a few hearts along the way. Although they had yet to refine themselves fully, Jon's exceptional good looks, scintillating smile and twinkling clear blue eyes, gave him a head start when it came to chasing the girls. That, and his attractively assertive personality. There is a certain energy given off by someone with Jon's high level of determination which has a pull all of its own. He would later be ruefully self-critical of his early sexual technique, but it didn't hold him back at the time.

He was a roguish, jeans-clad, leather-jacketed, red-blooded New Jersey guy, happily on the make at home in Sayreville or out east along the sandy beaches. Those few carefree summers would stand out in his memory in more ways than one. Fondly, Jon looked back, 'In the seventies, Asbury Park had a Ferris wheel. It had the palace and it had the boardwalk. It was a great place.' He added sadly, 'Now, it looks like Beirut.'

No amount of girl chasing, however, could deflect Jon from his principal passion. At 16, he began wangling his way into smoke-filled bars where he stood unobserved in the low-lit gloom, watching the acts, quietly absorbing through every pore the adrenalin-driven high of live performance. It was then only a matter of time before he felt ready to form his own band.

The first outfit Jon put together was called Raze; their debut appearance was at a talent contest held at Sayreville War Memorial High School. For their allocated three song set they performed 'Strutter', the 1974 single by Kiss which had failed to chart and so was probably unfamiliar to the panel of judges, the Top 20 hit of that same year, 'Takin' Care of Business', by Canadian band Bachman Turner Overdrive, and the dependable standard 'Johnny B Goode', Chuck Berry's most covered 1958 song. On the night, Raze failed to win anyone over, least of all Jon himself or his loyal parents. Tactfully, they took years to tell him, but that night they were quietly cringing at how bad the band was. Jon knew at this stage, though, that he was merely getting his feet wet, gathering experience.

From 1978 into the following year, Jon tried out a few scratch bands – loose informal arrangements which came and went on a short-term basis. It was performing that was important to him. He once reminisced, 'Playing the local bar was the coolest thing in the world. Playing a college was the big time!' Jon did play college fraternity parties but he was more interested in getting together a band with which to shine in the fabled Jersey shore clubs the Stone Pony and the Fastlane where his heroes like Southside Johnny and the Asbury Jukes played.

At this point, Jon performed cover versions of popular songs. But he sometimes itched to try out some of his original compositions. His guitar playing had become proficient enough to let him articulate his ideas. There were too few occasions, though, when a gig's atmosphere would allow him to slip in one of his own songs, and so he could not yet gauge whether he had any talent as a lyricist.

The name of the game was to stay in the swim. Jon's policy was to nail every booking he could, to play local support to whichever artiste was passing through the string of east coast clubs. He knew that the better the band he could form around him, the better chance he had to develop. His chances of doing just that improved when, in 1979, he put together a ten-piece rhythm and blues band he called Atlantic City Expressway. One member was David Bryan Rashbaum, whom Jon would later call on as the first enlisted member of Bon Jovi.

Three weeks older than Jon, David was born on 7 February 1962. He lived with his family in Edison, near to Jon's birthplace of Perth Amboy. Although an extremely talented classical pianist, he had deviated from that path after seeing the progressive rock band Yes, and had designs on becoming a rock keyboard player. David Rashbaum attended a different high school to Jon, but their paths had been crossing regularly in the last year on the local music circuit. They shared a love of the hectic, high-energy club scene. 'If you weren't actually playing, you jammed with someone else. But you were always in there,' recalled David.

For Jon it was a melting pot filled with an enormous sense of camaraderie, of common purpose, and was incredibly stimulating because of the kaleidoscope of musical styles and musicians who congregated to watch a show as well as to generously share the limited stage space. In clubs crammed with upwards of 100 people, it was inevitably a sweaty, near claustrophobic experience. But far from having a suffocating effect, the hothouse atmosphere bred an even stronger will in Jon to succeed. It was a tough environment in which to cut his musical teeth. The critical audiences, used to a high standard of entertainment, took no prisoners. From the moment a band took the stage they *had* to be good or they risked being crucified. Southside Johnny summed it up bluntly when he said, 'If you didn't go up on stage to kick ass, you got your ass kicked.'

On the face of it, the money on offer for each gig might have sounded alright at $100 in 1979. But by the time it was split equally between all ten members of Atlantic City Expressway, each one was really playing for loose change, particularly since they had to travel miles to get to and from Asbury Park. In this sense David Rashbaum was able to help the band out by co-opting the use of his father's works van in the evenings.

By playing so regularly, Atlantic City Expressway began gaining in strength and local popularity. With his thick hair waving down on to his shoulders and his slender build, Jon's attraction as a frontman was becoming obvious, too. But for many it was more the white-hot ambition radiating from the teenager and the commitment to what he was doing that left its mark. Although Jon would not know it for years to come, his hero Southside Johnny was now busy admiring him. It was a switch-around that led the older musician to state later that no matter how many guys were on the stage, regardless of what was happening, Jon was always the one the eye was irresistibly drawn to.

Jon's devotion to music led to him playing gigs to all hours of the morning, practically every morning. He would hang out in bars until 3.00 a.m., trundle home and still have to roll up at school by 8.00 a.m. He was playing in bars he wasn't legally old enough even to be in yet. But his parents saw this unusual lifestyle for a 17-year-old as further evidence of his determination to make his way in life through music and they were liberal enough not to try to put a leash on him. There was at least a comfort in knowing where he was. But primarily, they understood and applauded his drive. Carol Bongiovi remembered that on the day Jon announced to his family that he was going to be a rock star, his father immediately told him, 'Go for it!' It was a positive attitude which had a lasting influence on Jon.

At the same time though, Jon was causing his already frustrated teachers some new degree of consternation when in the middle of lessons he would, unsurprisingly, often fall asleep with his head on his desk. When he did manage to keep his eyelids open, he was counting the hours until he would be free to get out of school and into band rehearsal. There was no mystery as to where the nerve centre of his life lay.

His band's burgeoning local reputation was never more enhanced than when one night New Jersey's latest superstar, Bruce Springsteen, dropped by to see Atlantic City Expressway play at the legendary Fastlane. As was Springsteen's wont, he suddenly got up on stage beside Jon and joined in. This wasn't an isolated occasion – it would happen time and again. Jon and Bruce would jam on old rhythm and blues songs, and cover versions, and even rattle through a few of Springsteen's own compositions. But where Jon's friend Dave Sabo would remain blown away for years by the sheer memory of such events, Jon was less excitable. He thoroughly enjoyed it when Springsteen would bound up on stage beside him, and he would always consider that the star had shown him valuable encouragement. Jon has remarked that Springsteen definitely contributed to his becoming a star in his own right.

But, from the start, there was too bright a light burning within Jon for him to be in anybody's shadow. Jon had no intention of ever being the 'new anybody'. He was determined to make it as himself. Nor was he going to sit back and wait for life's opportunities to wash up at his feet. His philosophy was to go out there and actively hunt them down. He was willing to work himself and his band to the bone to find that break. With Bon Jovi years later, he would be exactly the same. At least one Atlantic City Expressway band member recognised the unusual degree of tenacity in their frontman. David Rashbaum later described how exciting Jon was to watch in live performance in these raw early days. 'If there is such a thing as star quality, then this guy has it all,' he declared.

How much of that raw electric spark was nervous adrenalin, despite the degree of arrogance that can only come with the fearlessness of youth, is anyone's guess, but few could have matched Jon's focus right then as he concentrated on honing his craft. Off stage he was just as avid in his determination to learn from people who had been on even the fringes of the music business. School was a distracting obligation that got in the way of performing. His real education came from talking to performers in the Fastlane, the Stone Pony et al. He was also busily sculpting his fledgling talent as a lyricist. Being a cover band had no future, and having songs written for him didn't appeal. Jon would go on largely to collaborate on songwriting, but at this stage he composed alone. He still infiltrated his own material into the band's song sets of cover versions, but it remained hard to foist original compositions on audiences easily critical of the unfamiliar. It was, though, a useful barometer as to what – to his own ears – worked, and what missed the mark completely.

In many ways 1979 was an unforgettable year for Jon. Looking back, he has fond memories of the full, chaotic and hyper existence he enjoyed even before becoming a famous rock star. He drove a Camero, a nifty little sports car which doubled as a passion wagon and a means to get him to his bookings. One memorable night, he got caught up in racing his Camero along the open road with another motorist who, Jon assumed, was heading to the same local bar. Suddenly his high spirits were doused when his car was forced to a halt by a team of New Jersey state troopers. Seconds later, the driver's door was yanked open and Jon alarmingly found a gun pointed at his temple. It seemed an extreme reaction to his speeding, he thought, until he discovered that he had inadvertently engaged in a car race with an unmarked vehicle in which state troopers were transporting a prisoner between two jails. The dramatic situation simmered down quickly enough when the cops realised that Jon was no threat. His natural charisma came in handy in placating the officers, to the extent that he invited them to that night's gig, and once off-duty they did just that.

Away from music, the most important personal turning point for Jon happened at school where he began making a special point of staying awake in history class; sitting next to him now was a dark-haired dazzler named Dorothea Hurley. With her long hair and strong eyes set in an oval-shaped face, she was attractively independent-minded too. Jon recognised in her a fellow rebel in her own quiet way, and he was instantly besotted. He recalled, 'She was the be-all and end-all for me – the cool girl in class, the one who would always arrive late'. The snag was that she turned out to be dating one of Jon's friends. The boyfriend went off to enlist in the navy, however, leaving the field clear for Jon. He couldn't understand why he had never noticed that this girl was in his grade before. He began by surreptitiously cadging her help with some test questions; this led to small talk and it developed from there.

Having previously enjoyed raiding the local maidenly preserves, Jon now fell head over heels in love for the first time. Dorothea Hurley came to feel the same about the vibrant, unusually driven 17-year-old. Jon was quiet, different to the other, overly macho types. They became high school sweethearts, a very attractive couple who would skip their high school prom for listening to music down by the night shore.

This shift was not the only change in his life, however. Jon began to feel that, exciting as Atlantic City Expressway had been, the band's days were numbered. He and the other nine members were coming to that crossroads in life where individual futures lie in different directions. Many a potentially successful band has splintered at the point where key personnel go off to university. David Rashbaum's classical piano skills were just too good to squander. At this stage he decided to walk away from plans to play in a rock band and headed for New York City, where he had been accepted as a student at the prestigious Juilliard School of Music.

Jon, too, now left Atlantic City Expressway, although his academic life ceased when he left high school. Work prospects in Sayreville for the unacademic were fairly depressing. A paint factory and a brick-making factory were the town's two major employers. Traditionally, the only way out of being sucked into the manual labour market, of having the chance to see anything of the world beyond industrial New Jersey, lay in joining the US Navy. None of these options inspired Jon.

Unsurprisingly, given his myopic focus thus far on his lodestar, he saw music as his way out. His aspirations had mushroomed beyond playing in regional clubs, although he did continue for a while to play the local pub circuit when he joined a band called the Rest, in which he sang and played electric guitar. But it would prove to be a short-term gig for him.

As Jon neared the end of his last year at school he was hungry to forge himself a bright future. He also had a deep reservoir of resilience. If others outside his close family circle found his fanaticism hard to comprehend, it was very straightforward to Jon. He wanted to be a major rock star and he was going to do whatever was necessary to achieve that goal. He has called it having blind faith in himself. One thing was already abundantly clear. However long it took him, ultimately he would succeed, for despite his youth he was already a distinctly hard man to keep down.

CHAPTER 2

A Relentless
Driving Force

IT DID NOT TAKE LONG for Jon Bon Jovi, now 18 and out of school, to follow David Rashbaum's example and head to New York City. There, he started work at Power Station recording studio in downtown Manhattan. This prestigious facility, where several top stars had recorded major albums, was co-owned by Jon's father's cousin, Tony Bongiovi. In his line of work, Tony was naturally always interested in where tomorrow's talent might spring from. So when he learned from John and Carol that their eldest son had determined ambitions in his field, he was intrigued enough to come to the Jersey music scene that summer to see the teenager play live.

At that point, Jon was coming to the end of his six-month stint in the Rest, and on the strength of observing him for one pub performance, Tony Bongiovi reckoned that he saw something worthwhile. He later recalled of Jon on stage that night, 'There was a magic there.' Even so, it was Jon who rang Tony soon after and asked if he could come and work at Power Station. Unfortunately, in under five years' time, the relatives would end up embroiled in a legal dispute over the extent to which Tony Bongiovi assisted Jon's career. That long-running sore lay in the future, however. In September 1980 Jon was only too thrilled that Tony said yes.

Jon's duties at Power Station amounted to those of a general errand boy. He swept floors, made coffee, went to the bank, placed bets for people and fetched hot snacks for hungry clientele. It was menial work that paid around $50 a week, but Jon was in his element. He did not mind running out for beer for David Bowie. He liked getting to work in time to collide with Mick Jagger arriving at the studio. And as a young guy pushing a broom, he manfully overlooked it when the odd, less even-tempered, diva would be unnecessarily bitchy to him. A few years down the track Jon insisted, 'It was great experience for teaching me how to treat being a star.'

Being at Power Station studio not only gave Jon a great first-hand opportunity to see the process of recording hit albums; he was also able to record demos of his own compositions. This mattered to him a great deal more than did nodding at celebrities in the corridors. He aimed to make joining their ranks a reality and, to this end, over the next two years he would write, record and produce scores of demonstration discs.

As a 'nobody' Jon had to make his demos on downtime – odd hours of the early morning when no one else required the facilities. He would be charged for the studio time, which often racked up to more money than he could comfortably afford on his wages, even though his salary did gradually increase. When he did run up a tab for these sessions, Jon tried not to worry too much about it. Making demos was essential if he was going to make the most of being at Power Station studio.

At this stage, Jon had no band. He threw his all into songwriting. He would finish his working day, then sit somewhere in the building writing lyrics, deep in concentration for hours on end while waiting for the chance to cut his next demo. He would mostly accompany himself, unless he could rope in any willing session guy still hanging around the place. Eager for a sounding board, Jon would play back his work for anyone who was prowling about the studio at 4.00 a.m. Any crumb of encouragement thrown benevolently at him was pounced upon. It was welcome nourishment. Even with his rubber-ball resilience, it could sometimes be hard maintaining super-high confidence levels as the months rolled out. Especially when by day the constant traffic of established stars at work graphically highlighted the enormous gulf which lay between where he was and where he wanted to be.

He had entered an extremely intense time in his young life when maintaining motivation was vital, despite the fact that his high creative productivity was going thoroughly unrewarded. It was difficult for him in other respects too, for he had been thrust into an entirely alien environment. Till now, even if he was jamming most nights in smoky east coast New Jersey clubs till near dawn, he had always wound his way home afterwards, if only for a couple of hours sleep. Now, things were very different.

Although Sayreville was not many miles away from New York, the very nature of Jon's lifestyle meant that he mainly stayed over in the city. Frequently, he literally found a floor to kip on at the recording studio. Other times, he stayed at Tony Bongiovi's apartment. His bed was a pull-out couch, but he would have to make himself scarce if his cousin was entertaining a lady friend. On those occasions, to give Tony privacy, Jon's choice was to vanish discreetly into a back room which had no bed, or to take himself off into the night to wander the mean streets of New York City. He was consequently often lonely during this period. He had no real acquaintances there except his cousin, and many a night he would get out of the cold by huddling down in some cinema seat alone, not taking much interest in the movie on screen. Walking the late night streets he would see so many guys his own age staggering about drunk, getting into fights or being sick in alleyways, and he knew that, by contrast, he was very different. He would feed on that fact, just as he would become fired up about his latest idea for a song. Yet he acknowledged much later that it was still hard, having truly no idea of where his future lay.

It must also have been hard to maintain his relationship with Dorothea Hurley, who continued to live at home with her parents in New Jersey. But they managed to stay committed to one another. It helped that Jon sometimes commuted between New York City and home, allowing the couple to get together. Even so, his frame of mind was often clearly coloured by the light in which he viewed his career prospects. His brother Anthony vividly recalled Jon paying some home visits when he obviously felt downbeat about his lack of progress. On the other hand, his dad, John, can testify to his son's unwavering obsession with songwriting. Not only did Jon scribble incessantly on notepads during the bus journeys to and fro, he even penned partial songs on his home bedroom walls.

What spare time Jon had for these trips began to shrink as he put together a new band. The line-up was inevitably pretty fluid, with constant personnel changes. The only permanent thing about it was the name Jon gave it – the Lechers. It was, essentially, a vehicle through which Jon could satisfy his need to be playing live, and it also gave him an outlet to try out his own songs. During the early 1980s Jon began playing clubs around Manhattan and Brooklyn, but he was often acutely aware of the shortcomings of his scratch band. When the Lechers inevitably faded away, the next band he put together appeared to have more substance.

He called this the Wild Ones; the big difference this time around was that two of its members were Jon's friends. His hometown mate Dave Sabo joined him, playing guitar. And notably, David Rashbaum, still studying classical music at the Juilliard School of Music, had begun turning his mind again towards rock. He agreed, therefore, to bring his considerable talent back to the fold. Gig-wise, the Wild Ones were consequently much more capable. They received a boost when Southside Johnny extended a helping hand to Jon by offering him the support slot on some gigs he and the Asbury Jukes were about to embark upon. By this time, Southside Johnny and the Asbury Jukes had racked up five albums, and Jon saw this generous leg-up for what it was – a chance to impinge on the east coast music scene in his biggest way yet, playing to much larger audiences. The exposure and the experience could only be good.

Inspiration also came from seeing new bands break in. Like many others at grass roots level in America, Jon was now taking notice of U2 – the latest band from across the pond to be playing their first US gigs. Fronted by singer/songwriter Bono, U2 had emerged from the aggressive nihilistic punk rock era. But while the band agreed with the principle of individualism, they flatly rejected the violence that was inextricably associated with punk. Instead, U2 strove to create an aura of hope. In the prevailing climate of mass unemployment and fast-spreading disillusionment in British society, Bono had declared that far from letting negativity take hold, U2's music was meant to be about getting up and doing something about it – uplifting sentiments which were mirrored exactly in Jon Bon Jovi's young heart.

Jon got the chance to see U2 in performance when the four-piece played a selection of club dates on America's eastern seaboard at the tail end of 1980. The resounding shouts for encores energised the newly launched recording stars busy playing out of their skins, and they pumped up a future rock star in the audience, who left that night eager to press his nose back to the grindstone. Such nights as those helped Jon to believe that he was right not to give up doing the soul-destroying round of the record companies, hoping to get remorselessly-pestered A&R guys to listen to his growing pile of demo tapes. Instead of posting tapes in, Jon felt that presenting them in person was the answer. But his persuasive charisma would only get him so far. It was clear that he was not yet armed with his best shot.

He kept at it, and at Power Station staff members, and now occasionally stars, were passing on constructive criticism coated with clear encouragement. They were much impressed with the staying power of the ambitious studio gofer. But Jon's soundest ally continued to be his own self-belief. He has revealed, 'I could never think of the idea of *not* getting signed.'

By the time he had been over a year at Power Station Jon was finding it increasingly hard to make ends meet, particularly with the drain that paying for recording time, still with no return, put on his slender finances. So from early 1982 he undertook a variety of extra jobs. These included working at a car wash and as a shop assistant; for a short while, he tried putting his winning personality to effective use when selling newspaper subscriptions to housewives door to door. He also put in a stint at a fast food restaurant and got his hands dirty and built up his muscles labouring at a junkyard. It was all mind-numbingly boring work, but it drew in much-needed cash.

On 2 March he turned 20, and had already been dreaming seemingly for ever about becoming a rock star. Unwittingly, he took his first major step towards realising that dream during the summer of 1982. With an ever-keen weather eye on the way popular music trends were shifting, Jon had been clocking the success of bands such as Reo Speedwagon. The soft-rock ballad group had been recording for almost ten years when in spring 1981 they finally achieved their breakthrough, with the album *Hi Infidelity*.

Pomp rock exponents Styx were regularly hitting the spot. So were adult-oriented rock bands such as Journey, powered by the strong vocal style of Steve Perry. When Jon's long-time favourites, the J. Geils Band, departed from their R&B base and landed their million-selling number one single 'Centerfold' in February 1982, it seemed as clear as day that a fusion of rock and pop held the key.

Hunched over his acoustic guitar, a pad and pen at the ready, Jon began to develop (with an acquaintance, George Karakoglou) a song titled 'Runaway'. Expressing a form of teenage angst, it told the tale of a lonely young girl who feels out of place at home and is drawn to the bright Broadway lights, searching ultimately for love. There was nothing profound or elaborate about the lyrics and there wasn't meant to be. It was aimed squarely at the teenage market. It was the sound Jon came up with that would form the first appeal. With a chiming keyboard opening, it swelled into an energetic, full-bodied thumping backbeat. An instrumental break three-quarters of the way through then led into a hearty repetition of the short but catchy chorus.

Playing 'Runaway' to himself over and over again, Jon wondered if this was it. At this point in 1982 he needed to get a foot in the door that would lead the way in to the business. Despite his extra jobs he was over his head financially, having by now produced around four albums-worth of demos. Still, he knew this was not the time to be squeamish. An extra special effort then was invested in creating the 'Runaway' demo. For it Jon was backed by four experienced, specifically-hired musicians – Frankie La Roca on drums, Tim Pierce on guitar and session man Hugh McDonald on bass (the same Hugh McDonald who now features on Bon Jovi albums and appears with the band on stage). Lastly, Roy Bittan (pianist with Bruce Springsteen's backing group the E Street Band) happily supplied the keyboard work. The recording was made at Power Station studio. Billy Squier agreed to produce the demo tape which, along with 'Runaway', included another three of Jon's original compositions. Jon furnished almost every record label on east coast America with a copy of this demo, credited to 'Johnny B', but it didn't elicit any interest.

Jon's bandmate in the Wild Ones, David Rashbaum, had faith in 'Runaway', and they performed the number at gigs around New York. Even though it usually connected with a live audience, it didn't look likely ever to become a bona fide record. By Christmas Jon could have been excused for banging his head on the nearest wall in frustration. And he wasn't too happy when his voice did finally feature on a released record.

In 1982 writer/director George Lucas was part way through the first trilogy of *Star Wars*, his phenomenally successful science fiction blockbuster movie series. Tony Bongiovi was producing an album called the *Star Wars Christmas Album* and Jon had sung lead vocal on the track 'R2D2 – We Wish You A Merry Christmas'. To Jon, the only good thing to be said of this effort was that he got paid for it – money which he promptly ploughed into an excursion to California to see if any west coast record label would be interested in his work. Accompanied by David Rashbaum, Jon set out to blanket the music men in Los Angeles, but here too his efforts fell on barren soil. So it was back to New York and back to the drawing board.

In late 1982, among the plethora of US radio stations clogging the airwaves, one was starting to stand out as being at the cutting edge – WAPP FM 103.5, broadcasting out of Long Island. Like record companies, established radio stations collectively constituted a bastion that was nearly impossible to breach. But Jon had a gut instinct that this one might be different.

WAPP's parent company was the Doubleday group, and this new radio station, aiming to make its mark, took pride in having a more youthful outlook than some of its long-established rivals. Jon just hoped that that freshness would extend to its disc jockeys being prepared to give a hearing to a young guy with nothing but his fierce determination and self-belief to recommend him.

Having staked out the radio station's reception area and identified Chip Hobart as his quarry, Jon took the upfront approach. Handing the DJ a copy of his demo tape, Jon asked for his opinion. Frankly, he said, he had been bum-rushed by everyone else. Hobart liked the tape, and it turned out to be excellent timing. As part of its assault on the public consciousness, WAPP was organising a talent contest called 'Rock To Riches'. Jon's 'Runaway' was entered for this contest and promptly won the regional heat.

The major consequence of this mini-triumph was that the WAPP executives then wanted Jon to let them put 'Runaway' on a station-sponsored album which would act as a showcase for local talent. There was no money on offer for this, which gave Jon some pause. 'To be on a homegrown record wasn't my aspiration,' he said later. If 'Runaway' had real potential, and he let it go on to this album, would it also snuff out any chance he had of obtaining a one-off single deal with a record label? Such deals had been commonplace for years, and although Jon wasn't wild about those either, he hadn't yet managed to land one. He had his doubts, but he decided to agree to its inclusion on the WAPP album.

In early 1983, therefore, 'Runaway' by John Bongiovi appeared mid-division on a playlist of similarly unsigned acts. The compilation album, titled *New York Rocks 1983*, consisted of, among others, 'She Got Free' by Mike Corbin, 'Outlaw (Josie Wells)' by the Southern Cross Band, and 'Jaded Heart' by Humans From Earth. WAPP's parent company quickly circulated the album tracks for free airplay on its other Doubleday-owned radio stations around the country, and independently 'Runaway' immediately began to be singled out by one DJ after another. It started to pop up all over the place. Listener requests to hear it again soared and, state by state, its popularity rapidly gained astonishing momentum. After all these years of Jon knocking himself out, suddenly there was an exciting buzz as 'Runaway' broke nationwide.

Jon has repeatedly called it 'a fluke'. It was certainly a highly unusual position to find himself in. The Wild Ones had never felt like a permanent setup. So while his song was taking off, Jon had no band and no management structure or official representation of any kind. Yet he suddenly had several A&R men for influential record labels avidly homing in on him – in some cases, the selfsame A&R people who had very recently shunned him. However it had come about, it was an exciting turnaround in Jon's fortunes. The front runners in the chase to sign John Bongiovi soon emerged as Atlantic Records and Polygram. Thrilled as Jon was, he knew that right then was the time to conceal his fervour, inasmuch as he did not immediately snatch at the first offer made to him.

Shrewdly, he took the view that against the welter of interest created by 'Runaway', any first bid would probably be a base offer and that there would be room for at least some manoeuvre. His apparent poise and confidence led Atlantic Records to be first on the table with an offer. Jon appreciated it, but on the advice of a lawyer friend, he promptly invited Polygram to better it. Polygram were happy to outbid a rival, and not just on the basis of the startling street level reaction to 'Runaway'. One senior record executive with the label, Derek Shulman, felt that Jon had intrinsically the kind of eagle-eyed drive that record companies look for in an artiste who has to compete in a crowded and cut-throat marketplace. Shulman said of Jon, 'I felt he had an unbelievable burning desire to be huge.'

Terms were duly agreed, and on 1 July 1983 Jon signed a record contract with Polygram; the records would be released on the music giant's Mercury Records label. Effectively, Jon was signed as a solo artiste, but it was up to him if he wanted to put a band together. The onus for the success or failure of such a unit would sit squarely on his shoulders. The upfront money that this record deal produced would actually enable Jon to employ musicians and pay them proper wages, which was both a relief and an exciting opportunity. He knew what he was looking for. They had to be guys who shared a common commitment and had ability to back it up.

By now, Jon was well versed in who was around and who was good. He also had a reliable radar for assessing someone's drive and determination. If those factors did not register high on his personal screen, he didn't want to know. The first person Jon called on was keyboardist David Bryan Rashbaum. He telephoned the skilled musician with the news of his record deal and told him that he was putting a full-time band together – was he interested in coming onboard? David, as he once put it himself, had worked his ass off to be selected for a place at the Juilliard School of Music. To give it up just like that could not have been easy, but he made the jump. Presumably used to his friend's exhaustive verve and optimism, though, in accepting the invitation, David also jovially warned Jon, 'If you're lying to me, I'm gonna kill ya!'

Next up was a bass player named Alec John Such. Born on 14 November 1952 in Yonkers, New York, he was an experienced studio session man whom Jon had also noted playing in cover bands around the Jersey clubs. Alec had held down bass duties with the Message until it broke up, when he switched to Phantom's Opera, a popular New Jersey band. He was now ready for another move and was happy to accept Jon's offer to join his newly forming line-up. Alec promptly suggested that Jon should consider a friend of his, Tico Torres, a drummer who had also played in Phantom's Opera.

Born Hector Torres on 7 October 1953, Tico was a musician Jon had admired for some five years. He was a strong drummer, a veteran who had worked with Lou Christie, had toured extensively, performed on various albums, played strip bars and had drummed with Franke and the Knockouts. Tico Torres took a call from Alec John Such, who suggested he should check out Jon and his band. Along with a couple of stand-in musicians, Jon was taking his fledgling outfit out on the familiar club circuit, gauging how it was piecing together. And Tico would well remember his first impressions of his energetic future boss. He said, 'The first time I saw Jon perform he was like a wild man and the girls went nuts. I wasn't used to seeing that.' Jon and Tico arranged to meet to discuss it properly, and soon the drummer was hired.

Jon was happy with his choices but knew that he still needed a strong lead guitarist. Jon's own guitar skills are far from basic, but they were not sufficient for the impact he ultimately hoped to make with his band. Jon's songwriting too was beginning to lean towards the kind of material for which he would require a musician who was capable of articulating that raw appeal.

Jon's Sayreville friend Dave Sabo would sometimes step in as guitarist, but it was never viewed by either party as a permanent arrangement. Dave's future lay with the band Skid Row further down the track. But for now he appeared in some club dates alongside Tico, Alec, David and Jon.

From his days in the Message, Alec remembered a lead guitarist named Richie Sambora. Tico Torres also knew Sambora through the local New Jersey club circuit, and so between them they urged the guitarist to come and see Jon's band play, with a view to joining their ranks.

Born Richard Stephen Sambora in Woodbridge, New Jersey, on 11 July 1959, Richie is a multi-instrumentalist who plays piano, trumpet and accordion as sidelines. He taught himself to play electrifying lead guitar by the tried and trusted method of doggedly listening to the likes of Eric Clapton and Jimmy Page on the radio, then tirelessly figuring out how to play along with them.

He started his career as a session musician in the late 1970s and has stated that one of the most useful lessons he learned during that time was that it was vital to be a good listener – that what separates the professional from the amateur is the ability to know just when to stand back and blend in and when to take to the light and shine. Great timing is essential. Today, Richie Sambora is one of the finest lead guitarists in the business. Back in 1983 he already had flair and had accumulated sound experience before he teamed up with Jon. As well as a stint in the Message, he had played with Duke Williams and the Extremes, and with the metal band Mercy.

Richie Sambora would collaborate with Jon as songwriter for Bon Jovi which, along with his considerable guitar skills, makes him a valuable asset to the band. But his initial entry was inauspicious, when Jon failed to take him seriously. Responding to Alec and Tico's urgings, Richie had traipsed along to one of the Jersey clubs where Jon was performing. Watching the frontman in action, Richie joined the already growing list of people who were knocked out by Jon's ability, focus and charisma. Sambora quickly concluded that Jon was the real deal, a star in the making. He also saw himself fitting in neatly with the band he was watching.

With unusual front, Richie buttonholed Jon afterwards, and following some small talk he made a blunt pitch to join Jon's band. He reeled off his experience to date and tried hard to impress upon the singer that he really was the final piece of the jigsaw. Years later, Jon recalled admiring what he terms Richie's 'balls in walking up to me that way.' At the time, though, Richie felt that he had blown it. It had not come naturally to push himself forward so boldly, and he felt that it had not gone down very well. Richie said, 'I rubbed Jon the wrong way instantly. He kind of went, "Who is this asshole?"'

It was no secret that Jon was looking for a lead guitarist, and consequently he had had several guys approaching him at gigs. That night he had been more interested in getting loaded up and making his getaway from the club. Luckily, Sambora was made of sterner stuff and was persistent. At another of Jon's gigs, he tried again.

This time, Jon gave in and invited Richie to a try out at a band rehearsal. Keen as mustard, Sambora arrived and met the other three members; he had come ready to impress. To warm up, the four musicians set about jamming, and by the time Jon arrived, having been unexpectedly delayed elsewhere, the band had a satisfyingly full-bodied sound which hit him powerfully the second he walked through the door. Richie can now laugh at the ease with which Jon then capitulated and said, 'Okay! You're in!'

The line-up was now complete, though when Jon discussed the band with Polygram, the record label had one or two ideas about restructuring. Jon flatly refused to implement them and the subject was dropped. The label did, however, insist on a couple of points. As was common enough practice, Alec John Such and Tico Torres, the two older group members, shaved some years off their ages for PR purposes, to bring them more into line with the band's figurehead. Then there was the matter of Jon's name and, subsequently, the band name.

Jon rejected mortifying suggestions to saddle him with monikers such as Johnny London or, worse, Johnny Lightning. But after some discussion he did agree to de-ethnicise his name. In a variation of his real Christian and surnames, therefore, it was now that John Bongiovi officially became Jon Bon Jovi. As far as the band name was concerned, the idea of calling it Victory was briefly floated – label executives themselves abandoned that. To capitalise on the popularity of 'Runaway', Polygram preferred to call the group after the renamed artiste they had newly signed – hence, Bon Jovi.

Bon Jovi's first task as summer 1983 progressed was to gain experience working together. All five men were good in their own right, but as a unit they had some ironing out to do. Tico Torres frankly felt that their initial gig together sounded 'like shit'. The reason was easily detected. The four musicians around Jon had been used to doing their own thing in their own way, or with other singers. No one doubted, however, that the talent was there to become a fine, cohesive band. Their plan to work up an impressive live act was tested at times, when after cramming themselves and their equipment into an overloaded station wagon, they would arrive at some venues to find, dishearteningly, that they were playing practically to themselves. At one gig later in the year at the New Jersey club Xanadu, when the audience only outnumbered the band six to one, the atmosphere was so soporific that Richie ingeniously blamed it on the punters having overstuffed themselves with Thanksgiving Day turkey! It was a teething time for the band. But in another sense it gave them a breathing space in which to formulate a truly complementary blend of their individual talents.

With the record deal in place, and plans to cocoon Bon Jovi into working on their debut album at the prestigious Power Station recording studio, it was inevitable that the next stage would be to acquire formal management. Music managers were already casting their beady eyes towards Polygram's newest signing, and Jon was being robustly wooed by well-established firms, eager to add him to their illustrious rosters. But in autumn 1983 Jon opted to go with Doc McGhee, a rotund, balding figure who spoke with a Chicago accent. Right then, McGhee was making waves with Mötley Crüe who, fronted by vocalist Vince Neil, were notorious for their over-the-top stage antics. Mötley Crüe had signed to New York City-based McGhee Entertainment Inc at the end of the previous year, and their second album, *Shout At The Devil*, released in September 1983, would eventually go multi-platinum.

That autumn when Doc McGhee, newly acquiring a public profile, set his sights on Bon Jovi, his brash, though hardly original, pitch to Jon was that he could make his band the biggest in the world. As a streetwise New Jersey guy, Jon was not necessarily bowled over by this clichéd line, but he felt that McGhee's timing was right. Jon could see what was happening with Mötley Crüe, and his own band was on the cusp of launching themselves on to the market.

What was essential to Jon was that the guy had ambition. At that point Doc McGhee often wore about his neck a miniature gold disc on a chain. Of course, he had no gold disc to his name, and Jon would enjoy ribbing the manager about the naff necklace. But he liked the optimism it symbolised. Jon needed a manager not to talk big but to think big, and he felt he had found that with Doc McGhee who, on a personal level, aimed to push hard to become big league as a rock band manager. In one way, Jon's attitude was understandable. He and Doc McGhee were both just setting out on the path to hopeful stardom, and both had the essential thing in common – that unquenchable fire in the belly. What Jon could not know at this time was that McGhee had been involved in drug smuggling activities sometime during the previous year – criminal offences that would not come to light for some years.

As 1983 wound to a close it was an excitingly hectic time. With Bon Jovi's debut album scheduled for release early in the new year, the band had to take time out from laying down the tracks to involve themselves in their first official publicity photo shoots. Although Bon Jovi had far more substance to them than the music critics would originally give them credit for, they slotted into the hair band bracket at this time. All five wore their hair long. Each member, too, was a looker, which made the image-makers' job easier.

Tico, David and Alec were all eye-catching in their individual ways. But Richie, with his height, dark hair and almond-shaped liquid eyes presented the biggest competition to Jon's striking looks. A frontman normally has his closest on-stage rapport with the lead guitarist, and Jon and Richie were obviously the perfect foil for each other. That said, it was clear that Jon himself was major pin-up material – even if they now look back on their early publicity shots and cringe. When the veteran performers were asked during the promo for *Bounce* what advice they would pass on to up-and-coming bands today, David Bryan (the keyboard player shortened his name to make it more showbiz friendly) quickly quipped, 'Steer clear of wearing Spandex!'

The wider public's first sight of Jon Bon Jovi saw him poured into eye-wateringly skin-tight leather trousers and almost wearing a shredded scrap of a T-shirt which exposed his seriously hairy chest. With a fringed jacket, the overall look was dominated by his heavy, full-fringed, shaggy, long fair hair. His piercing blue eyes, strong bone structure and that letterbox smile were, however, his most captivating assets. And from the beginning, his posters were destined to plaster countless teenage girls' bedroom walls and ceilings.

That was fine. It was a valuable part of the whole package. Behind the photogenic grin, though, as the band's relentless driving force Jon felt a weight of responsibility already on his 21-year-old shoulders. But that was counterbalanced by his inner confidence. He knew that his four hand-picked band members were all in it for the love of playing music. Each one wanted to make a success of Bon Jovi. And Jon? He had enough white-hot ambition for them all.

The career he had longed for was at last about to get under way. The idea that in 2003 Bon Jovi would be celebrating 20 years in the business, having seen off most of their contemporaries, didn't enter their heads right then. Theirs would be no overnight success – it would take a massive amount of time-consuming commitment. Although Jon was not shy of delivering the hard work, it would exact a personal price that he had never anticipated having to pay.

CHAPTER 3

So Much Passion and Pain

IN JANUARY 1984 Bon Jovi's eponymously titled debut album was released in America. Initially, it sold in excess of 350,000 copies and subsequently went gold. The album had benefited from the experience brought to it by one of its co-producers, Lance Quinn, who had worked with Talking Heads and Aerosmith among others. It was a blend of hook-filled melodies and anthemic rousers, giving a foretaste of the soaring power ballads which would soon become Bon Jovi's trademark. Of the nine numbers featured, all but one were written by Jon. On two of those eight songs he collaborated with David Bryan, and on four with Richie Sambora.

Lyrically, Jon had no lofty ambitions to save the planet, or to comment on where society's moral compass was going awry in the greedy 1980s. The album was written from the perspective of Bon Jovi being just five fresh young guys from New Jersey. It set out to speak to teenagers in their own language about what mattered to them close to home. Jon's awareness of the unrewarding, preordained path of life that is most people's lot came later, bringing with it a philosophy that urged people to do their best to get out from under. This would be one of the effective cornerstones of his songwriting.

For now, he concentrated on the subjects of young love and carnal lust. He continued to compose on guitar and had come up with tales of destructive relationships, of foxy ladies and of love lost. A debut album that largely reeked of adolescent hormonal yearnings was setting itself up for attack by the rock critics, but it came away relatively unscathed. The glancing blows from that quarter were saved for when Bon Jovi took the material out on the road.

Perhaps it was because Jon alone was signed to Polygram that the album looked at first glance like a solo work. Jon was the only band member to be pictured on the front sleeve. Standing in the middle of a deserted, well-lit street at night, he looked all of his youthful 21 years, and not particularly threatening, despite his intent stare and ready-for-anything stance. The message this artwork sent to the other four in the band can only be guessed at. What mattered more immediately was that their first album managed to make it to number 43 in the US charts. Released later in spring in the UK, it did less well and stalled at number 71. However, the first single from the album – a re-recorded version of 'Runaway', released in February – had by then cracked the US Top 40, dropping anchor at number 39. Exciting times lay ahead.

Before that though, came the cringe-making experience of their first promotional videos. These days Jon will admit loud and clear that his idea of excruciating torture would be to be forced to view these embarrassing early offerings. The first video was for 'Runaway', and it was shot over three days in a big, draughty, long-abandoned warehouse in New Jersey at a cost of around $60,000. As a new signing, Bon Jovi had no option but to be steered by the record company's marketing people, and therefore had no creative control over what was happening. Scenes were filmed which didn't involve the band. Jon said later that half of the time, 'We couldn't see what the fuck was going on!'

Jon's first sight of the completed video came when he and the band arrived at manager Doc McGhee's office for a private advance viewing. As very much a hands-on guy, Jon was nervous enough at being denied involvement every step of the way with this video. But he was still naturally excited too, aware of a building anticipation at seeing themselves on screen. As it turned out, his most vivid memory at the end of the short video clip was of the total silence in the room. One or two PR guys present valiantly talked it up, but the band sat shell-shocked, in deep dismay. Jon's unvoiced verdict on what he had just witnessed was, 'It's shit!' Moreover, despite all the ebullient talk from the record company's side, privately Jon felt that the crappy video had ruined his song.

'Runaway's video was the first in a series of god-awful Bon Jovi promo films. They would not be in a position to get their act together in this area until their third album. Right then, Jon had no option but to grin and bear it. And there was another, even less attractive, side to the affair. Although Jon did not realise it at the time, standard business practice was for the record company to recoup the full cost of making a promotional video – offset against the band's share of record royalties.

Luckily, a diversion from the deep disappointment over the 'Runaway' video debacle came swiftly, in the shape of the band acquiring its very own tour bus. It was essential that Bon Jovi get out on the road to start connecting with a far larger live audience than they had done to date. Sardining themselves and their equipment into one station wagon had to be a thing of the past.

Jon gleefully recalled his unqualified delight at this development: 'I remember the day we got our first tour bus. We rode on it to a gig in our hometown. We got in it at 4.00 p.m., and hung out there until midnight, when we went on stage. Afterwards, we jumped straight back on it!' It felt to Jon like the big time had already arrived. In his mind that night he was, he has admitted, a superstar.

Jon came back to reality long before Bon Jovi's second single, 'She Don't Know Me', released in May, petered out in the US charts at number 48. This tepid performance only reinforced his belief that gaining live visibility was the key. Bon Jovi had already notched up a memorable support slot when they opened for Texas rockers ZZ Top at Madison Square Garden. This distinctive trio, recently winners of *Billboard*'s award for Best Group Performance Video for 'Gimme All Your Lovin', in early 1984 were on the brink of their world tour. Securing support duties at this high-profile New York City gig had given Jon and the others a big boost.

It was undeniably difficult to know just where Bon Jovi should attempt to fit into the current smorgasbord of musical styles. Pretty-boy pop was at its height, personified by outfits such as the George Michael/Andrew Ridgeley duo Wham. Flamboyant gender-bender performer Boy George, fronting Culture Club, was receiving massive media attention. And even Queen had adopted drag for a one-off video to accompany 'I Want To Break Free'. At the opposite end of the spectrum, heavy metal veterans Judas Priest and blues-influenced hard rock exponents like Whitesnake were still making their presence felt. Def Leppard, one of the most popular metal bands of the 1980s, had arrived with a vengeance from England, having set the charts ablaze with their monster hit album, *Pyromania*.

Bon Jovi's power ballads were more mainstream soft rock. Yet Richie Sambora's lead guitar work was certainly capable of roughening the edges, and Jon's glamour and high-energy style injected the necessary bombast. It meant that they chose to lean towards the harder end of rock, specifically the emerging metal scene. Style-wise, they developed their adopted image to suit – figure-hugging leather or satin trousers, studded belts, ripped vests, and bright scarves tied decoratively around an arm or a leg.

Jon's curled shoulder-length hair attracted swipes from the music press of 'poodle perm pop'. Just as dressing up and wearing fake jewellery was not part of the New Jersey psyche,

Jon did not take naturally to black eye-liner or, worse still, lipstick for live performances and photo shoots. It felt by turns fun and foolish, but Jon believed that it was necessary to achieve the required visual effect, and although that would alter over time, for now he took the band down this path. That their public image was very different to the jeans and leather jacket guys they were in real life, was just showbiz.

Jon also knew that it was only by going out on the tour circuit that they were going to discover just who their fans were. At the outset, Bon Jovi fans would be mid-to-late teenagers who formed a spreading base which would strengthen and grow up with the band; remaining unswervingly loyal to this day. Finding friends among the music press corps was more difficult. Indeed, it became clear fairly early on that some sections were prepared to dismiss Bon Jovi as lightweight – which only acted as a spur to Jon.

He decided that, as a way of proving that they could more than hold their own, Bon Jovi would deliberately range themselves against the most uncompromisingly hard rock acts in the business. It was a healthy defiance and, to a man, the band were ready to let battle commence. There was, however, an unhappy downside to their plan to tour until they dropped – it was inevitably going to wreak havoc on individual personal relationships.

This was Jon's time. He had to do this. There could be no question of not going on the road. Dorothea Hurley had been his girlfriend for too long not to understand. But in both human and practical terms it would have been difficult for her to view the prospect with anything but sad misgivings. It naturally wasn't what she wanted for their relationship, and Jon must have seen that. Had they met when Jon was a wealthy rock star, able to accommodate an entourage, following her lover from city to city, saying 'Wow!' from the wings would have been no life for an independent-minded young woman.

As it was, even had Dorothea been prepared to go on tour with Jon in 1984, it would have been impossible. The life of a support band is not one of dignified comfort. In addition to money being tight, Bon Jovi were five guys single-mindedly fired up to work their ticket. With her own life to consider, Dorothea was understandably not prepared to sit at home and wait for Jon to wind his way back eventually, whenever that might be. And Jon couldn't ask that of her. After much distress and heart-searching, four years into their relationship the couple parted – to all intents and purposes, for good.

It would have come as no comfort to Jon, but he was not alone in experiencing this kind of love-life wrench. Drummer Tico Torres and bass player Alec John Such were both already married, and the pressures brought about by making this all-out commitment to Bon Jovi contributed to those marriages ending in divorce.

Putting aside personal problems, like the rest of the band, Jon soon had his hands full when they set out to spend what was left of spring and a chunk of summer playing support to the Scorpions. Formed in Hanover, West Germany, in the early 1970s and fronted by vocalist Klaus Meine, this hard rock band (whose aggressive style was distinctive for its heavy use of their native accent) and Bon Jovi were Mercury Records stablemates. In April 1984 the Scorpions' album, *Love At First Sting*, was their most successful yet, and Bon Jovi joined them for the US arena leg of their world tour, which kicked off in Philadelphia in March.

Over the coming four months Bon Jovi played in 28 cities across 15 states at major venues such as the Municipal Auditorium in Nashville, Tennessee, and the Memorial Coliseum in Jacksonville, Florida. Early on, they paid a return visit to New York's Madison Square Garden. Every step of the way it was a tough slog. It's not in any headliners' interest to help their support band to outshine them. As was par for the course, the Scorpions did not overexert themselves to smooth the passage for the New Jerseyites.

At outdoor gigs, Bon Jovi had no lighting rigs, which would have been pointless anyway since it was still daylight when they played. But frequently they were offered no soundcheck either, and were sometimes left tight for stage space and PA facilities. These handicaps were not taken into account by some critics, keen to review Bon Jovi in live performance. In *Kerrang* the band was quickly damned as anonymous; the knife went into the material, which was described as 'bland, unexciting, foot-tappingly melodic stuff, tailor-made for US radio airplay'. Jon shrugged off the poor notice. He would never be swayed by reviews, either good or bad. He could use his time much better to develop his stagecraft.

Vocally Jon could be melodic, plaintive or downright raucous. With his untamed look, and usually encased in black leather, he cut an eye-catching figure who was a supple mover. His hunger for success was intense. It shone in the determined gleam in his eyes and was projected by his uncompromising body language. Surrounding his high-energy performance, Tico and Alec were a powerful hard-working rhythm section. David Bryan's keyboard skills were becoming an integral part of the whole sound and Richie Sambora put the rock into Bon Jovi. They were enthusiastic, and patently had immense belief in their own ability.

At this stage, reaching out to a vast audience of their own faithful followers and drawing an ecstatic response from an audience was their key aim. Reality was that they had to work hard not to be demoralised at the outset of a gig when, with almost an hour to go before the start of the headliners' performance, they would often walk on stage to find the auditorium barely a quarter full. When people did file in, audiences tended to split into two distinct categories – idly indifferent or heatedly hostile. One of Richie's clearest memories of those days is of having missiles thrown at them. David Bryan has remained astounded at the lengths that some people in the crowds went to, to try to intimidate them. He revealed that from the stage he could see it coming when fans teamed up to lift increasingly heavy objects, just so that they could lob them at Bon Jovi, who kept performing regardless.

There is no doubt that in their desire to take it on the chin, Bon Jovi went out on some seriously mismatched bills. They were the warm-up act for headliners who spewed aggressive lyrics inciting all kinds of carnage. Which meant that the punters who had paid to enjoy that sort of act had a matching mentality. There was, therefore, a gaping gulf in style between the night's turns. And the onus was always on Bon Jovi, as support band, to bridge it. Every night, it was sink or swim time.

The uphill struggle and the nightly abuse they suffered brought out the fighter in them all. Ultimately, they made it their goal to win over the hearts and minds of the most difficult audiences. They by no means always succeeded, but their individual sense of purpose was strengthened by that collective desire to win through. The valuable by-product of these testing times was that it bonded the members together, until they were much more than a rock band. They became family, a brotherhood who believed that if they stood shoulder-to-shoulder then they could conquer everything.

One band publicist later reflected that at the time it had seemed like Bon Jovi versus everybody. Manager Doc McGhee certainly knew how tough it was for the young band. He had confidence, however, in their resilience. Tico Torres summed matters up when he described the band as a gang, ready to take on the world. And while their self-belief and tenacity brought them through pretty hairy moments, they were also acquiring experience and being exposed to much bigger crowds.

Away from the stage, outside their familiar environment, the Bon Jovi guys also stuck together socially, plunging headlong into the lurid indulgence synonymous with rock and roll, as groupies galore began gathering backstage. Jon once remarked, 'It never failed to surprise me how forward some girls are.' Coming off stage, firing on all cylinders and with the adrenalin still pumping, he was pretty forward himself. As a free agent, he had reverted to his former footloose ways. Only now it was the girls, and lots of them, who were doing the chasing. Looking the way Jon does, it's a fair assumption that he enjoyed the lion's share of the action either in backstage recesses, motels or the tour bus.

Virile publicity photos of Jon Bon Jovi were firing teenage girls' fantasies. He was captured in snakeskin or leather, his jacket slipping off one shoulder, a studded leather belt slung low around his slim hips as he struck poses, often cherishing a guitar like a possessive lover. Not many 22-year-old unattached guys would worry about becoming an object of devotion to a growing army of young, pretty, uninhibited women. But in a way Jon did, for it was vital to him that Bon Jovi be appreciated for its music. He was aware of his looks, and of the help they gave, but deep down it bothered him that the band's attraction should rest on his pin-up pull. So much in the music business is facade, hype and marketing, and as he fast became the primary lightning rod for this side of things, this was an underlying anxiety for Jon from an early stage. To the best of his ability, he used what influence he was permitted by the record company to decline requests for interviews with fluff, teenybop magazines. Never otherwise slow to speak to anyone who would listen to him talk about his band, he hoped to fence off that section whose journalists were more interested in who styled his hair, or if his taste in girlfriends ran to redheads. He wanted Bon Jovi to be taken seriously.

Live performance remained the best arena in which to set out their stall. So, having survived playing support to the Scorpions, when that obligation ended in mid July at the Coliseum in Charlotte, North Carolina, three weeks later Bon Jovi warmed up for Whitesnake before turning their attention to what would be their first British tour. They were backing Kiss this time, and opening night was on 30 September 1984 at the Brighton Centre.

Critically, they got off to a mixed start, when Jon was dismissed by one reviewer as a 'juvenile Steve Tyler', while another declared that Jon was the 'unembarrassing, acceptable face of pop metal.' Comparisons to Aerosmith's singer didn't faze Jon. He remembered having watched Tyler perform around the New Jersey clubs, and didn't argue with the notion that subliminally he had absorbed certain aspects of the flamboyant frontman's style.

Playing in Britain for the first time felt pretty special to Bon Jovi; so did playing support to Kiss. Jon had not forgotten the effect Kiss had had on him when he'd gone to see them as a young boy. It seemed like a dream that here he was with his band, sharing the bill. As far as Kiss was concerned, there was one material difference now. The previous autumn the group so synonymous with visual theatrics had stopped using their trademark face make-up. After ten years in the business Kiss were enjoying a second wind of popularity with the success of *Lick it Up*, and with their explosive stage antics they made for energetic headliners.

This was an entirely different experience to the Scorpions tour. For a start, Kiss vocalist Gene Simmons made a special effort to be welcoming to their support band. Indeed the whole of Kiss showed an unlooked-for degree of indulgent interest in Bon Jovi. Jon and the others responded gratefully to this generosity, and it created a positive backstage atmosphere. Of course, on stage – as is the duty of any self-respecting support band – Bon Jovi set out every night to blow Kiss away, to poach their fans. It produced a good, value-for-money package which Jon thrived on. The tour moved to Cornwall, then up to Manchester and Tyneside, among other places, and paid a fleeting visit to Scotland, before winding its way eventually to London for two nights in mid October at Wembley Arena.

Because there was now no combative energy to be repelled from the audience, on a professional level Jon could at last sense the benefit of being able to imbue his personal performance with the full passion he felt for his lyrics. He could appreciate, too, the corresponding strength and nuance with which his band interpreted these musically. On stage, that intensity gave Jon a raw vibrancy for that 45-minute slot, which couldn't help but communicate to audiences and began at last to start building a Bon Jovi fan base. Some rock journalists, too, were now beginning to spot his star potential.

As yet, though, no one was remotely living the life of a star. Bon Jovi were working hard, but they weren't earning much money. To keep costs to a minimum they were sleeping three to a room. Jon bluntly confessed that they were practically staying in 'whorehouses', since those dives were within their minuscule budgets. None of that mattered. Bon Jovi were only too thrilled to be living the experience and looking forward to telling their friends in New Jersey all about it. After their spin round Europe the band headed back to the States, where the pressure was on to write material for their follow-up album.

For the past nine months, home had been the open road. Coming off tour in the new year, Jon went home – not to mum and dad, but to Sayreville, where he moved into a two-bedroomed apartment and was promptly joined by the rest of the band. It was claustrophobic and sometimes a bit desperate, when on top of a complete lack of privacy, a continuing dearth of funds frequently left them all starving. To alleviate the problem, Jon's father made regular missions of mercy to the apartment, laden with home-made meals for five, courtesy of Carol Bongiovi, who suddenly seemed to have acquired four more sons. He brought extra thick blankets, too, since it was winter time and freezing.

There was one bonus element, however, to the overcrowded setup. At least everyone was in place for intensive discussions about their second album. Jon had been given a mere six weeks to produce the material, and the question uppermost in his mind was – lyrically, what should they be aiming for? He admitted, 'We didn't really know what was expected of us.' It made sense then to fall back on their own experiences. The last year had not brought the desired level of success, but it had wrought some significant changes, and the ten tracks that were pulled together throughout January and February 1985 reflected those.

Jon was sole composer on three of the numbers, and for the rest he again collaborated with one or more members of the band. This song collection embraced tales of love-cheats, of soulless one-night stands, of desire and of failed commitment. A depiction of a tough and lonely life branded itself on to the three-way composition, 'The Hardest Part Is The Night' and disturbed confusion-riddled 'Only Lonely'. It could be argued that the essential theme had not altered much from their debut album. But the difference lay in the increasing maturity and the harder edge inherent in the lyrics.

Tico Torres's retrospective opinion of this work was that it was a thoroughly depressing album, articulating as it did the core unhappiness which at least three of the guys were still struggling with, over their individual broken relationships. Doc McGhee declared in hindsight that to read those lyrics was to want to weep. But they had met the deadline imposed by the record company, and studio work could commence.

By spring 1985 Jon had come to a fork in the road with his father's cousin, Tony Bongiovi, as they became locked in a dispute that would see them sever connections for several years. In the circumstances, the Power Station recording studio was out. So work shifted for Bon Jovi's follow up album to the Warehouse studio in neighbouring Philadelphia, where there was one line of continuity in that they again recorded under the auspices of producer Lance Quinn. This time around, Jon insisted on an increased involvement in the actual production of the new album. At times, it threatened to set Jon at stubborn odds with Quinn, but they were both working towards the same end and ultimately respected each other's position.

Jon would also stand his ground on points such as the sound he drew from his guitar work. The last time around, he felt he had been too malleable in his all-out willingness to take any direction. For this album Jon sought a grittier overall sound, and wanted to develop his vocal range for certain songs. He had been closely studying what he termed the 'real screamers' in music. He already admired gutsy singers like Little Steven, and had become ever more impressed with U2's Bono. He would retain his own individual sound, but he wanted it infiltrated when necessary with that gravelly, grating rasp.

Listening to the final mixes, Jon was not completely convinced that they had achieved everything that they could have with their second album, and not only because of the strict timetable they'd had to adhere to. But there was an elusiveness about what was missing. That was probably because Bon Jovi were, in fact, in the throes of an identity crisis. Jon wanted a voice in the marketplace but he didn't believe that his band had found a niche into which they fitted completely. And the question was – had they come up with an album of songs which would help them establish a niche that they could call their own?

The answer to that appears to have been, no. All around him Jon heard super-confident projections about how this new album was going to do great business and have spin-off hit singles. But to his own way of thinking, it would be a realistic achievement if it could go gold. *7800° Fahrenheit* did earn Bon Jovi a gold disc, but even that aspiration had briefly looked beyond their reach when the first single, 'Only Lonely', released in April, stopped at number 54, and the next cut, 'In And Out of Love', soon after creaked to a halt at number 69.

The second album arrived in May 1985, and in America it bettered *Bon Jovi* by six places, managing to reach number 37. Again it looked like a solo album, with only Jon's face looming dramatically through an orange and blue wash depicting flames on the front cover. Clever lighting highlighted no more than his eyes, nose and part of his left jaw to stylish effect.

The singles' accompanying videos continued to be horrendous. But they did move up a notch in another respect. Although the reviews were again mostly negative, one of Britain's most popular heavy metal magazines, *Kerrang*, praised the new work for being altogether more abrasive. It also ran a lengthy feature interview with the band and put Jon Bon Jovi on the front cover. Pictured in a black leather jacket, leaning forwards on a pool table in a darkened bar, Jon stared half quizzically at the camera. Between his clenched fists on the green baize of the table lay a black Fender Stratocaster guitar. The headline was 'Bon Jovi Some Like it Hot!' The exposure provided by Jon's face staring off shop shelves around the country must have contributed to this album's vastly improved performance in Britain, for it rose to number 28. And although the next single, 'The Hardest Part Is The Night', released late summer, stuck at a lowly 68 in the UK, it nevertheless marked Bon Jovi's first appearance in the British singles chart.

Jon's solo appearance on the magazine front cover, coupled with a full page shot, again of him alone, at the start of the *Kerrang* feature, further cemented his status as the band's figurehead. Although forthcoming to inter-viewers, Jon was also noticeably more reserved than, say, Richie Sambora – more watchful and almost wary. Intrigued journalists could not accuse Jon Bon Jovi of being resistant to interviews, but they were often left slightly unnerved at the level of inner control in someone so young who was the boss of a band.

The weight of responsibility on Jon doubtless played its part in his markedly more sober approach during PR. It was hard to goof around when he knew that he had mounting debts. The new album's performance was clearly not enough to start lifting that burden, and recording and video costs for

7800° Fahrenheit only added to that pressure. Nothing deflected his determination to plough on, though. There was even an element of relishing the challenge of going fearlessly for broke. They *were* broke! They had nothing to fall back on. The only way left was forward. Jon believed that because things were so far out on a limb, it would make achieving their goal so much more rewarding. He never worried that his band-mates did not share his belief. They had already proved their commitment. Richie summed up their position at this point as being one of honest hunger, adding on a personal note, 'Anyway, if I wasn't a musician, what the fuck would I do with my life?'

Because of the performance of their new releases, they had quickly acknowledged that for now Bon Jovi were facing another round of playing support gigs. Jon refused to give way to the bogey that his band was destined to be stuck in this rut, and steered them to his birthplace, Perth Amboy, where they embarked on studious rehearsals in a club called The Seven Arches.

Bon Jovi was lined up for a major tour in summer backing Ratt. But when the band took to the road again in April 1985, after a one-off gig in Munich, they headed from Germany to the Far East, where their album sales already made them headliners, and where Jon's personal popularity was colossal. Doc McGhee confirmed, 'Johnny broke in Japan before he did in America.'

They played dates in Tokyo, Nagoya, Osaka and Sapporo before returning to Europe to trek through France, Sweden, Finland and Holland, prior to arriving in Britain for their first UK headlining tour. With opening act Lee Aaron, Bon Jovi were scheduled to play five theatre and club dates spread over Manchester, Birmingham, London, Newcastle and Edinburgh; the most memorable of these was an appearance on 23 May 1985 at London's Dominion Theatre. All the UK venues had reassuringly sold out and, with each gig, Jon's reservoir of confidence was topped up. But he still felt aware that Bon Jovi could be teetering on a knife edge. In the cut-throat music business, where expectations are quickly set high, how long would the record company stay interested?

It was becoming increasingly obvious that the time a band was given in which to prove itself was shrinking alarmingly; the industry was littered with stories of good bands with potential being prematurely cut loose. For Jon, the night at the Dominion Theatre represented a vital moment in which they needed to pull out all the stops. For this gig his parents had come to the UK capital to see them play. Before taking the stage, Jon urged his band-mates to put on an extra specially ear-bustin' performance for his folks' benefit. 'That way, they'll think we're famous in Britain.' he said.

It became a stand-out gig, but initially for all the wrong reasons. They had scarcely settled in to the performance when a technical glitch made the microphones go dead. That embarrassing hiccup had no sooner been sorted than the sound cut out again. Three times, the band were suddenly plunged into very public trouble. As the saying goes, if you can keep your head while all around are losing theirs, it sets you starkly apart. That night, when by the third cut-out people in the wings and backstage technicians were practically in collective meltdown, Jon abruptly left the stage. The band, and the bewildered audience sitting agog, had only a short time to wait. Then the singer reappeared toting his 12-string acoustic guitar, and proceeded to rope the crowd into a rousing, almost old music hall style singalong while the problem was being ironed out. His charisma and infectious warmth won over the audience who had paid, it seemed now, for the role-reverse privilege of singing back to the frontman at the top of their lungs. Eventually they were enjoying themselves so much that they were almost disappointed when the fault was rectified, allowing the gig proper to get underway.

In the circumstances, with the semi-hostile British music press present, this single headlining gig in the UK capital could have made Bon Jovi a laughing stock. As it was, Jon's cool professionalism earned him firm respect as critics applauded the 23-year-old's deft handling of every band's nightmare scenario. The depth of the response he had drawn from what could have been a feisty crowd had not gone unnoticed either.

Roughly four weeks after the UK trip ended, Bon Jovi embarked on a six-month stadium tour in support of Ratt. Ratt had been enjoying album chart success in America and were still giant arena headliners. But they could doubtless have done without an energised Bon Jovi nipping at their heels. Bon Jovi's confidence in handling such famous venues as the Cotton Bowl in Dallas, the Nassau Coliseum in Uniondale, New York, and New Jersey's Meadlowlands in East Rutherford, was high, and fully justified by the excellent audience response they elicited. It's been said that that response was sometimes too good for Ratt's liking.

Bon Jovi were not being given any great favours by the headliners. There was nothing unique about that. But as the tour went on and continued to be successful for his band, Jon began to feel that they were becoming a less and less welcome presence on the bill. This feeling may have been entirely wrong, but, like a red rag to a bull, it only intensified his desire to make an outstanding impression. He later told journalists that Bon Jovi were 'even more determined to kick their [Ratt's] ass every night.'

On 17 August 1985, Bon Jovi and Ratt stepped briefly out of the tour schedule to appear at the Monsters of Rock festival, the annual heavy metal thrash held at Castle Donington in Leicestershire, England. ZZ Top headlined, with Marillion, Metallica, Ratt and Magnum making up the rest of a bill on which Bon Jovi ranked third. Thrilled to be involved in what was an important event on the musical calendar, Bon Jovi faced a 50,000-strong crowd, having employed a photographer on stage to capture the moment for posterity. Richie Sambora reckons that it was that show which gave him a glimpse of things to come for Bon Jovi. As they left, it was Jon's expressed ambition to return to Castle Donington some day soon as headliners.

Photographs from Donington were meant to act as a spur. Not that Jon needed pictorial proof that he was a bona fide rock star. Even if their two albums had not yet catapulted them to stellar stardom, in some ways he was living the life of a rock god. They all were. Richie unequivocally owned up to the band leading a lifestyle he described as, 'Sex, drugs and rock and roll in full force. If you want to talk percentages, let's talk 100,000 per cent,' he said, adding, 'There wasn't a lot of sleeping going on in my room during these years.' Excepting the drugs bit, Jon was also running the gamut during this whole period. With inelegant frankness, he once put it, 'I had my share of fucking my way through Hollywood. It was like nothing you ever imagined, or can be prepared for.'

When the Ratt tour got back on track after the Monsters of Rock festival, it soon hit America, where they criss-crossed the States for three solid months. On stage, responding to the burgeoning hysteria of nightly audiences was a blast. Spare time was spent in the grip of the sort of excess that had been the staple diet of rock stars for decades. But a shake-up was on the way.

In October 1985, the American matinee idol Rock Hudson died of Aids. This revelation sparked off an intense public awareness of a ravaging disease hitherto not widely recognised. Although at this time the medical profession knew little about the fatal illness, enough was known to ring alarm bells. One of the three high-risk categories quickly identified was those who had unprotected sex with multiple partners.

Looking back, Jon stated, 'We got to enjoy the last hump of wild abandoned fucking and drinking. On a tour bus in 1985 I remember reading a magazine and going, "What's this thing, Aids?"' In a sense it *was* the last chance saloon before the Aids spectre cast a long, deadly shadow over promiscuous behaviour claiming millions of lives worldwide, including high-profile casualties such as Queen's Freddie Mercury.

Right then though, Jon was a rampant young rock star on the loose and telling himself he was having a great time. He maybe chose not to party quite as hard as some, but he played the game and started to taste the social sphere where the worlds of rock music and film overlapped. There, he enjoyed the company of beautiful starlets who came and went. Then Jon met and became involved with New York-born actress Diane Lane, whose recent film credits included *Touched By Love*, *National Lampoon's Movie Madness* and the stylish 1984 Francis Coppola gangster film *The Cotton Club*, in which she had co-starred with Richard Gere, Bob Hoskins and Nicolas Cage. They met backstage at a gig, and the instant attraction was mutual. The relationship would be brief, but long enough not only for the pair to be seen socially together, but also to appear photographed in intimate poses in glossy magazine layouts. They looked a glamorous, attractive couple, but it was not destined to last. That was partly because Jon realised fairly fast that it was not fulfilling for him – any of it, not just the relationship with Diane. The whole jet-set lifestyle was just not him. 'I tested the famous waters in '85', said Jon. 'The movie star girlfriend and the big parties. But I didn't like it.'

The tour ended on New Year's Eve 1985 at the Sports Arena in San Diego, California. By this time, at the crucial point of live contact between artist and audience, Bon Jovi were unmistakably thriving, and their fan base was steadily swelling. Jon hoped they had done enough to show those holding the purse strings that Bon Jovi could yet be a very sound commercial investment if they would just keep faith with the band. The five young men themselves, though, were in a strange situation. There is no doubt that essentially they all wanted to keep going, to try to kick down that door to another level. But these past two years had been a rough, sometimes draining ride. Physically demanding, the tough support slot on the tour circuit had opened their eyes. They had been learning fast, often the hard way, and amid atmospheres of hostility from out front and from backstage. They had shown their mettle and come through it. But they were tired, and frankly had little or no money to show for all their hard work.

Jon was acutely conscious that there is a point where an artiste can slip between the cracks, never to be seen again, and he was anxious for that not to happen to his band. By now he was also intent on distancing Bon Jovi from the thrashing, head-bending rock bands' bracket. His lyrics spoke directly to the man on the street; they would soon start becoming ever more inspirational at grass roots level, and he still wanted them to have their own identity.

Even while high-rolling his way through America, he had never taken his eye off his ultimate aim – to make Bon Jovi massive. But right then the worrying financial burden resting solely on his shoulders meant that behind the screaming adoration, the frantic bustle at autograph signing sessions, and the magazine layouts, the truth was that as a business Bon Jovi was struggling. On a personal level, too, within the band the past couple of years had taken their toll with the two divorces and relationship break-ups. Tico Torres called this period 'about as down and dirty as you can get.' And Jon had come to certain conclusions about the way his off-stage life had been going.

Although he'd resisted acknowledging it for some time, he had missed Dorothea Hurley badly. As the last few gigs wound the tour up, he was increasingly champing at the bit to get home. Home to a way of life in which he felt at ease, and home to see if he could resurrect the love he and his high school sweetheart had found so special for so long. Hardly had his feet touched the ground at Sayreville then, before Jon was heading out to the Hurley family house to persuade his one true love to come back to him, to give their romance a second try.

Whatever Dorothea's personal life had been after breaking up with Jon, she was clearly still susceptible to his charm when he got her alone at her parents' home. Jon later recalled lightheartedly how he came on as the soulful, pleading, hopeful suitor, cheekily grinning, 'And she fell for it.' But while Bon Jovi's wild antics had not come to an end, Jon was sincere in his belief that Dorothea was the woman he wanted to spend his life with. He was on the cusp of stardom, which would bring enormous rewards and added pressures. Having reconnected with his girlfriend, as the new year dawned he felt ready to make the push that would take him and his band to where he wanted to be.

CHAPTER 4

Spiralling Success and Superhuman Stamina

AT THE START OF 1986 when Jon Bon Jovi and Richie Sambora knuckled down to start writing a new batch of songs, Jon had no illusions that this third album could be anything other than do-or-die for the band. He knew that if they could not make that great leap up into a different league this time, then, at best, Bon Jovi risked surviving for a few years trapped in the theatre circuit, at worst, faced becoming a set of fast fading skid marks down music's memory lane. And they did not exactly have the most auspicious surroundings in which to be especially creative.

As part of their renewed commitment to one another, Dorothea left her parents' home, and she and Jon rented a small apartment together on the Jersey coastline. Richie had moved back in with his parents, as the rest of the band made their own individual arrangements. Every day, Jon drove in his white Datsun 280Z to the Sambora house in Woodbridge, having picked up some pizza on the way. Arriving just after noon, he would let himself in with the house key Richie had given him and proceed to wake up the guitarist. Said Jon, 'I'd say, "C'mon! We gotta do something productive today!"

Richie's parents were out at work, so they had an empty house in which to get down to business. The house itself squatted at the end of a dead-end street, right next to a swamp, which meant that the low-ceilinged, concrete basement where the pair made their base was prone to flooding and was perennially damp and cold. Torn insulation hung from the overhead pipes, and the old washing machine vibrated noisily against a brick wall. By the meagre heat of a two-bar electric fire, their fingers often numb, Jon and Richie sat with their acoustic guitars balanced on their thighs, trying to create melodies and come up with inspiring lyrics. A basic cassette tape recorder captured their various ideas, some of which would run out of steam, while others seemed to hold possibilities. The cut-off point was 6.00 p.m., when Mr and Mrs Sambora came home. Leaving Richie to his evening meal, Jon would then return to Dorothea.

Doing this daily became an almost ritualistic exercise during which, by the dim electric light in the airless basement, they began to draw increasingly for inspiration on their recent experiences, their own circumstances and aspirations. By dint of discussing just what they had been through personally and professionally, they started to feel that they were on a different track to previous compositions, that something of substance was evolving.

That proved to be especially true of the song that would become 'Wanted Dead Or Alive', a number Jon later took to referring to on stage as, 'our national anthem'. He and Richie had already talked exhaustively about the itinerant existence of the touring musician, of bowling into a town to earn some money and tangle with the women, before taking off into the night. But this time, Jon began to connect that rootlessness with the lives of the old Wild West outlaws, forever staying just one step ahead of the law. Jon's romantic streak and his overflowing enthusiasm for this concept communicated so precisely to Richie that the guitarist suddenly picked out of thin air a distinctive intro which had all the right overtones. Excited, Jon declared, 'Now, we're talkin'!' and within three hours 'Wanted Dead Or Alive' was nailed.

Pleased as they were with this one song, Jon wanted to pull out all the stops. He decided that it might be beneficial to draft in an outsider, a third party who could inject new blood into this writing process. After asking around, he was put in touch by a Mercury Records executive with New Yorker Desmond Child, a lyricist not so well known in 1986 as he is today, but someone with whom, as it proved from the start, Jon and Richie found a stimulating chemistry. Their collaboration began when Child drove out to Woodbridge, New Jersey. His initial impressions were of a colourless, industrialised location and a small nondescript wooden house at the edge of an ominous-looking misty marsh.

This lacklustre, fairly depressing environment was offset, however, by the near static electricity given off by the vibrant pair he had travelled miles to meet. The dynamics were right between the trio from the second they sat down to talk that afternoon in the basement. Listening carefully, Desmond Child intuitively assessed how the two young men felt about where they were at, how they saw themselves developing musically and which path they had already found opening up before them. After almost two hours of discussion he came up with a title, 'You Give Love A Bad Name.'

Jon's eyes, Child later described, immediately gleamed as he flashed a wide smile. Jon promptly sang out what was actually the title of a song from Bon Jovi's debut album, 'Shot Through The Heart', ad-libbing 'and you're to blame.' Automatically, the three then chorused Child's title, 'You give love a bad name.' Child recalled that as silence fell and they looked at each other, they knew it was a special moment. From that point on the song, which to Jon was a tongue-in-cheek swipe at what a beautiful woman can appear to be, compared to what she is in reality, developed so rapidly that it almost wrote itself. It would become a Bon Jovi pop metal classic.

They could hardly have got off to a better start and, on a roll, the three-way symbiosis quickly produced another future hit, 'Livin' On A Prayer'. Again, so tuned in were the men to the tale of a fictional young couple with nothing but inherent guts and ambition to pull them out of poverty, that the song came together in a single afternoon. 'Livin' On A Prayer' would become the first proudly blue-collar anthem to be forever associated with Bon Jovi. It could not help but strike a universal chord with the masses, because the lyrics came from a genuine understanding of what it is to struggle. And they nakedly stoked the urge to battle one's way out – a very gritty, working-class ethos.

Judging by these two numbers alone, they had patently shifted up the required gear. Confidence bloomed and the creative juices flowed even faster. It made for an incredibly energised and very emotive time for Jon. He wanted urgently to seize the moment. He was up against the wall financially, and desperately needed to bring the brotherhood through the testing times and to make worthwhile the sacrifices they had all endured in the name of their communal belief.

It was easier, too, to maintain a round-the-clock focus, because away from the cauldron of creativity in that basement, Jon was not confronted with any distracting pressure from Dorothea for them to marry and start a family, as most of their hometown peers were doing. Conventionality was never their thing. Jon would always openly admire Dorothea's innate self-possession, which he partly attributes to her involvement in martial arts – she has become a black belt in karate. She was a lady who would clearly carve out her own path in life. But her commitment to supporting Jon in his cause was now absolute, and that supplied him with a solid base from which to operate. His dream was their dream, and they would sometimes drive around New Jersey's more affluent areas, gazing out of the car windows at the opulent houses, seeing how the other half lived and wondering if there would come a day when they could afford a luxury home.

Buying a fancy mansion set in lush acres would be a by-product of success for Jon. His principal motivation was to prove himself right. In his head he had believed for ten years in his ability to become a successful rock star. As he approached his 24th birthday in spring 1986, he took the next step towards attaining that goal. After an intensive period of productivity, with and without Desmond Child, which provided a pool of about 40 songs, the band booked time at Century Productions, a small recording facility in Sayreville, to start making demos.

Perhaps it was because it was so vital to be right that Jon was, oddly, the hardest to be totally convinced about some of their material, now that they were out of the basement and working in a recording studio with the rest of the band. Even with its catchy, soaring chorus, 'Livin' On A Prayer' momentarily gave him pause. Was it really that good? Playing devil's advocate, Jon felt that he had to challenge his belief in the songs. For it may have been born out of a brew of claustrophobic excitement and desperation. His uncertainty did not reign long. When he voiced his doubts about 'Prayer' to Richie, Sambora stared at his co-songwriter as if he had suddenly sprouted a second head, before declaring stoutly that it had number one written all over it. Although smiling, Jon knew his friend's vast capacity for optimism. So, to be sure, they agreed to solicit a second opinion. At Mercury Records the marketing department personnel were eager to hear Bon Jovi's latest offerings. Instead, the band chose to try them out on local teenagers who hung out at a nearby pizza parlour. Although the work was far from finished, the band would periodically take a break and drift round to the busy café clutching their demo tapes and a portable tape deck, to invite some blunt criticism from a sample of their target audience.

With two gold albums under their belt and in their own stomping ground, they were obviously local celebrities. But the New Jersey psyche being what it is, Jon was confident that they would still get an in-your-face, unvarnished opinion of the songs. And they did. There was no effusive sycophancy. As Jon later revealed, the thumbs-up for a number came more in the shape of comments such as, 'Well, it doesn't suck.' High praise indeed, but enough to allay the anxiety that tunnel vision could have been an unwitting enemy.

By late spring, once the material had been heard at this still raw stage by the record label executives, proper recording work could commence; this time with producer Bruce Fairbairn at the helm. Canadian-born Fairbairn had produced *The Revolution By Night*, the 1983 album by the guitar-laden, heavy rock band Blue Oyster Cult. But it was his work with Loverboy that had attracted Bon Jovi's attention. Both Jon and Richie appreciated a certain sonic sound Fairbairn had brought to some records; a quality they anticipated might complement their own basically power-filled songs. For his part, Bruce was keen to work alongside such a committed outfit.

A stickler himself, Fairbairn could have no doubts about the band's appetite for work. But to concentrate their minds even more, he suggested that Bon Jovi should seek fresh fields in which to record this all-important third album. Perhaps the producer also felt it would be advisable to shift Bon Jovi from their New Jersey moorings to a place he himself was more familiar with, so as to increase his control over proceedings. At any rate, the band agreed to decamp to Vancouver in British Columbia, Canada, where they quickly got underway with recording sessions at Little Mountain Sound Studios.

Bruce Fairbairn also brought in Bob Rock, a studio engineer with whom he had worked before. For the first time ever, Bon Jovi felt that they were, studio-wise, in the grip of a taskmaster. Fairbairn certainly opened Jon's eyes with his ultra methodical approach to every step in the proceedings; it was an attention to detail that dovetailed neatly with Jon's own attitude. Every day, they worked hard from entering the studio till about 11.00 p.m. But just as they worked hard, so they partied hard when they were unleashed on to the late night streets.

Bon Jovi's two months in Vancouver would go down in the band's folklore as a binge of unparalleled off-duty decadence. Not far from Little Mountain Sound Studio, they had rented one of the middle units in a condominium, which was a pink stucco building with tacky plastic flamingo birds piercing the ground in the communal front yard. The two-bedroomed apartment quickly became a tip. Tico Torres admitted, 'There was soon garbage everywhere.'

Neighbours were driven crazy by the volume of the stereo blasting music out till all hours of the morning. That's when the five were at the apartment. Most of their leisure hours were spent in the city's lurid red-light district. They tended to favour about six different seedy establishments. One in particular, a small showroom pub called No. 5 in Orange Street, brought the group back again and again. In this joint the salacious delights on offer for the attentive clientele included saucy strippers who would scissor their shapely legs around the top of a gleaming pole and slide slowly, suggestively, down from the ceiling to the stage. At this point they would strip naked, then step into a specially constructed shower stall to writhe about, soaping themselves intimately.

Lap dancers were one thing. But this? Jon recalled, 'It was total nudity', pointing out that these Vancouver beauties lathering up were doing things that no New Jersey girl did – at least, none that he had ever come across. He liked the atmosphere, he said. It was just the place to chill out apparently. Frankly, their first experience of the No. 5 strip shows floored the five rock stars, who thought they had already seen it all. 'We just about lost our tongues', Richie

Sambora confessed, admitting with equal candour that they made an instant pact to come back every single night. Other adult attractions featured messy female mud wrestlers falling out of the skimpiest of bikinis, and go-go dancers who were only too happy to come back to the band's apartment to provide background entertainment while the guys drank and played cards.

What with the music, the drinking and the sounds of high spirits coming from the centre flat in the otherwise respectable block of apartments, it was not long before their name began to be bandied about Vancouver. Whether Jon restricted himself to just looking at the women is not clear. For a particular period of time, starting from his reconciliation with Dorothea, it would never be entirely known if, or when, Jon strayed from the straight and narrow in the fidelity stakes. And he played his own part in muddying those waters.

In years ahead, he would tell journalists openly that he was in town to play a gig, get laid and get gone. He would also confess to having sometimes fallen off his pedestal, would publicly tell audiences over the mike that he had sometimes given Dorothea cause to kick his backside. But he has always been careful to give no specific details of any unfaithfulness. About the wild social aspect of this Vancouver excursion, all he would say in general terms was that when they went home once the trip ended, they all had a hard time being believed by the women in their respective lives.

Regardless of the excess going on outside the studio, the band were committed to creating a special album this time. When it came to recording 'Livin' On A Prayer', Richie introduced the talkbox, a device which allows a guitarist to form word-like noises by channelling the sound through a tube leading to a mouthpiece set alongside the microphone. It added a distinctive quality that made people sit up and take notice, though it wasn't a new contraption – talkboxes had been around since the mid-1970s. Richie had used one when he played in a school band and, somewhat shyly, he had produced it for use in this number now. He had envisaged exactly how to make a difference to the sound of 'Prayer'. But when he started up, the rest of the band thought he was clowning, and laughed at him. Bruce Fairbairn, however, liked the unique touch it added, and so the talkbox became an integral part of the song's sound, making 'Livin' On A Prayer' instantly recognisable from its first note.

During these eight weeks there was only one track that presented any difficulties – surprisingly it was 'Wanted Dead Or Alive'. It had swung together so fast in the Sambora basement, but capturing it in the studio proved elusive. Fairbairn knew how recklessly the guys were behaving during their off-duty hours, and while none of them ever showed up at the studio drunk or unable to work, he had made it obvious from the start that he took a very conservative approach to recording sessions which kept the five within strict boundaries, something they completely respected. As frustration over this one number mounted, the producer could see that the band was becoming as tight as a drum, particularly since they were planning to make 'Wanted Dead Or Alive' the title track.

Before heads could sink any lower, Fairbairn stopped the session one evening and surprised the guys by taking them out for a meal at which he actually encouraged them to crack open some wine. He was quietly monitoring their consumption, but it was all it took. Steered astutely back to restart the session, Bon Jovi was suddenly buzzing. David Bryan let loose with his vision that they should see the track in cinemascope, so to speak, that what it lacked was the atmospheric qualities which conjured up vast open, inhospitable spaces and the tangible threat of danger and death. It was a mood his band-mates locked into, and by the second tape they had nailed it. Prone himself to being a taskmaster, Jon registered how their producer had taught him a valuable lesson that night.

The euphoria of capturing 'Wanted Dead Or Alive' further fuelled the idea of naming the album after this track. So it was a logical step when they visualised a Wild West look to the album cover. Caught up with the romance of it, the band all grew beards, obtained the requisite long coats, holsters and battered cowboy hats and headed up into the Vancouver mountains to a deserted mine shaft with photographer Mark Weiss.

To Bon Jovi, 'Wanted Dead Or Alive' meant masculine moodiness. They were keen to appeal to male fans in their quest not be perceived as pop metal pretty boys. Overall, the album material was actually a fine blend of tough and tender songs, but they wanted to promote the more rugged aspect. The concept evolved into a cover design like a wanted poster from days gone by, depicting five individual lean, mean, desperado faces. Sporting a beard and moustache, and with his long scrunched hair peering out from under the worn brim of his hat, Jon was actually fairly striking in this get-up. In fact, they all looked like Hollywood versions of the Younger Brothers.

Weiss was a good photographer and a friend. But somewhere, somehow it became clear that what had originally seemed a great idea was starting to slip. When Doc McGhee was tipped off by Tico Torres that the band were dressed up as cowboys for this shoot, his response was stark. 'You're from New Jersey, for Christ's sake!' he spluttered, 'Not cowboys. Get the fuck out of there!' They would kick around with different looks, at one stage departing so far from the macho image that Jon concluded they looked like girls! That was a nonstarter. Abandoning the Wild West idea, they headed back down the mountain to rethink their strategy in the familiar surroundings of the No. 5 showroom pub.

Chalking up another piece of Bon Jovi folklore, the actual title of their third album was born out of their debauched surroundings. Doc McGhee is said to have spotted a traffic sign on the road leading to the mountains, which warned motorists of slippy conditions when wet. But the moment the manager put the suggestion of *Slippery When Wet* to Jon sitting in the strip joint, it took on a whole new connotation when, before his still not jaded eyes, yet another erotic blonde slid teasingly down the pole, undressed and headed languorously to the shower stall. Richie recalled exchanging looks with Jon, grinning and agreeing that it sounded about right to them.

With a totally different album cover concept to work on, photographer Mark Weiss headed back to New Jersey, ready to find himself a buxom beauty to take centre stage. It wasn't hard. As soon as he patrolled the Jersey beaches and boardwalks he found plenty of potential candidates willing to be photographed in a torn, tight, wet T-shirt for a rock album cover.

While the new artwork was under way, time was up for the band in Vancouver and the recording sessions were over in the nick of time. The residents at the condo complex had been fast losing patience with the on-going nocturnal antics of the boisterous rock stars. Besides the noise and the rubbish (now stacking up outside, since the flat was near wrecked inside), the neighbours were often made nervous in the early hours of the morning by the furtive jangling sounds as one or more of the band scaled the security gates and fences to get into the grounds, having lost their key for the umpteenth time. Bon Jovi would never earn a reputation for loutish, destructive behaviour, but during this one brief phase they went a fair way to making a start. As it happened, they made good the mess they had caused by paying to have the apartment completely redecorated and new carpets laid before they were visited by the Vancouver police, who asked them firmly to leave.

With the upcoming record releases, thoughts turned quickly to videos – till now the perennial thorn in their side. Haunted by past disasters, Jon was understandably intent that they pull themselves out of that particular mire. The key player in the rescue was video director Wayne Isham, whose whole approach turned previous efforts on their head. Jon made it clear that they would brook no conceptual nonsense anymore, no B-rate storytelling promo films. Like the others, what he yearned for was to be seen as themselves. Simplicity itself, Isham's idea was to film them in live performance but, crucially, to present them as major stars already.

He scouted out an abandoned auditorium in downtown Los Angeles which was ideal for what he had in mind. Isham then had an impressive stage setting put together, which incorporated an elaborate lighting rig geared up for special effects, and had Bon Jovi written in huge slanted lettering all along the stage floor. Filmed from virtually any angle, the band name stood out boldly. A call was put out over a local radio station for anyone who wanted to come along and make up the fictitious gig crowd. Admittance, of course, was free and Bon Jovi promised to play for the audience between takes. The combination was perfect. The band, fired up by the whole idea, were itching to perform out of their skins, and an enthusiastic crowd of teenagers showed up ready to rock. 'It just exploded!' said Wayne Isham. And indeed the exchange of energy was electrifying. In their element, Bon Jovi let rip. Jon conveyed a mix of strut and fun. He was by turns sexy and playful, bombastic yet tantalisingly natural, and the band camaraderie shone through strongly. Before he viewed the final cuts, Jon knew that they had at last been captured as they really were.

Confidence levels had been topped up high, but they were not yet the headliners that their new videos projected. Even so, this seemed almost academic to the band in July 1986, when they faced the reality of stepping back into the support role, opening for Judas Priest. In a way it was a retrograde step. For here they were battling again for hearts on a grossly mismatched bill. Judas Priest were leather-clad veterans chiselled out of the early 1970s hard rock mould. Vocalist Rob Halford's flamboyant stage act included such theatrics as invading the stage on a Harley-Davidson.

Bon Jovi, though, were experienced in devising ways to upstage larger-than-life headliners. Anyway, as they toured Canada they were bolstered by the building anticipation of their upcoming album release. This suffered a setback that put Jon into a spin the moment he returned home. He had not been shown how the *Slippery When Wet* album cover artwork had been developing, and was appalled when he did get first sight. The raunchy, busty babe on the front could be construed as a very rock-oriented image. But although some songs were racy, others romantic, and passion in its various forms certainly saturated the album, major tracks like 'Livin' On A Prayer' were more indicative of Jon's vision for the band.

What really got him was the colour scheme. 'The damn cover was *pink*!' he exclaimed later, the passage of time unable to dilute his disgust. As a New Jersey guy there was no way he could tolerate having a sugar-pink border on the album sleeve. Immediately, the cry went out to the record label that this artwork could survive only over his dead body.

There were only four weeks until the album's release date. Left in no doubt about Jon's irate sentiments, Mercury Records magnanimously agreed to provide a new album cover. The snag was that Jon had to come up with his preferred replacement artwork in one day. If he couldn't do that, the only option would be to delay the release. Galvanised, Jon rushed over to Mark Weiss's New Jersey studio, arriving like a whirling dervish. Weiss had been forewarned by phone of the problem, but was at a loss as to what they could conjure up between them in the space of a day. Jon demanded a black refuse bag, and Weiss watched as the singer flattened it out, liberally sprinkled water on it, then used one fingertip to scrawl *Slippery When Wet*. Jon said, 'Quick! Photograph that!' And that was it.

Mercury Records accepted the idea, and it was a last-minute save as far as Jon was concerned. Because the release date was so close, 300,000 copies of the album with the pink cover had already been shipped for release in Japan. Mercury Records more than proved their commitment to Bon Jovi when they destroyed half a million copies of the unloved version held in their warehouses.

Slippery When Wet with its new cover was released in mid-August 1986, having been preceded earlier in the month by the first cut off the album, 'You Give Love A Bad Name'. The single would peak in Britain at number 14, providing Bon Jovi with their first major UK chart breakthrough. But that achievement was easily eclipsed by the single's popularity in the States. US radio adored it and gave it massive airplay, to the delight of both the band and the record label. It was instant reward for the latter's faith in Bon Jovi, and more than recompensed them for the costly debacle over the album cover when 'You Give Love A Bad Name' steadily winged its way to number one in the charts. There is always someone ready to rain on your parade, though, and the band took some fairly hefty critical broadsides.

Perhaps taken by surprise by the skyrocketing performance of the new single from a band towards which they had always been tepid, some reviewers were decidedly uncomplimentary about Bon Jovi. The critics' attitude would occasionally irritate Jon immensely, especially when someone would take a song title and make a puerile play on words with it. *Rolling Stone* delivered the put-down that Bon Jovi were 'a third generation smudgy xerox of Quiet Riot'. David Bryan was so affected by the swipe that he kept the review and framed it, confident that one day the influential rock magazine would have to change its mind about the band. In fact, nine months later, Jon Bon Jovi in full rock star pose dominated the front cover of its 500th edition.

With their single and the album snowballing, Bon Jovi honoured their continuing touring commitments by supporting the band .38 Special on a US arena tour, commencing in September. In Britain *Slippery When Wet* lodged at number six, but in America it just kept rising. On a nightly basis the band could also see the signs, not only in the increasingly wild audience response, but also in other ways, such as the sudden hike in their front-of-house merchandising sales figures. Doc McGhee rubbed his hands the harder it became to keep pace with demand for the album.

By late October 1986 *Slippery When Wet* had gone platinum, taken pole position in the US album charts and held on to it for a massive 15 weeks in all. It was undeniably Bon Jovi's defining moment. When the album hit the top, the band received the news in Iowa, having earlier opened for .38 Special. They were crammed into a room at a local Holiday Inn and their response was to get into a group hug, something akin to a rugby scrum where all five heads are bent together and, with their arms around each other's back, they form an impenetrable circle. They then proceeded to get blind drunk.

For the first six months *Slippery When Wet* sold a million copies a month, going on eventually to exceed the 14 million mark worldwide. By November 'You Give Love A Bad Name' notched up as Bon Jovi's first million-selling single globally. By then the second cut, 'Livin' On A Prayer', had soared to number four in Britain and was destined to duplicate its predecessor's achievement in America by seizing the top slot in the singles charts. Bon Jovi looked unstoppable. Certainly, they were nobody's opening band now. They began travelling between gigs by chartered Lear jet. Initially, it was a treat organised by Doc McGhee. Then the tour's promoters continued the practice, happy to pick up the tab for the luxury arrangement because the tills were jangling.

By November 1986, Bon Jovi were big enough to strike out confidently on their own. Jon had always been aware that a band usually gets only one true window of opportunity to make that leap up to major league headliners. Fans in their droves had to be baying at the doors and queuing round the block to get into venues. Empty seats night after night would quickly cause disgruntled promoters to pull the plug and turn their backs on them, perhaps forever.

By the time Bon Jovi completed a month-long headlining blitz of Britain and Europe, any fears on that front were firmly scotched. Their fan base was exploding, and for those keeping a shrewd eye on the demographics, it was working out at a 60-40 split, in favour of female fans. The hallmark of any band which goes on to enjoy a long shelf life is a good solid proportion of male fans at its base, topped up with a higher percentage of female followers.

Bon Jovi got mobbed wherever they went. Fighting their way to and from the stage, all five were just about torn to pieces. Girls in the grip of lusty hysteria for Jon would expose their breasts for him to autograph, before seizing his head with both hands and pulling him forward to kiss him. On stage, Jon whipped up a frenzy as a colossal tour of America rolled out from mid-December. As the year drew to a close, Jon Bon Jovi was *the* top sex symbol in rock, and his intoxicating combination of sizzling sensuality and playful fun was developing apace

Revelling in the proof that they had reached their goal by being who they really were, and not by trying to fit in with prevailing trends, on stage Jon often favoured leather jackets and patched jeans, torn at the knees. Or long leather fringed coats which, with his long hair and flowing scarves would create a swirl of energy around him as he rushed about the stage, getting down and dirty to the music. A Bon Jovi concert was a dazzling, blood-pumping, breathless event. Never more so than when Jon stunned the audience by literally soaring up off the stage during 'Livin' On A Prayer' and 'flying' over their heads.

This show-stopping spectacle was achieved courtesy of theatrical wires, almost invisibly attached to a body harness worn under his coat and operated by pulleys on the roof of the auditorium. One second Jon would be belting out the song, punctuating the lyrics with a fierce clench of a fist, a sudden knee jerk or sharp kick. Then his run across the stage would suddenly take him clean over the edge and up into mid air, far out into the theatre, to loud gasps of shock and delight. In a shower of sparks, carrying his microphone stand pointed forward, he looked like a superhuman rock god.

The stunt required a deal of trial and error to get used to taking off and landing with flair so that it wouldn't look stupid. The crucial piece of equipment was the harness, which Jon stepped into like a paratrooper getting kitted up, pulled up behind his back, over his shoulders and fastened at his waist. Alec and Richie tried out these harnesses too, and at times in practice sessions there were mid-air collisions when they would bump off each other, their legs pumping thin air, their arms flailing.

On the night, though, it was always perfect, dramatic and effective; familiarity never bred contempt. Even after pulling off this stunt countless times, Jon still experienced mixed emotions. At one point he revealed, 'I'm getting to be a cocky son-of-a-bitch on this thing, but I get scared every time. Flying without a safety net, man? You fall, and it's all over! You hold on to this thing and your knuckles are white and you're thinkin', "Jesus! Why am I doing this? Please God, don't let me fall!"'

The reward for the risk was the initial look of awe on the fans' beaming upturned faces, and the thrilled smiles that showed they felt thoroughly entertained. During this whole period and for some considerable time to come that is what absorbed Jon's every waking thought – how to ensure that the band's two-hour stage set each night gave as much stimulus and pleasure to the audience as possible.

The other all-important reward was money. Jon Bon Jovi was never going to be the kind of rock star who finds out once or twice a year how much the record company says he has earned and is due to be paid. Having shouldered the financial burden, and aware that he had started out green in some respects, he now attended closely to every financial detail. He was in regular conference with those handling the business side of the band and was meticulous in studying the real-life corporate mechanics behind the glitzy glamour. At last, after years of scraping by, hard cash was finally beginning to flow their way. Tico Torres still unashamedly salutes the day he received his first cheque for $100,000. Although he needed to cash it, he did hang on to it for a while, just for the pleasure of looking at it.

The spiralling success was all the sweeter because they had struggled together to earn their breakthrough and had done it the hard way. Nothing has ever been handed on a plate to Bon Jovi. Although Jon is very much the boss, there is no doubt that, far from stardom establishing the five as confident, self-sufficient individuals, it actually served to meld the fraternity even closer together. Unlike any other rock outfit, perhaps, the bigger they became, the more firmly they closed ranks. They really trusted only each other, along with a very small select number of satellite others.

Rock bands are generally notorious for accumulating a thicket of nefarious hangers-on, from which betrayal of all kinds can stem. No one in Bon Jovi would tolerate such an entourage. They were also all too aware that fame would make them the focus of intense media attention, and a pact was made there and then never to let leaks develop around the band. This strict code saw anyone external to the band and the chosen inner circle as an outsider. Certain sections of the media nicknamed the setup 'the Jersey Syndicate'. Jon openly mused whether it was the old Italian/American-New Jersey heritage kicking in as self-protection, and joked that it came from an over-exposure to *The Godfather* movies. But he was solemnly serious that whatever went on in the band was not to be spoken about freely.

Loyalty is a concept that has always been very dear to Jon Bon Jovi. So much so that in 1986 he had a limited number of diamond-studded gold pendants specially made; he gives these on rare occasions to those people whom he considers to be close friends, worthy of his trust. Jon's youngest brother, Matt Bongiovi, wears his pendant with glowing pride, and has maintained that the medallion means so much to those in the band's organisation that to be presented with one by Jon, and thereby made part of the select brotherhood, is enough to make rough and ready guys emotional.

The valuable pendants form the outline of the Superman badge and sport two slanted S-shapes that match the *Slippery When Wet* logo. Sticking with the Superman theme, as Bon Jovi became the biggest band on the planet, Jon got himself a Superman tattoo high on his left arm. He said he felt superhuman, which was hardly surprising. Quite apart from the ear-ringing adulation greeting him every night he walked on stage, and his emulating the comic strip hero by flying over the audience's heads, his seemingly endless stamina was carrying him through a mind-blowingly tough schedule. Exhilarated, drenched in sweat and with his heart thumping by the end of a gig, Jon would look out over the crowd, slightly bemused at the sight of sheets unfurled over balconies with giant messages such as, 'We'd die for U Jon'. He engendered a deep devotion that was sometimes frightening in its intensity.

The Slippery When Wet tour already amounted to their longest stretch on the road, and life was fast becoming a blur of performing, travelling, photo sessions and media interviews, at which 90 per cent of the time Jon was the main focus. Jon invariably also arrived at venues ahead of the rest of the band to consult with everyone from promoters to on-site technicians, to make sure that everything was as it should be. After that, he had to perform. Jon adores performing. He has admitted that he doesn't know what he would do if he were never to get on stage again. But when witnessing the crush waiting outside venues, the eager faces of those at the front of the masses pressing against the windows and doors, the pressure would build up. The toughened glass often muffled their yells. Jon knew well, though, what was expected of him.

In the dressing room and the backstage corridors he would psyche himself up by doing exercises to flex his muscles, would slap brick walls with his palms and frantically dodge about shadow-boxing before joining the other hyper band members to face the delirious crowd waiting in the auditorium. A raw chemistry nightly energised band and crowd alike in an exhilarating shared experience that provided an addictive rush. By the time the new year arrived though, this had become extremely debilitating. Yet there was no stopping the juggernaut.

During the award season, in early 1987 Bon Jovi's meteoric rise was publicly acknowledged when at the annual American Music Awards the band took the trophy as Favourite Pop/Rock Band and also won the People's Choice Award as Band of the Year. Later in the year, Bon Jovi lifted the Best Performance Award for the video of 'Livin' On A Prayer' at the fourth MTV Music Awards ceremony, held at Universal Amphitheatre in Universal City, California. Although Jon welcomed the recognition, the level of responsibility he carried increased all the more. 'Everything moves twice as fast,' he said at the time. 'You have to sell even more records, become not just big but huge, become smarter, understand the business side even more.' Driven by demand, the tour schedule of sold-out shows became a killer.

Jon could have begun to apply the brake, but he wouldn't. Although tired, the band were just as keen to carry on. Richie Sambora later laughed about their bravado attitude that they could handle anything and keep going. He also pointed out that being alongside a guy with Jon's ambition meant that you had to be prepared to keep up. The comfort in which they travelled had taken another step up; now they crisscrossed the States in a Grumman G-I airplane with the band name emblazoned in huge lettering on the fuselage. But the extra dates that the plane helped them to accommodate added to the cranked-up tension.

In a practical sense, too, Jon began to find the luxury confines on board a bit overpowering at times. And by January 1987 after a gig in Phoenix, Arizona, he opted for once to separate from the band and be driven alone in the tour bus to San Diego in California for the next gig, so that he could catch up on some much-needed sleep.

He was a young man, not yet 25 years old, who worked out and was physically fit, but he was driving himself too hard. A measure of how shattered he had become recently showed itself when, in an uncharacteristic burst of temper, he lashed out and hit someone. The incident happened at a radio convention, where the drink had proved better quality than the dinner. The Dom Perignon champagne went down too well on a near-empty stomach, in a tired and stressed-out body ready to snap. All it took was a passing remark from a stranger to light Jon's short fuse. 'So I hit him,' said Jon. 'I couldn't believe it. I kept going up to him and saying, "I'm sorry! I'm sorry!"'

With crossing different time zones and experiencing extreme shifts in the weather, Jon's body clock was also knocked for six. From playing on the snowbound east coast in the grip of winter, the band had then transplanted itself to desert country where temperatures were nudging 80 degrees. Jon's system decided spring had arrived and he was promptly plagued with allergies which made his throat start to seize up. Calling in unknown medics on tour has always been a dodgy area for rock stars, and Jon had had his share of quacks who were only too willing to respond to a call from the band's management, but also only too quick to assume that the celebrity patient was a drug addict. As the problem worsened, Jon was in the grip of agony and anxiety over his voice. He needed to sing well, and for that reason he began accepting offers to take cortisone. Later, the crushing pressures of touring drove Jon to have regular steroid injections, something he soon looked back on with regret.

In time he would find a better way of handling matters; for one thing organising his own personal touring physician who was skilled in various healing arts, including acupuncture. But for now, he was in trouble. Although his exhaustion was starting to show itself to the media, Jon was loth to complain. When pressed as to whether high-pressure fame was taking its toll, he retorted, 'We worked our asses off to get where we are today. Everything's cool.'

Just before Bon Jovi were to take the stage before 15,000 fans corralled into the San Diego Soccers' home stadium, one out of town radio station crew belatedly intruded backstage, demanding a live interview with the frontman on the spot just at the time when Jon, like the rest of the band, was mentally concentrating on readying himself for the show. Before anyone could refuse on the grounds of it being sacrosanct time, a not-so-veiled threat is said to have been issued by one of the radio crew that to reject their request could result in that station never playing a Bon Jovi record again. If true, it's doubtful that it would have made any detectable difference to the band's fortunes. Everyone wanted a piece of Bon Jovi. For six months prior to early 1987, they were the band most requested by MTV viewers.

As the massive tour continued through California and Nevada to Texas and beyond, one persistent matter niggled away at them all. That was the pin-up image, now in such manic overdrive that they all had to disguise themselves if they wanted to venture out of doors. On the rare occasions when the band took time out to attend public events, it usually ended in chaos. In February, the tour hit Florida; after playing St Petersburg, they hung around next day to take part in a local charity softball match at the Al Lopez Field. The game got under way, despite the massed ranks of Bon Jovi fans on the sloping spectator benches working themselves into hysterics at the sight of Jon. Then all hell broke loose when restraint evaporated and they stormed on to the pitch. It was game over as the singer was tackled to the ground and vanished under an avalanche of weeping, overwrought girls.

The next night, at the Civic Center in Fort Myers, determined fans battered through the perimeter gates with such force that the venue doors were opened early to avoid a potential disaster. And during their final Florida gig in Jacksonville, girls in the audience started removing items of clothing and throwing them on stage. Near knee-deep in knickers, the band played valiantly on, Jon deftly dodging a shower of frilly garters with invitations and telephone numbers pinned to them.

It was partly in an effort to bolster their appeal to male fans that the band disagreed with the record company's choice of the next single from *Slippery When Wet*, and instead advocated the release of 'Wanted Dead Or Alive'. The cowboy-ethos rock ballad had the kind of gritty connotations to appeal to guys. Released in April 1987, the single reached number 13 in Britain but peaked six places higher in the US.

The video for 'Wanted Dead Or Alive' was shot on tour and the footage gave the biggest signal of the breakdown in health that was afflicting the whole band. Dressed up in a long silver coat, Jon wore scarves tied around his head, was weighed down with tons of junk jewellery, and had his guitar slung down by his side. It looked dramatic, but could not disguise the fact that he was a total wreck. Live on stage, he certainly looked different to the face which shone out from the front cover of *Rolling Stone*'s 500th issue in late May 1987. Alongside the title 'Hot Throb: Bon Jovi', Jon, clutching the lapels of a black leather jacket, looked clear-eyed and brimming with health.

As the band barrelled through Indianapolis, Kentucky, Ohio and Michigan to Chicago, Illinois, the main problem again became his voice. It wasn't just allergies now. He was experiencing severe voice strain, and on top of the serious discomfort to his vocal cords, it also had a very lowering mental effect. Usually sitting some way detached from everyone else, as the band travelled between pit stops, Jon spent hours preoccupied and quiet. Jon recalled, 'All I could think about was, "I can't sing another note. I'll never hit the high notes on 'Prayer.'"' It darkened his mood even more to know that there were several months to go yet, months that were choc-a-bloc with gigs.

Some help was at hand. David Bryan and Richie Sambora, who sang back-up vocals anyway, would step in whenever they realised their friend was in trouble. And the crowds' unending devotion would give Jon a lift. Ultimately, he had to enlist a vocal coach to help him get through the rest of the tour, and had to tough it out. But he was more unwell than he would admit. The steroids were hurting, not helping him. He was bloated, yet losing weight and desperately trying to hide the ravages. Some nights he was violently sick minutes before going on stage, knocking his guts out to perform as if everything was alright, and heading for the basin to vomit the second he was off.

As the band approached one complete year on the road, Jon privately admitted to suffering severe fatigue. Yet at gigs, in an almost reckless denial of his condition, he would leap off stage into the audience, risking worse physical injury than having his clothes torn and his body scratched by clawing fingernails. Jon didn't really confront the full extent of his health problems until he was given photographic proof.

During the first half of August, Bon Jovi played a succession of gigs at Madison Square Garden, New York, Meadowlands in East Rutherford, New Jersey and the Nassau Coliseum in Uniondale, New York. He was accustomed to receiving a variety of gifts from promoters and the like. But then he was presented with a framed photograph of himself taken at this time, which he had every intention of hanging proudly on a wall when he got home. Until he took a good long look at it, that is. Appalled, Jon stared unblinkingly hard at the ashen face with sunken eyes ringed with black. 'I looked fuckin' dead!' he later admitted.

Relentlessly, the Slippery When Wet tour promptly left America for Britain, where the sentimental ballad, 'Never Say Goodbye' had recently reached number 21 in the singles chart. Bon Jovi were in the UK to fulfil a dream by headlining at the annual open-air Monsters of Rock Festival held at Castle Donington, Leicestershire, on 22 August 1987. It was the first time that this UK one-day rock event featured only American acts; the other performers were Anthrax, Dio, W.A.S.P., Cinderella and Metallica. It was while Metallica were performing that the headliners arrived in some style in two helicopters with 'Bon Jovi' emblazoned on the side.

In typical British summer style the rains had come, turning the field into a mud bath for the 65,000 rock fans. But it wasn't the inclement weather which dampened the show for Jon. Although thrilled to be back as top of the bill, he exhibited all the brittleness that comes of trying desperately to hide his true worn-out state from those around him. 'We shouldn't have been there,' Jon later reflected candidly. 'I was really too ill. I couldn't sing and we looked like death. It's a shame, because I don't look back on that Donington fondly, and I should.'

Although the crowd thoroughly enjoyed Bon Jovi's performance, for Jon there were a couple of hiccups. First, his planned spectacular arrival on stage by sliding down a rope from the overhead lighting rig to the mike went unnoticed, because the guy working the singer's spotlight wasn't on station in time. Then the encore was slightly marred. The band summoned several fellow music stars from backstage and the audience to join them for a rendition of Grand Funk Railroad's 'We're An American Band'. But while the likes of Iron Maiden's singer Bruce Dickinson, plus Gene Simmons and Paul Stanley from Kiss were happy to oblige, when Jon approached Metallica's vocalist James Hetfield and drummer Lars Ulrich to take part, he felt himself to be snubbed.

Quitting Britain for Australia, then Japan, the tour finally ended in Honolulu, Hawaii, on 16 October 1987. In 16 gruelling months Bon Jovi had circled the globe, playing 200 sold-out shows. Towards the end of 1987 they had made the multi-platinum *Slippery When Wet* officially the biggest-selling hard rock album of all time, so far. Having grossed over $28.5 million, the band members who had been flat broke at the outset, ended the backbreaking tour as rich young men. The difference in Bon Jovi's status in the space of two years was astounding, and Jon had every reason to allow himself to take his foot off the pedal just a touch, even for a little while. But it wasn't his way.

Now that his band had hit the top, Jon's determination to consolidate that position was absolute. In such an ephemeral world as rock music he feared that Bon Jovi, though here today, could still be gone tomorrow. He declared, 'Next year, I plan to be better. I want a bigger record, to do more shows.' Jon's urgency to accelerate Bon Jovi's success was understandable. But he launched himself and the others, metaphorically, on to a track that would indeed soar to even greater heights, but would also plunge them headlong towards derailment.

CHAPTER 5

The Physical and Emotional Burnout

ALTHOUGH SHATTERED AT THE CONCLUSION of the Slippery When Wet tour, Jon Bon Jovi refused to rest for long. Almost immediately he forged ahead with writing new material for the next album. This time, when Richie Sambora arrived daily at Jon's home, they would vanish to an upstairs room to work. The mantle of world champions can be a heavy one, and despite brisk creativity producing 17 songs by Christmas 1987, Jon was worried. Listening to the demos of this first collection, he knew that though one or two shone through there was, glaringly, no big hitter among them. Worse, one song sounded nearly identical musically to 'You Give Love A Bad Name'. 'To be honest,' he said, 'I panicked.'

Professionally, it meant everything to Jon to prove that *Slippery When Wet* was not a fluke one-off. Having moved up the property ladder with Dorothea into a better house, he wanted to be able to sustain that. He has admitted that when occasionally the pressure got to him too badly, he would stalk about the house shouting that he needed some hot songs to pay for the place. Richie, ever the more placid of the two, would reassure Jon that they'd soon get into the groove.

Sambora's laid-back confidence was helpful, but Jon was only truly convinced once they had put together a second batch of some 14 new songs, during the early weeks of 1988. By now, he and Richie had re-teamed with songwriter Desmond Child, and the old magic brought a flood of potential hits. It was easy for critics to accuse Jon and Richie of needing Desmond Child to raise their game as lyricists, but that wasn't true. 'I'll Be There For You', for instance, a fresh Bon Jovi/Sambora composition, was destined to add to their haul of number one hits. It would have been sheer folly to overlook what the proven chemistry between these three songwriters was capable of producing.

Song ideas had been percolating mentally for a long time. There was always the danger with stepping straight off an exhaustive tour into songwriting sessions, that creative thoughts would be stifled by having repeatedly performed a certain range of songs for months on end. But, equally, new experiences on and off stage were bound to infiltrate too. In the case of one of their strongest new numbers, 'Bad Medicine', inspiration had suddenly sprung upon them. Several weeks before, the band had been invited to film a commercial for Japanese Fuji tape, and Richie recalled standing atop a tall building, knee-deep in black water (meant to represent a sea of recording tape) thinking, between takes, about the fraught personal relationship he was in at that time. Suddenly, he said to Jon, 'I've got this idea – "Bad Medicine".' Jon's head swivelled round immediately, the title alone already conjuring up a song theme. This raucous, hard-rocking number would become the first of a litter of hits to spin off the new album, but it was another composition, 'Blood on Blood', that would be Jon's favourite. It was a blatant ode to camaraderie between guys – in this case, Jon's old hometown mates named in the song, with whom he speaks of having made a life-long Musketeer-type pact. He makes no apologies for his penchant for writing about blood-brother sentiments, nor for the rousing musical style such songs require. 'Why have half measures?' he has asked. 'I love all that majestic shit.'

With his brief early jitters well behind him, Jon was now in flat-out working mode. He even found time to continue something he had been doing throughout the previous year – writing songs which were tailored to other artists; to date he and Richie had provided material for Jennifer Rush and Cher to record. In April 1988, Cher, with whom Sambora was now romantically involved, released the single, 'We All Sleep Alone', which had been co-written and co-produced by Jon and would reach number 14 in the US.

Jon and Richie had involved themselves with producing the band Loverboy. Jon had also been able to make good on a promise made long ago to hometown friend Dave Sabo, that whichever one of them made it in music first would help the other on to the ladder. While Jon had gone on to scale the heights with Bon Jovi, the guitarist, who had once played temporarily in Jon's fledgling bands, had himself joined or formed a succession of bands. Jon had kept an eye on Dave's endeavours, but had not stepped in with any assistance until Sabo got together with four other musicians as the promising heavy metal band, Skid Row.

In 1987 Jon and Richie set up the New Jersey Underground Music Company, whose primary function was to deal with the publishing royalties arising from specific areas in their songwriting activities. Skid Row had entered into a contract with the New Jersey Underground Music Company which, though beneficial to them, later became problematic. However, in early 1988, Jon's interest in his hometown friend's band led to this locally popular outfit being signed to McGhee Entertainment Inc. Soon afterwards, Skid Row landed a recording contract with Atlantic Records. Jon used his considerable influence to trumpet the virtues of this new band every chance he got in media interviews. And he provided them with valuable exposure by hiring them to play support to Bon Jovi on part of their next tour.

It pleased Jon to be able to help Dave Sabo in this way. But not everything in the garden was rosy. A most unwelcome distraction occurred when some criminal activity in Doc McGhee's distant past finally caught up with him. At the start of 1988, McGhee had pleaded guilty to his part in a drug smuggling offence dating back six years, involving the shipment from Columbia into North Carolina of 40,000 pounds of marijuana, which had been intercepted by US Customs. In April 1988 this became public when the courts handed down McGhee a five-year suspended prison sentence, plus a $15,000 fine and extensive community service. His jail term was suspended, provided he established an anti-drug charity.

This offence had taken place before Doc McGhee's involvement with Bon Jovi. But since he was the manager of the hottest rock band in the world right then, this conviction obviously drew the media to Jon like moths to a light. Jon made it clear to journalists that he in no way condoned what Doc McGhee had been involved in before he knew him. Yet he also let it be known that he was not about to abandon his beleaguered manager, despite the lures being thrown out to him. 'It looked like a phone book of fucking managers trying to woo me,' Jon revealed, but he insisted that not for a second did he consider dumping McGhee. In fact, he had been prepared to attend court, if necessary, to show his intention to stick by the manager.

This intrinsic loyalty was part of the glue that held so much together for Jon, upon whom the burden of responsibility continued to grow heavier with success. That responsibility took different shapes. He was no longer in dire financial straits. Instead, though only just turned 26, he headed a lucrative organisation that was becoming bigger all the time; consequently the circle of people whose fiscal welfare depended on him widened.

Jon also felt the weight of expectation surrounding Bon Jovi's next move. Although to a large degree he was ready to meet the challenge, there was a lurking fear that having reached the top, the only way to go now was down.

With the furore over Doc McGhee's drug conviction still reverberating, Jon was glad to go with the band in early May to Canada where, back at Little Mountain Sound Studios in Vancouver, they began recording the new album with producer Bruce Fairbairn in charge again. For three months, into early summer 1988, they developed enough material for a double album. Jon quite fancied the idea but Polygram knocked it on the head at once.

Jon was toying with calling the album *Sons Of Beaches*. When it came to whittling down the pool of songs to the final dozen, once again Bon Jovi were keen to harvest the opinions of the kids. No New Jersey pizza parlour jury this time. Instead, they were either teenagers known to the producer, or intrepid fans who, having discovered the band's presence at the recording facility, had taken to camping in the street outside in the hope of meeting their heroes. On occasions, Jon wasn't above waylaying passers-by and inviting them to step into the studio to listen to tapes and give their verdict. The band didn't always agree with their market research guinea pigs, but it was an interesting exercise. Said Jon, 'Some loved us, some hated us and some didn't give a shit either way.'

The band's express aim this time around was to telegraph that there was more depth and nuance to their material than was so far widely acknowledged. The result was a hard-rocking album that showed maturity and was at times soulful. The lengthy intro to 'Lay Your Hands On Me', with its tribal beat and rhythmic chants, ensured an unusual opener; it was immediately followed by a second thrasher in 'Bad Medicine'. Other rousing numbers included 'Blood On Blood', '99 In The Shade' and 'Homebound Train'; the last almost a kick-back to 1970s Led Zeppelin-style hard rock. The counterbalance to these testosterone-driven powerhouse

Half a million people crammed into New York's Times Square on 5 September 2002 to see Bon Jovi headline at the concert to kick off the new NFL season. Midtown Manhattan had been shut down since the afternoon and Jon later said, 'We caused one helluva traffic jam that day'. (GETTY IMAGES)

With the blistering success of the *Slippery When Wet* and *New Jersey* albums and world tours, by the end of the second half of the 1980s Bon Jovi had conquered the rock world. On the face of it, they seemed invulnerable. In truth, they were about to implode under the strain. But the brotherhood would revive. (REX FEATURES)

Bass player Alec John Such's departure from the band in 1994 pared Bon Jovi down to a four-piece. The following year they released *These Days*, at that point their darkest and most accomplished album. (REUTERS)

Arriving at the Desert Sky Pavilion in Phoenix, Arizona during their global One Wild Night tour. Too often Bon Jovi had seemed destined to feel like the comeback kids in rock music. But the colossal triumph of *Crush* in 2000 silenced their critics. (REUTERS NEW MEDIA/CORBIS)

Long-time friends, the complementary contrasts in their individual personalities make for a stimulating songwriting partnership between Jon Bon Jovi and Richie Sambora. (REX FEATURES)

Jon and Richie with their respective wives, Dorothea Hurley and actress Heather Locklear. Jon met Dorothea in high school. He was in the middle of the backbreaking New Jersey tour when he persuaded her to run off with him to Las Vegas to marry on 29 April 1989 on the steps of the Graceland Chapel. (FRANK TRAPPER/CORBIS SYGMA)

Despite all the obvious trappings of wealth, Jon has never deserted his working class roots. A single-minded, tenacious man, he has always been the hub of Bon Jovi. (REX FEATURES)

Jon accepts VH1's Music Video of the Year Award in Los Angeles in November 2000 for 'It's My Life', the tour de force song from *Crush*. Its pounding potency and stirring passion makes it Jon's own signature tune. (REUTERS NEW MEDIA /CORBIS)

Any Bon Jovi live gig is a high-energy, exciting and adrenalin-driven experience. Jon in full throttle wows the crowd on the One Wild Night tour in 2001. (REUTERS NEW MEDIA/CORBIS)

Jon's acting ambitions have always been geared towards the film world. However, he accepted David E. Kelley's (centre) offer to guest star for nine episodes of TV's *Ally McBeal* appearing as the love interest of the quirky lawyer, played by Calista Flockhart. (REUTERS/FRED PROUSER)

When Jon was asked to pen the music for the 1990 Hollywood movie *Young Guns II* it was the solo creative outlet he had badly needed at the time. His stirring single 'Blaze of Glory' became the movie's theme tune and earned Jon a Golden Globe Award as well as an Oscar nomination. The song's dramatic video was shot on top of an awe-inspiring canyon mountain range. (NEAL PRESTON/CORBIS)

Charismatic and dynamic, Jon Bon Jovi is an inspirational figure to many. Beneath his famously handsome looks he is a natural born survivor with the kind of grit which has taken him and his band to where they are today, still energising millions on their worldwide Bounce tour, retaining their faithful following and attracting new devotees every day. (REUTERS/ETHAN MILLER)

numbers came in the shape of the heartfelt ballad, 'I'll Be There For You', and 'Born To Be My Baby', a soaring song similar in sentiment to 'Livin' On A Prayer', in that it concentrates on a working-class couple's mutual devotion and their ambitions.

Two cuts made it on to the album because they were among the fans' preferred choices, despite Jon's strong inclination to omit them. One was 'Wild Is The Wind', about a dissolving relationship, on which both Desmond Child and lyricist Diane Warren had worked. The other was 'Stick To Your Guns', a collaborative effort between Jon, Richie and songwriter Holly Knight. The husky 'Living In Sin' was the only number on this album written solely by Jon, and was an attack on different generational attitudes to marriage. The anchor track was 'Love For Sale' – a standout number because of its heavy bluegrass style overlaid by agitating harmonica and highlighted by the lively vocal end banter between Jon and Richie. Richie reckoned that everything revealed in these lyrics reflected who Bon Jovi were. There was no clearer signal of this than when it came to naming the album.

Jon had got far enough with the idea of calling it *Sons Of Beaches* to have come up with a montage design for the sleeve. But now he ditched the whole concept and decided instead to call the album *New Jersey*, not so much after the state as to signify an attitude, one that was all about knowing and being proud of one's heritage.

What Jon had not anticipated was the propensity seemingly everywhere in the music media to tie him in with New Jersey's other rock ambassador, Bruce Springsteen. It would go on for years and lead Jon, when his patience became threadbare, to speak out. 'The biggest mistake I made in my career was calling an album *New Jersey*,' he said feelingly. 'Because suddenly everyone's comparing me to this guy, making out we're drinking buddies, when we're not. I get fucking sick of it.' Jon had nothing against Bruce Springsteen, and still admired his music. But the press wouldn't let it go, so it continued to needle him into outbursts. He would reasonably point out how many other famous people also hailed from New Jersey. Springsteen, Jon declared, 'didn't buy the whole state, doesn't own the name.' But it was to no avail.

New Jersey was released in September 1988. Destined to go multi-platinum, it was Bon Jovi's second consecutive number one album in America, and their first chart-topping position in the UK album charts a month later. Hard on *New Jersey*'s heels in Britain, the single 'Bad Medicine' stopped at number 17. Weeks later, it lodged at number one in the States, just before the band was due to embark on a mammoth world tour. Punishingly, in the next 16 months, they would perform 230 shows in 20 countries.

Jon's urge to break previous Bon Jovi records now had the perfect breeding ground to come to fruition. But while he was raring to go, he also tried to be mindful of what had happened on the last tour. As well as getting into shape for the upcoming trek by jogging and working out at the gym, he had taken some vocal coaching in the hope of avoiding the painful voice strain suffered last time. Band rehearsals too had occupied much of his time. He also honed his guitar skills and sought tuition to improve his harmonica playing. All the while, the band had the chance to see what the critics were making of their new releases.

Jon had already accepted that Bon Jovi were probably never going to be the critics' darlings, but on the whole that was no big deal to him. Even so, there were clearly still occasional exceptions. Tico Torres revealed, 'I get a kick out of seeing one man's view. But Jon hates bad reviews.' Richie Sambora made the salient point: 'Critics get the records for free. Kids *buy* the records. We depend on our public to be our barometer.'

When the tour commenced on Halloween 1988 at the RDS Hall in Dublin, Ireland, all the indications were that they had a tiger by the tail. The fans were brimming with excited anticipation, and Jon was so wired that first night that he had to suppress a powerful urge to unceremoniously usher their opening act, singer Lita Ford, prematurely off stage so that he could face his public. He had so much adrenalin coursing through him, he felt almost on fire. The tour roared off through Europe, quitting Ireland for Germany and Switzerland before hitting Italy in mid-November. After France, it took in the Netherlands and Scandinavia. Every step of the way, determined to prove worthy of their crown, Bon Jovi left sold-out audiences soaked in delirium and themselves high on performing.

Truly, it was a spectacular show. 'Flying' was out this time. But audiences got just as big a thrill when, after a deafening introduction courtesy of Tico Torres and David Bryan, suddenly in a fizzing shower of sparks and a swirling cloud of smoke Jon, Richie and Alec would shoot up through three separate trap doors in the stage floor, each individual hydraulic platform making them appear simultaneously before the startled crowd as if by magic. Long, mechanically-operated runways would reach out high above the audiences, allowing Jon to get closer to the back of the packed venues, to press the flesh.

Poured into soft leather trousers and long patchwork coats, Jon's sexuality ran even more rampant this time during such numbers as 'Lay Your Hands On Me', when he would provocatively ignite a surge forward to the lip of the stage by demented girls itching to respond literally to the invitation. Equally, he created the desired romantic effect with the meltingly sentimental, 'I'll Be There For You.' But the show wasn't exclusively geared to turning on the girls. The droves of hyped-up guys in the audience were swept away on the back of the bruising hard-rocking anthems, and they also responded thoroughly to the very visible on-stage display of masculine camaraderie

Jon and Richie had devised a routine in which they would charge towards each other from opposite sides of the stage, each swinging an arm which, when they met in the centre, would lock together and hold. Choreographed to a fine art, it was a most effective demonstration of unity and friendship. The blatant brandishing of their brotherhood mentality helped deflect the media from its past habit of tagging Bon Jovi 'pop metal pretty boys'. The organisation's nickname, 'The Jersey Syndicate', was becoming more widely known, and Jon talked in interviews of the real bond between the five. He openly pitched a person's sense of loyalty to friends as being more valuable than cultivating business links. 'Because,' he said, 'when your back's against the wall, you know who's gonna be there for you.'

Some took the view that, spectacular as the shows were, there was a sameness to the band's overall look and sound – that not a great deal seemed to have altered between the Slippery When Wet tour and this new one. The obvious reason for that was that they had allowed themselves so little downshift time in between. It was a charge which Jon, particularly with hindsight, did not in essence deny. He knew that his relentless drive to press on after the end of the Slippery When Wet tour had suffocated the chance to sit back and assess matters. While he felt it vital that Bon Jovi songs stayed true to themselves and their fans, Jon argued strongly that he and Richie *had* matured as lyricists; certainly that they had moved on substantially from where they had started out.

Another element still ingrained in Jon at this time, was his inability to resist adding extra dates to the already crammed tour schedule, in response to the fans' voracious appetite to see Bon Jovi live. Rashly sidelining memories of the super-exhaustion suffered last time around, Jon was determined to satisfy them. In time, this contributed to the mosaic of pressure that would build up within the band. But in late November they were distracted by a short detour to the land of America's old enemy – the USSR.

Accompanying the band to Moscow for the three-day stay were manager Doc McGhee, a video crew headed by Wayne

Isham, and a handful of Polygram executives. They had gone to the Russian capital to formulate an ambitious plan to stage, in summer 1989, the very first rock concert to be held in Lenin Stadium. And to work out a deal with the State-owned record label Melodiya to release *New Jersey* in the Soviet Union.

Rock stars had performed in the USSR before, but in the new climate of *perestroika* (economic reconstruction) and *glasnost* (public accountability) under President Mikhail Gorbachev, it was suddenly possible to expose the communist youth to a Western rock band in an officially approved manner. The Soviet government felt able to countenance Bon Jovi as their country's first foreign superstars because they were not a politicised band. That meant that although on arrival at the airport the band were shown to a special holding area while their documentation was thoroughly examined, the atmosphere was nevertheless friendly and good-humoured. Even when, to the officials' surprise, the terminal building came under unexpected siege from thousands of teenagers clamouring to meet the band.

Negotiations had yet to be finalised to bring out *New Jersey* the following year, but black market copies of the album had been circulating and doing remarkable business considering that the price per album was 150 roubles – roughly three weeks' wages for the average Russian at the time.

Limousines and a police escort were laid on to take the band from the airport to their designated hotel, where a sea of excited fans were lying in wait outside. To avoid unseemly public scenes by their citizens, the Russian hosts immediately diverted the cars and took Bon Jovi instead to the offices of one of the people closely involved in arranging this unique visit, Stas Namin, manager of the Russian rock band Gorky Park. Gorky Park were to appear on the bill of the planned 1989 rock event, and there was a pre-existing link between Namin and Jon Bon Jovi. Months earlier, while in the US, the Russian musician had contacted Jon to ask his help in composing some English songs. With Richie, Jon had agreed.

In Moscow, besides a little touristy sightseeing (Jon made a night excursion to Red Square), the band packed two press conferences into their limited time. At these Jon made it clear to the country's media that Bon Jovi were not there as political ambassadors. What further appealed to the authorities was Bon Jovi's intention to use their proposed Lenin Stadium event to promote an anti-drug message. Conforming to the terms of his court sentence earlier in the year, Doc McGhee had set up MADF (the Make A Difference Foundation), a non-profit-making anti-drug charity to which proceeds from the stadium gig would be donated. Other bands slated to feature on the bill included Mötley Crüe and the Scorpions. More would be added, as indeed the event itself would grow in size.

As the short visit drew to a close, Jon was confident that they'd made progress. Meanwhile, on a personal note, he'd also had a chance to revise his thinking about the Soviet Union. He admitted soon after that his preconceived opinions had been shaped by Cold War teachings that America and Russia were eternal enemies. Movie influences had even played a part. 'It wasn't what *Red Dawn* led me to expect' he said, referring to the violent 1984 film directed by John Milius about a thwarted Soviet invasion of America. By the time Jon left Moscow, he had high hopes that a successful big-scale Western rock event might help to open up a better understanding between the youth of both cultures.

Bon Jovi headed from Russia to Britain to pick up the tour on 2 December at Glasgow's SECC. Newly released was the single, 'Born To Be My Baby', which, though halting just outside the UK Top 20, got to number three at home. This British leg of the tour concentrated on three venues. After packing out the NEC in Birmingham, the band arrived in London for the first of their four dates at Wembley Arena. As a top echelon band, Bon Jovi now drew superstars to watch their gigs. Attending that first Wembley Arena concert was Queen guitarist, Brian May. Richie Sambora had admired May's guitar skills ever since he had gone three nights out of five to see Queen open for Mott the Hoople at the Uris Theater on Broadway in 1974. 'I was knocked out.' said Richie. 'Queen were absolutely fantastic and Brian made a big impression on me. I was just a teenager at the time, but I never forgot it.'

During the encore at the Wembley Arena, Bon Jovi invited musicians present at the gig to come on stage. Richie recalled, 'Brian May, Elton John and a whole bunch of guys had come that night, so we just called them all up to jam with us. We played the Beatles' "Get Back" and a couple of other numbers. It was one helluva jam. But what was really cool was something which happened after the gig. Brian gave Jon and me some really sound advice, which was not to work our asses off so hard that we forgot to take time to smell the roses along the way. That's what he felt he and Queen had often done, and he couldn't get over strongly enough to us how important it is always to try to be there – to live the moment and savour it, because all too soon it'll be over and you'll have missed clean out on enjoying it.'

Jon recognised the value of this sage advice, but he wasn't yet ready to slow down. There was over a year of the tour still to go. This kind of globetrotting was hard on relationships, but Dorothea could choose to travel with Jon for spells, or visit him at various pit-stops, as she did when the band were in London. So far, Jon's voice was also holding out. Still haunted by the problems which had beset his vocal cords last time, he would sometimes be buzzing in the wings waiting to go on stage, praying at the same time that he would be able to hit the high notes. 'If I can't sing, I hate it,' he said, maintaining in a more dramatic mood that there were times when he believed that for every night he could perform at his best, he would be prepared to shave a day off his life.

When not performing almost nightly, Jon was keeping his finger on the business pulse and was reassured to know that with *New Jersey*'s sales going through the roof, and the booming interest in their back catalogue, their finances were buoyant. Yet he was in no danger of letting this wealth go to his head. He was more relieved than anything. He still woke up on the road, pleased that he had no worries about paying the band's hotel bill.

It was not so easy for him when he tried to be generous to his immediate family. He had lately managed to get his father to accept a gift of a car, but wanted to do more for parents who had always been loving and supportive. But he had their strong sense of pride to surmount. John and Carol Bongiovi did not find it easy to accept lavish gifts from their famous eldest son, and they resisted him flat out when Jon felt there should be no need for them to keep on working. Jon remembered that his grandparents had worked their fingers to the bone all their lives, and he yearned to ease life for his mother and father. Whether it was tongue-in-cheek, or a desperate effort to persuade them to give up their full-time jobs, Jon threatened to buy out the respective businesses which employed them, and then sack them as a way of getting them out of the labour force. But they had a sovereign answer. Jon said, 'They just told me to shut up and remember where I came from.'

On New Year's Eve 1988, having left Europe, Bon Jovi commenced a four-date Japanese excursion with a gig at the Tokyo Dome. Then, a fortnight later, they embarked on the first of two colossal US/Canadian legs of the world tour, kicking off where the Slippery When Wet tour had ended – in Honolulu, Hawaii.

Jon said, 'I've always said, we're a bar band who just plays big bars.' And certainly the singer still made as much one-to-one contact with audiences as possible to continue that communion between them. But there was a certain amount of self-effacing modesty sewn in there. Bon Jovi were stadium fillers, and Jon's own star was inexorably in the ascendancy. In early February 1989, Jon again dominated the front cover of *Rolling Stone*. Labelled 'Bon Jovi: Rock's Young Gun', Jon, barefoot and dressed in black, complete with black stetson, was pictured standing before a majestically rearing white stallion. And he was constantly deluged with requests for a piece of his time.

Although he was now well acquainted with the media game, stardom had not much altered Jon in interview situations. Journalists were still often perplexed by his friendly, yet watchful manner. To some, he was an enigma – handsome, charismatic and accommodating, yet often too unexcitable to suit rock writers. He could still be disconcertingly frank, and had no qualms about drawing the boundaries of what he was prepared to discuss. Religion and politics were almost always ruled out. To put the whole area of idolisation into context, he declared, 'I have more respect for what Mikhail Gorbachev is doing, pulling down the walls, than I have for Bob Dylan, who was one of the geniuses. Gorbachev is trying to save the planet. Now *that's* important.' His answer to those who, in faintly derogatory tones, called him a goody-goody type, was to muse aloud just how bizarre life had become when a rock star had to practically apologise for not being a dope-head or a crazed maniac.

Bon Jovi's almost inhuman concert schedule would scarcely have allowed for their frontman, or any band member, to go off the rails as, with Skid Row opening for them, they hopped across states in a kind of blur. Still, when Jon was caught doing something illegal, harmless though it was, it made front-page news. His 'crime' was that he had been picked up by police for trespassing when he, Dorothea and two other people had found their way on to the ice at New York City's Wollman Skating Rink in the early hours of one March morning.

Despite such capers and having Dorothea in closer attendance, as the tour wound on its way, the strain began to tell. At times it seemed as if they had been on the road for years nonstop; once again the emotional high of performing, followed by endless travelling and promotion was becoming a pernicious combination. Jon maintained that while stars may complain of feeling pressure from the public and the press, in reality it was preferable to being ignored. But he would not be so sanguine about pressure by the end of the year.

For now though, such was the extent of the public adulation for Bon Jovi that on 15 March 1989 when they played the Meadowlands Arena in East Rutherford, New Jersey, the Mayor of Sayreville made the homecoming gig even more special by handing the group the keys to the city. The Mayor of New York had also declared that day to be 'Bon Jovi Day'. It was heady stuff which propelled the five through the next six weeks until, towards the end of April, they played two shows at the Forum in Los Angeles. Even for a band that had achieved so much success, they had reached an exciting pinnacle. Their new single, 'I'll Be There For You', made a modest 18 in Britain, but it gave the band their fourth number one US single. There was a gigantic Bon Jovi billboard on the world-famous Sunset Strip and both Forum gigs had been breathtaking experiences.

It left Jon elated. 'I was on top of the fucking world,' he recalled. He and Dorothea went out celebrating. He was in perpetual motion the whole time, going to a tattoo parlour, where he had the top of his right arm permanently decorated with a steer's head design. Then they headed to a casino, where his luck at the tables made him feel invincible. His euphoria still hadn't found its limit, and suddenly he surprised Dorothea with the words 'Hey! Let's get married!' Bemused and excited, his long-time love at first bombarded him with 'When? Where?'

To her shocked surprise, Jon wanted to wed her within hours and in secret. Sceptical that he was thinking straight and meant what he was saying, she told him frankly that he was 'full of it'. Jon, however, insisted, 'Now!' adding that they could fly to Las Vegas, get hitched and be back before they were missed. So, like eloping lovers, they dashed off to Las Vegas where, on the steps of the Graceland Chapel on 29 April 1989, they were married by Reverend George Colton. Of course, they had no proper rings and so used two cheap plastic ones. There were no bridesmaids, no best man, and the ceremony was over in five minutes. But they were deliriously happy. Jon rang his parents' house at 3.00 a.m. to break the news to them. Carol Bongiovi took the call, fearful at first that something bad had happened for her son to be waking them up in the early hours. But seconds later, Jon's delight-filled voice asked long-distance, 'Would you like to say hello to your new daughter-in-law?'

News of Jon Bon Jovi's sudden marriage was soon splashed over newspapers, where it was revealed, 'The bride wore black leather and so did the groom!' The romance of the secret nuptials caught the public imagination, but behind the scenes, Jon came under serious fire when he and his wife returned to the fold. The fact that he had not told the rest of the band, Doc McGhee, anyone in fact, went down very badly. It felt like a rebuff, and some were most unhappy with the stealth of it all.

Jon acknowledged that he had 'pissed off' many people close to him and he felt the heat of that collective displeasure acutely for a couple of days. Then he decided that it didn't matter what people thought. He and Dorothea had married for themselves and no one else. He also resented any knee-jerk attitude that because of his sex symbol status, he had had no business getting married. Perhaps Doc McGhee's first thoughts *had* focused on how his star being married would affect that valuably potent status, but that was his job as manager. Dorothea had never sought any public profile, and would continue not to do so. However, nothing cools a fan's ardour so fast as realising that her dreamboat, fantasy pin-up is a happily married man and not available, as he projects on stage.

Jon was happy to be married, but increasingly disgruntled in other respects. Being smack in the middle of an exhaustive tour, a honeymoon break was clearly out of the question. It was straight back to what was turning into a grind for everyone.

In May, a series of dates in Canada was spliced into the US itinerary. And although Jon enjoyed some off-stage time in Vancouver in the company of his friend, Def Leppard frontman Joe Elliott, by the time Bon Jovi hit Toronto in early June, he was feeling low enough to confide in another friend, Southside Johnny. He said, 'I called Johnny, feeling really sorry for myself. I told him, "We're in Toronto for three nights and I'm so bored of this fucking band!"' The older man heard him out, then highlighted none too subtly the sharp difference in their positions. Jon was playing these huge prestigious venues, while he was appearing at the Stone Pony club. Not to mention the huge disparity in their respective bands' record sales. It might not have been exactly the response Jon wanted to hear at that moment, but it was the touchstone he needed to help him find some perspective again. But the peaks and troughs would continue.

One definite peak was reached on 11 June 1989, when Jon realised a long-held dream by playing the Giants Stadium in East Rutherford, New Jersey. Although his hectic life hardly allows him a lot of time to indulge it, Jon has retained a deep passion for American football, especially for the NFL's New York Giants. When he can, he enjoys watching games, visiting the team in the locker room and sometimes meeting his favourite players socially. His desire for the Giants to win every game has even led him, on occasion, to intervene if he spots a player reaching for a beer on the night before a match. Small wonder then, that when Bon Jovi played the sold-out gig on the Giants' home turf, it left Jon choked with pride.

By July 1989, 'Lay Your Hands On Me' managed to secure the number seven slot in America, and matched their previous single's performance in Britain by getting to 18 there in August. That month was made memorable by the two historic gigs at Moscow's Lenin Stadium on 12 and 13 August 1989. Melodiya brought out *New Jersey* the day before (making Bon Jovi the first American rock band to have an official album release on this Soviet label). The giant rock event, filmed by several international TV crews, was now christened 'The Moscow Music Peace Festival.'

As had already been agreed, all proceeds were to go towards programmes to help combat alcohol and substance abuse in Russia and the US. The line-up consisted of Ozzy Osbourne, Mötley Crüe, Scorpions, Cinderella and Skid Row, with Russian groups Gorky Park, Nuance, CCCP and Brigada S also in attendance. A plane carrying all the musicians, plus a large chunk of the Western world's showbiz media headed for Moscow. The irony was that although Doc McGhee's MADF sponsored the concert, some artists on board relieved the boredom of the long flight by indulging in some serious alcohol abuse of their own. Skid Row's Dave Sabo described his band as getting 'absolutely shit-faced.'

From the moment the plane touched down at the airport, all eyes were on Jon Bon Jovi. He emerged from the aircraft first, before a blinding bank of flash photography and TV camera crews. He drew almost all of the attention at the madhouse affair that was the international press conference; this niggled some of the other rock stars, who felt they were being ignored. By the time it came to group photographs of all the bands jostling together, smiling and joking for the press, the truth was that, behind the scenes some individual egos were clashing big time over the order of play, and particularly over the notion of Bon Jovi as the event's headliners.

When it came down to it, Bon Jovi was not only the biggest band in the world right then, but Jon had been very closely involved for months in putting the whole event together. The bands had all been given equal-sized billing on the posters promoting the festival and had been treated the same with regard to the arrangements for the trip. But Jon was adamant that Bon Jovi would close. As it happened, he came up with a piece of pure theatre that would have stolen any show, when he made his way to the stage for Bon Jovi's set from the floor of the stadium. Appearing unexpectedly among the crowd, wearing a Red Army greatcoat and military cap, he strode down the central aisle flanked by bodyguards. The TV cameras zoomed in on a surprise grand entrance that screamed out to be topped by an especially vibrant performance.

Within days, Bon Jovi returned to play some dates in Britain before crossing back over the Atlantic. As the relentless treadmill took them through Canada, then home to America, Jon began to fear that he was becoming zombie-like. The real problem, however, came from an unspoken enmity that had crept in between the band members and taken root. They were undoubtedly exhausted, more than road-weary, and had had enough of living together in such constant close proximity. But sometimes Jon felt that there was something else wrong. Being strained and tense himself, he couldn't figure out what it was, but the friction was palpable.

Outside disruptive influences didn't help the sense of trouble in the camp. By now, it was well known that Jon headed the organisation, and because of this he was often on the wrong end of rumours regarding the demands he made on his band. Erroneous stories began to bounce from one publication to another. A classic example was when America's *National Enquirer* repeated a floating rumour that Jon had insisted that Tico Torres and Alec John Such lose weight, even undergo liposuction. Years later, Jon could laugh at these false claims, but at the time they compounded the growing tension within the close-knit unit.

None of that strain showed itself, however, when Jon and Richie made a special impact in early September as guest performers at the annual MTV Video Music Awards. The event was transmitted on national television and performed before an audience of their peers. For their set, both wanted to express something different, and decided to perform playing only acoustic guitars. The idea was to strip down what they famously did on a grand scale, to showcase the unvarnished way in which they had originally created such hits. Said Richie, 'We wanted to show people that Bon Jovi wasn't a hair band, that Jon and I were songwriters and real musicians.'

Two hours earlier, they had played 'Wanted Dead Or Alive' and 'Livin' On A Prayer' for the staff and technicians at the auditorium, willing to let these people decide which number they should perform. Dick Clark, the show's producer, said they ought to perform both songs, which they did, sitting on stools with no flash, no razzmatazz. The new acoustic renditions were in such startling contrast to the rafter-rattling electric style familiar to the audience, that it brought a stunned hush to the crowd. The purity and soulfulness of their singing, the enunciation of these well-known lyrics in slightly altered keys was also captivating. Oddly, Jon misread the audience's quietness and assumed he and Richie had bombed. It wasn't until the glowing reviews and plaudits in the next day's newspapers that he realised how well it had actually come off. That single performance was ultimately responsible for MTV launching what would become their massively popular 'Unplugged' series.

The perfect public unity was a mirage, however, and it was back to the reality of a stressful life on the road. Increasingly, almost helplessly, the band members were becoming isolated from one another offstage, and all of them were drinking too much. Even long-distance, Jon's family sensed that things were not right for him, that although he would try to hide it, he was in fact deeply unhappy. All Jon would admit to during anxious telephone calls was that he was exhausted. He, too, had thrown up defensive barriers.

It took years for the band to expose the truth about this depressing time. As Sambora pointed out, they had become thoroughly sick of the sight of each other. And Jon revealed that they'd reached the stage where they knew so much about each others' lives that there seemed nothing left to talk about. They actually needed to get away from each other, but they were tied into many more months of roadwork yet.

Plus, problems were accumulating with the lead singer of Skid Row, their backing band on this US stretch. Canadian-born Sebastian Bach had a reputation as a dynamic and provocative frontman. This was good for enlivening the audiences packing out the stadiums, but in the latter stages of this leg, things were turning sour. Bach had developed a problem with the terms of the contract Skid Row had entered into years earlier with Jon and Richie's New Jersey Underground Music Company. The needle he felt about this was now spilling out on stage in remarks about the headliners. This discomfited and bewildered the Bon Jovi faithful and increasingly infuriated Jon, hearing these comments from the wings.

Naturally, it was undesirable to be bad-mouthed by the paid support, or at least by the support band's singer – the rest of Skid Row continued to enjoy harmonious relations with Bon Jovi. Inevitably, considering the already abundant tension, Bach's persistent public digs ended up provoking a physical altercation between the singers one night when Sebastian Bach steamed off stage at the end of Skid Row's set, straight into an enraged Jon Bon Jovi. The US gigs were drawing to a close and soon the bands would part company as road partners. But the trouble between Sebastian Bach and Jon Bon Jovi went on to become a thorny legal issue, only brought to a conclusion in the mid-1990s. Before that, however, Bach had spoken volubly to the music press about his feelings, and this naturally gave rock journalists a new bone to chew on.

By the end of 1989 music magazines, in fact, were close to running stories of a suspected dislocation of the much-vaunted Bon Jovi brotherhood, giving Jon yet more grief. It was piling on from all angles. Emotionally and mentally, Jon felt on the rack; physically, he suffered recurring pain from an inflamed injury he had sustained earlier in the tour. While dashing around the stage he had fractured a tibia, but in order to carry on performing he had only had it strapped up .

Bon Jovi marked the one-year anniversary of the New Jersey tour by starting the Australia leg in Brisbane. New Zealand gigs capped their excursion Down Under before they headed to Europe at the beginning of December, to blaze through eight countries, winding up in Germany just before Christmas. The next stop was Britain for the third time on this globetrot, where they were committed to their biggest number of London gigs yet, when Wembley Arena dates were added to a string of nights at the Hammersmith Odeon. Jon spent Christmas Day 1989 in a London hotel room with a hangover from celebrating on their plane trip into the country the night before.

Their latest single, 'Living In Sin', had by now clocked up a Top 10 hit in America, although it stalled at 35 in Britain. It's likely that its performance went practically unnoticed by the band since, by the time they hauled themselves to South America in the new year, communication had broken down so much that they were barely speaking to one another. They played such imposing stadia as the Maracana in Brazil's Rio de Janeiro and San Paolo's Morumbi, but they were really on autopilot. By the time they staggered into Mexico to complete the tour, the crushing workload had almost buried Bon Jovi. Richie Sambora later declared darkly, 'We almost lost a couple of the band members during that tour.' And while it made their manager miserable to witness the disintegration of what had been a uniquely close five-way friendship, he was powerless to prevent the slide. No one talked collectively anymore; everyone saw himself as an individual unit. In Doc McGhee's experience that was usually the death knell for a band's future.

Having notched up more hits and played to millions, Bon Jovi had achieved what they had set out to do – they had consolidated their pole position in the rock world. But the cost seemed to be very high. Looking back, Jon acknowledged,

'There was a time from '83 till '90 when everyone's sole heartbeat was the band. It could have killed us, because we were so burnt out.' Just how matters had come to such a drastic pass was not entirely understood. There was more to the breakdown than the colossal workload. But Jon was definitely in no condition now to fathom any of it out. When the last note rang out on the last night of the tour, the band quit the stage. Then, without so much as a farewell to one another, they promptly headed off in their own separate directions. Bon Jovi, in Jon's own bleak words, 'were dead.'

CHAPTER 6

When It's Hard to See a Chink of Light

JON BON JOVI WAS A PHYSICAL AND EMOTIONAL WRECK. In the three and a half years since *Slippery When Wet* had jet-propelled Bon Jovi to the top, life had rushed by so incredibly fast that his feet had scarcely touched the ground. His self-imposed, relentless momentum had sustained him on that dangerous high-rolling course far beyond what seemed humanly possible. By the time he staggered off the New Jersey tour, the painful price was plain to see.

The man who came home to Dorothea was spent, brittle, and had acquired a vivid aversion to confined spaces. He would panic within seconds of finding himself shut in an elevator, and had little or no control over this unreasoning reaction. On one occasion it could have cost him his life, had it not been for the swift reflexes of his worried wife. Jon has revealed that 'She stopped me jumping out of a moving car, one time.'

Unsurprisingly, that was the point at which Dorothea decided Jon needed to seek professional help in overcoming his problems, and she encouraged him to consult a therapist.

The prospect of opening up to a stranger about what was tying him in knots was not particularly alluring to someone normally so self-contained. But, recognising he was in trouble, Jon was prepared to give therapy a shot. However, the first session was his last. Having turned up late, he was just about ready to unburden himself when the therapist, with other people to see, called time, requesting he schedule another appointment. Momentarily thrown, Jon gathered his exposed emotions together and grimly decided on Plan A – he would sort himself out.

Clearly, a large part of his recovery process would entail stepping back from the rock star life. That prospect, strangely, didn't feel as repellent to him as he might have suspected because, for the first time in years, Jon had no desire to write new Bon Jovi songs. Yet inactivity was not an option. It was almost a godsend then when, in spring 1990, Jon was made an offer he couldn't refuse.

Hollywood screenwriter John Fusco had adored the 1987 hit, 'Wanted Dead Or Alive', which had proved inspirational for him while penning what became the 1988 blockbuster Western *Young Guns*. Now, two years later, while shooting was underway for *Young Guns II*, Fusco approached Jon out of the blue, originally to ask permission to use 'Wanted Dead Or Alive' in the sequel. Jon was flattered. However, once the men truly focused on the song in this context, it became clear that while the punch line and overall tone seemed perfect, the actual lyrics were not really suitable. Jon promptly offered to write a new song; Fusco was delighted.

Furnished with the skeleton of the new film's plot, Jon eagerly set to work and came up with the proposed song fairly quickly. It was called 'Blaze of Glory', and reeked of reckless anti-heroism and the fatalistic defiance of the wanted outlaw. Confident of the song getting a good reception from the filmmakers, Jon was armed with it when he picked up on an invitation to come out to the movie location in Santa Fe, New Mexico.

Young Guns II, continuing the lawless adventures of the fabled Billy The Kid and his gang, and starring Emilio Estevez, Kiefer Sutherland and Lou Diamond Phillips from the first film, plus Christian Slater, was directed by New Zealander Geoff Murphy. The action-packed movie was to be darker than its successful predecessor, and Jon's atmospheric Wild West tale of a world-weary, ultimately doomed young gunslinger could not have been more appropriate. To his delight, it was decided that 'Blaze of Glory' would be the movie's main theme tune. Moreover, on the strength of that one song, the film-makers wanted Jon to work on a whole soundtrack.

To this end, hanging around the set was supposed to be beneficial to him. Jon had his acoustic guitar and a note pad with him to jot down his ideas and impressions. But that wasn't an all-day occupation, and his excitement at being on a film location underwent a sea change when the rest of the time he found himself standing about, doing nothing and freezing cold, despite being muffled up against the desert winter. Jon had travelled to the New Mexico location alone, a state he was neither used to nor comfortable with. But he quickly compensated for this by making friends with some of the cast members, particularly with lead actor Emilio Estevez. Said Jon, 'I hung out with him a lot and took a real liking to him.'

The more the two talked, and the more Jon heard about the best aspects of an actor's life, the more the showman in the singer was attracted to this other world. When the actors were needed back on camera and Jon was left feeling like a spare part again, he became easily disgruntled. Noticing this, the film crew roped Jon in as an extra. The idea of the Old West drifter, lonesome, independent and living on the edge, forever just a whisper from capture, had always been attractive to him. He needed little encouragement then to get dressed up in full cowboy regalia for the part offered

Since the mid-1980s Jon had been in the sights of many a

movie maker, but to date he had turned down every one of the several film scripts sent to him for consideration. He didn't yet see himself diversifying into acting, and that remained true even when he went before the cameras in *Young Guns II*. It would stretch it even to term Jon's appearance a cameo role. The scene in which he took part involved prisoners busting their way out of a jail, which in fact was a caged pit dug in the ground.

No sooner do the convicts launch themselves out of prison than they are sprayed with gunfire. Jon's unnamed character takes a hit square to the chest, copious fake blood spurts about and he completes a 30-second round trip by falling down dead, back into the pit. As his scene was being filmed, the crew good-naturedly teased the star by chorusing loudly, 'Shot through the heart ...' Later, Jon repeatedly had to play down his last-minute inclusion in the film. It was not, he stressed, his acting debut, which was still years away. Right then, his pressing need was to make progress with the movie's soundtrack, and his visit to the set had given him enough seed material.

Once Jon left Santa Fe, he headed to Hollywood. He'd decided to record the songs in A&M Studios in Los Angeles, and so made his base in an opulent mansion, which he nicknamed Disgraceland, in the Hollywood hills. It was convenient for his needs, but his personal taste in wall hangings was less extravagant than the house owner's. While he was there, he temporarily obscured them with masses of Elvis Presley posters. Bon Jovi had sampled the wild excesses of Tinseltown before. To Jon, Hollywood was definitely another name for Babylon, a place to go crazy and where fame could drive a man insane. But this time around, he allowed nothing to distract him from developing his batch of inspired new songs.

Just a few weeks earlier he would never have imagined he could feel this invigorated again. It was undoubtedly unsettling to be in a recording studio without the rest of Bon Jovi, but he had decided to lure a few special guest musicians to help him with the soundtrack. Among those happy to be involved was the British guitarist Jeff Beck, Jon's first choice to handle the lead guitar work on 'Blaze of Glory' and other tracks. At the recent annual Grammy Awards ceremony, Beck had won the trophy for Best Rock Instrumental Performance and he was just preparing to go on tour. The 45-year-old Surrey-born musician had often attended Bon Jovi concerts; he was so keen to respond to this request that he flew to LA and was in A&M Studios before Jon himself arrived one morning.

Elton John, in America for the release of his latest hit, 'Sacrifice', was already in Los Angeles. As a long-time fan of the English entertainer, Jon was thrilled when Elton agreed to contribute the piano work on a couple of numbers. But if Jon was one for heroes, he was not alone. The legendary 1950s wild rock 'n' roller Little Richard was already acquainted with Jon, having played on part of the New Jersey tour; he responded quickly to the frontman's call to join the growing group of select guest musicians. The veteran performer was Jon's father's idol and Jeff Beck was dumbstruck on being introduced to Little Richard.

The album also benefited from the impressive keyboard skills of Benmont Tench from Tom Petty's Heartbreakers. Jon himself played 12-string acoustic and electric guitar, piano and harmonica. With the exception of 'Guano City', Jon was also responsible for all the lyrics and music for the other ten tracks. And he co-produced the album along with experienced west coast studio man, Danny Kortchmar.

In the process of recovering from the gruelling album-tour-album cycle, working on a new album ought to have been the last thing Jon got involved with. In fact, he had a ball. Because the film's plot provided all the modelling clay for him, he considered this to be the easiest album he had ever put together. He discovered that writing a soundtrack was a wonderful outlet, one he anticipated seeking some other time, when he needed to strike out on his own.

By a long way, the album's stand-out track was 'Blaze of Glory'. 'You Really Got Me Now', on which Little Richard played, was distinctive for its honky-tonk piano style. Actor Lou Diamond Phillips sang backing vocals on 'Justice In The Barrel', the album's longest track. And Jon played the guitar solo in the heavily orchestral ballad, 'Santa Fe'. Probably Jon's fondest memories are of working with Elton John, particularly on the emotion-ladened ballad, 'Dyin' Ain't Much Of A Livin''. Jon had composed this song on the piano, all the while absorbed with the notion that it sounded intrinsically like an Elton John song. The older star ended up singing harmony with Jon on this track, as well as playing piano.

Skilfully tailored to the film's content, the whole album – a collection of hard rockers, ballads, even a pseudo-religious revivalist number – conjures up mental images of desperate saloon bars, summary justice and gun-toting dusty outlaws who drink hard liquor and live short, lonely lives in which a man's gotta do what a man's gotta do.

Pleased with the product, Jon now had to film a video for 'Blaze of Glory'. He roped in director Wayne Isham, who had distinct ideas of what would work. Jon had confidence in his friend and was game to follow Isham's hunches. One hunch led to Jon, Wayne and a film crew deliberately stranding themselves high on a tabletop section of mountain so that they could make the most dramatic use of last and first daylight out in the vast, awe-inspiring wilderness. They turned the whole experience into a mini-adventure, camping out on site to wait for these optimum moments. In the two limited windows for filming Jon, dressed half Indian/half cowboy style, threw himself into performing the song. With swirling aerial shots and interrogating close-ups, and once spliced with silent action excerpts from the movie, it turned out to be one of Jon's most effective videos.

When work was completed on *Blaze Of Glory*, Jon was a bundle of excited anticipation at its release later in the year. When he arrived back on the east coast, the experience had given him a taste for working with other artistes. It was timely that Polygram now offered Jon the chance to set up a record label. The records would be distributed by Polygram but Jon would have a free hand when it came to choosing the artistes whose work would be released on the new label.

Ever family-oriented, Jon drafted in his two brothers, Anthony and Matt, to partner him in this venture; they named the label Jambco, which stands for Jon, Anthony, Matt Bongiovi company. Early signings to this fledgling label were the singer/songwriter Billy Falcon and Canadian-born artiste Aldo Nova.

In the early 1980s Aldo Nova had seemed an emerging force in music when his debut album, *Fantasy*, went platinum in the States. He had contributed to Jon's demo of 'Runaway' in 1982 at New York's Power Station studio, but had since somewhat fallen out of the public eye. Aldo and Jon had teamed up on and off, writing songs during the late 1980s. And now, in spring 1990, they had been so industrious that Nova had a healthy pool of co-compositions from which to consider pulling an album together.

Blood On The Bricks, described as excellent by *Raw* when it arrived the following year, would become the first release from Jambco Records. Aldo Nova openly praised Jon, crediting the star with having removed his sense of lethargy. 'Who knows where I'd be without Johnny,' he said. 'He really did work his heart out and played a big role in the album.' Billy Falcon's album, *Pretty Blue World*, followed soon after, while Jon was still learning the ins-and-outs of running his own record label.

As spring 1990 unfolded Jon received many requests from artists keen to enlist his songwriting and/or production skills. The American duo Daryl Hall and John Oates's new album, *Change Of Season*, listed Jon Bon Jovi among its co-producers, and their ballad, 'So Close', co-produced by Jon and Danny Kortchmar, peaked at number 11 in the US singles chart.

And so, as part of his healing, the gradual process of temporarily divorcing himself from the role of high-profile rock star continued. Never more so than when, in early summer, Jon hooked up with his friend Southside Johnny, joining him and the Asbury Jukes on a short tour of the east coast club circuit. Since Jon had never deserted his roots, this was not an exercise in reminding himself of where he came from. It was a genuine, low-key busman's holiday, which thrilled him. Gone were the jet travel, the plush hotel rooms and such luxuries as the travelling wardrobe personnel. It was back to lugging about his own amp, guitar cases and luggage, to squeezing into one van with a ten-man band and to bunking up overnight in cheap motels.

Even while he was content to play rhythm guitar and sing backing vocals, it's hard to imagine Jon Bon Jovi not attracting a storm of attention as the tour took in over a dozen cosy watering holes. But Jon got a lot out of the experience of not being in charge, not out front. Slapping his beer glass on top of his amp, he concentrated on enjoying the gigs and the ride until the tour ended with a show in Asbury Park.

It hadn't been hard for Jon to melt back into the New Jersey club performer scene. Despite his superstardom, away from Bon Jovi tours where security measures are required, he's as regular a guy as is possible in the circumstances. Off duty, he has no truck with personal bodyguards, adopts no pseudonyms when registering at hotels and has never been a prima donna. If recognised in the street, he doesn't throw tantrums about invasion of his privacy. 'It's no hassle to sign an autograph or pose for a few seconds for a snapshot,' he's maintained. Nor has he ever considered himself better than the guys who come to see the concerts, and has openly stated that in lots of bars around the world there are probably local entertainers with a better singing voice than his.

His attempts to keep a low public profile, however, ended in July 1990 as the movie *Young Guns II* premiered in American theatres, and the soundtrack album *Blaze Of Glory* was released. It shot to number three in the American album charts, soon claiming one place higher in Britain. By the year's end, it was certified double platinum and went on to sell over three million copies worldwide. The title track single, 'Blaze of Glory', stopped at number 13 in the UK but seized the top slot in the US charts. And as the album looked certain to attract awards, the plaudits rained down on Jon's solo achievement.

Although it had not been designed as such, the blistering triumph of *Blaze Of Glory* and its number one hit spin-off single was effectively a warning shot across the bows for the rest of Bon Jovi. It is inconceivable that the other four band members, busily pursuing their own individual lives, were not also keeping a weather eye on what Jon was up to solo. It would be surprising if insecurities did not begin to creep in now, the paramount question being – does he really need us?

The personal triumph had restored Jon's self-confidence. But he was not prepared to trumpet the soundtrack as a solo breakaway album. Indeed, on *Blaze Of Glory*'s liner notes, having thanked various people including his family and Dorothea, Jon wrote, 'This album is for Richie, Alec, Tico and Dave – still the baddest band on God's earth.' The music media, however, saw things differently, and the album's glittering success was tarnished a little for Jon by the mushrooming speculation that it marked the end of Bon Jovi, or at the very least signalled a serious doubt about the band's long-term future.

Press talk of damaging rifts within Bon Jovi had first cropped up even before the New Jersey tour had ended, back in February. At the time, no one officially corroborated the rumour mill's innuendos of splits and imminent defections. But it had increased the internal strain already being felt by all involved. The British tabloid newspaper, the *Sun*, had run a story suggesting that the situation between Richie and Jon was so tense that the guitarist might be on the verge of leaving. Not for the first time in such circumstances, somebody had simply got their wires crossed. But this kind of talk had been sufficient for Jon to be inundated by hopeful guitarists offering to fill a non-existent vacancy.

Prior to that, when Bon Jovi were still playing their final gigs in Mexico, Tico Torres was erroneously quoted in one of the rock magazines as saying that he had quit the band. So Jon was thought to be hunting for a replacement, and he was promptly snowed under with audio tapes, photographs and introductory letters from a plethora of ambitious drummers. Furious and frustrated, Jon had chucked all the tapes and accompanying literature out of a top-floor hotel window before ripping into Tico, the first chance he got, in irate and colourful terms about what he had read.

It came as news to the buttonholed drummer that he said he had quit the band. According to Jon, it appeared that Tico had been relaxing in a bar, and while in conversation with some strangers he had been trying to speak the lingo. Whatever Tico had thought he was saying in his far from perfect Spanish, had suffered in translation. Jon had been close to tearing his own hair out. Now, five months later, things were no happier. Jon bluntly dubbed the dismal state of affairs, 'a whole fucking fiasco', growling to journalists that many things had been printed that had been taken way out of context, and the resulting damage had stoked a fire that no one in the band had wanted. How it had come to be so bad was a puzzle, but they were still not talking to one another

To escape from it for a while, Jon took off on his Harley-Davidson on a three-week motorbike ride across America from Texas to California. Joining him on his cross-country travels were Dorothea, Doc McGhee, Wayne Isham and half a dozen other friends. Dorothea rode pillion with Jon, and the five-bike cavalcade hit the road early every morning, riding until early evening and stopping overnight at roadside motels. Although Jon had toured for years, he felt that only now was he really seeing something of his own country. He probed back into America's past, too, taking an interest in the Indian reservation culture. And he found the hours riding the open road helpful, in that he had time and space to clear his head.

It was a therapeutic sojourn, but it didn't help Jon for long. Once he returned home, his spirits were in danger of sinking low again. Inactivity quickly bored him, and music press talk that Bon Jovi were finished still darkened his mood. It's hardly surprising. Bon Jovi had been Jon's great drive, his full-time focus for so long. How could he just glance over his shoulder to see if it could still be there? There is no doubt that he wanted to keep the band together, that in his mind the separation was merely a hiatus in proceedings. There was too much history invested in the band. They had struggled together from having nothing. Surely, they could resolve their problems together too. His loyalty to his four band-mates was as powerful, he said, as the allegiance he felt towards his immediate family. Yet it would take some time before any of them really knew if Bon Jovi had a future. Enough had been written about them having problems to have convinced the individual members that whatever basic umbrage they felt was now magnified many times.

It was against this backdrop that Jon set out on a fairly short, but packed round of promotional duties throughout Europe in support of *Blaze Of Glory*. When, midway, he landed in London it is hard not to conclude that the star was in a strange frame of mind. He was certainly not his normal self during at least one major magazine interview. The usually controlled frontman seemed to have been replaced by an impostor. The Jon Bon Jovi who sprawled ostentatiously on a sofa in one of the capital's top clubs with his booted feet propped up on a coffee table grinned behind dark glasses about feeling like shit, looking like shit but said that he didn't give a shit. And he positively crowed that, during what spare time he had in London, he intended to get drunk and laid, not necessarily in that order. What's more, he would be repeating this lusty ambition every night for the remainder of the tour.

When asked what his wife back home might have to say about this publicly stated intention to be unfaithful, Jon declared in equally high-octane mode that he would deny it if the magazine printed his words, which, of course, they did. With untypical crassness, Jon ended the same interview with the nugget that he was headed to a particular trendy London nightclub, 'because it is full of the most amazing pussy.' When quizzed years later on these statements, Jon explained that though he might have talked about chasing women while alone on tour, he did not actually follow through.

Discovering an uncharacteristically slack-mouthed Jon Bon Jovi had probably pleased the journalist. But what the whole over-the-top blasé pretence indicated was that he was on a knife edge, and not overly comfortable with the music press in general right then. Portraying the stereotypical assholic rock star, uncaring and on the make, could have been an act to protect his inner vulnerability over his band's internal relations from showing itself to the very set of people who were doing Bon Jovi a disservice.

In October 1990 'Miracle', Jon's second and last solo cut from *Blaze Of Glory*, was released. In America it scored a number 12 hit, and in Britain it levelled out the next month at 29. In just over another month's time, a miracle was probably going to be needed, in the circumstances, to get Bon Jovi through a very tough test. They had a long-standing commitment to play a series of dates in the Far East around the turn of the year, also a concert on New Year's Eve at the Tokyo Dome, to be broadcast by MTV.

In early December then, the five reconvened to rehearse in an awkward atmosphere. They were conscious that the music press were on high alert for any potential fireworks or visible crack lines, especially when the band made its first public appearance for months on 23 December at a charity gig at the Count Basie Theater in Red Bank, New Jersey. They also held a press conference, through which they hoped they could put to rest doubts about the band's unity. However, when they flew out to Japan for the New Year's Eve bash, it became instantly obvious that all was far from well within the band. The tension between Jon and Richie, in particular, was overwhelming.

Hopes of concealing the unspoken animosity evaporated the moment a rock journalist and a photographer were given access to the band. *Rip* magazine were to do a cover story on Bon Jovi and had been invited to catch up with the band in Japan. Journalist Lonn Friend, on the trail of discovering if there was any truth to the rumours of an internal band crisis, flew out with the inspired cover line, 'Bon Jovi Dead Or Alive?' already branded on his mind.

In the event, the photo session for the cover itself signalled the extent of the problem. As Ross Halfin, the experienced photographer accompanying them, later attested, during the journey to the shoot's location and throughout the 90-minute session, Jon and Richie completely ignored one another. Not a single word was exchanged. The magazine's ready-made concept for the cover shot gave a clue to part of the trouble. As Lonn Friend revealed, the firm remit from their editor was to have Jon resplendent and dominantly to the fore of the picture, with Richie behind him, looking over the frontman's shoulder. Jon was unaware that this figurative and literal state of affairs was gnawing away at the musician, and it would be some time yet before it came to light.

The roller coaster carried on after Bon Jovi left the Far East and each man went his separate way. For Jon, some good things were happening, although the pleasure they brought was blunted by the unhappy state of the band. In mid-January 1991, 'Blaze of Glory' won the prestigious Golden Globe Film Award for Best Original Song For A Motion Picture. Attending the lavish ceremony with Dorothea, Jon had arrived for the occasion in formal dinner dress but he hadn't expected to win. When his name was called, he quietly cursed in his wife's ear, 'Shit! I don't believe it!' Nine days later, on 28 January, Jon once again collected a trophy for the hit song when it won the American Music Award for Favourite Pop/Rock Single of 1990.

The following month this achievement was complemented when 'Blaze of Glory' received a Grammy Award nomination for Best Original Song In A Film. Around the same time, in the equivalent category, the work also attracted a coveted Academy Award nomination. Ultimately, Jon didn't win the Grammy or the Oscar. In the case of the latter, on the night of 25 March 1991 at the 63rd Academy Awards ceremony, the accolade for Best Original Song In A Movie went to composer Stephen Sondheim for 'Sooner Or Later', which featured in the 1990 remake of *Dick Tracy*, directed by and starring Warren Beatty.

Jon performed 'Blaze of Glory' during the ceremony and Richie accompanied him. But this professional on-stage pairing before the world's cameras did not mean that all was well between them. When the evening ended, Jon was more despondent about the state of his and Richie's fractured friendship, than about having dipped out on carrying home the famous gold statuette.

From the outside, Jon's world continued to look successful and happily carefree. In reality, where it counted (apart from his happy marriage), it bumped along on the bottom. He and Dorothea took to spending a lot of their time in California, living in Malibu for what Jon later termed 'the grey summer'. By his own admission, there he sank into a demoralising daily routine of flaking out on the beach, drinking more than was helpful to his already miserable frame of mind. It wasn't supposed to have worked out this way. He had made his teenage dreams more than come true. But the place where the mind-blowing whirlwind of the last four years had set him down, seemed to be empty and ugly. Every day Jon sat for endless hours, swigging from a bottle, lost in a maelstrom of emotion – dejection, disillusionment, confusion and anger. To lose now what Bon Jovi had striven to achieve would be an infernal waste.

Repeatedly backtracking his thoughts to the end of the New Jersey tour when no one in the band was talking to one another, Jon still failed to fathom what had gone so wrong. Bon Jovi had not fallen victim to the familiar pitfalls which cause fatal schisms in bands. No one had been cheated financially. None of the guys had moved in on another guy's girlfriend or wife. And they were not a drug-ridden, degenerate band rendered incapable and on the slide. It made no sense. When anger at the frustration of it all was added to the confusion, it sent Jon round and round in anguished mental circles. Watching her normally dynamic, busy husband loafing about, drinking and troubled, must have been hard for Dorothea, but she was powerless to solve his problems.

These months were not a period of inactivity for every Bon Jovi member. David Bryan, for example, put his musical talent to work on material for the instrumental soundtrack to a horror film called *Netherworld*. Richie Sambora, meanwhile, struck out on his own with his first solo album. Eric Clapton guested on one track, 'Mr Bluesman', and the ten songs comprised an impressive, mainly blues-oriented collection. On this album, Richie placed less emphasis on his signature guitar playing and promoted himself more vocally, showing that in addition to the melodic, harmonising skills he employed on Bon Jovi records, he possessed a fine blues singing voice. In August 1991, Sambora's first solo single, 'Ballad of Youth', was released. It struggled on both sides of the Atlantic, managing only number 63 and 59 in the US and UK charts respectively. Its parent album, *Stranger In This Town*, on Mercury Records, followed soon after, halting at number 36 in America, though making the Top 20 in Britain.

Watching the five former friends individually bob about almost aimlessly compared with their usual joint dynamism, manager Doc McGhee decided to try to take control of the situation. Getting the band back together for the Japanese trip months earlier had not exactly been a roaring success, but that did not stop him hoping that things could be different now. At the upcoming annual MTV Video Music Awards in early September, Bon Jovi were to be honoured with the Michael Jackson Video Vanguard Award, and McGhee worked overtime to get all five to agree to show up at the Universal Amphitheatre in California's Universal City to collect it. It was a plan that would backfire, with unlooked-for repercussions for the manager.

On the night, Bon Jovi begrudgingly turned up at the venue, but the atmosphere was taut. 'I wouldn't sit with them,' admitted Jon. 'They wouldn't sit with me.' As Jon waited to be called on stage, it festered in his mind that he had allowed himself to be talked into accepting a trophy which stood as a Lifetime Achievement Award. In his jaundiced opinion right then, that was a joke. Bon Jovi had made four albums; the two latest had catapulted them to stardom. It was hardly a lifetime's work; he wasn't even 30. The band weren't on good terms and yet had agreed to appear on stage together and take part in a charade that was designed merely to boost TV ratings, Jon now decided, as his bad mood worsened.

The band congregated on stage and the frontman was clearly in grim humour as each member accepted his trophy. Jon then told the theatre and TV audience, 'This is not an award for anyone else but our fans', making it patently clear what he thought about the whole thing by walking off stage and promptly handing his trophy to a startled young woman standing close by, telling her to keep it.

If Doc McGhee had somehow missed the ominous storm signs gathering at the show, when he joined Jon in the back of his limousine after the ceremony, he was left in no doubt of the star's acute displeasure. The larger-than-life, one-time disgraced Doc McGhee was a friend, and in eight years of managing the band's affairs he had worked hard to fulfil his initial boast to make them the biggest band in the world. Jon openly acknowledges that. But their relationship had been changing, and the clash which erupted in the car leaving

Universal Amphitheatre that night was just the catalyst that brought matters to a head. Doc McGhee has since admitted that the situation between himself and Jon *had* been disintegrating and that the fault for that probably lay more with himself than with Jon. The upshot was that Jon fired Doc McGhee.

Hindsight would prove that this low, depressed point was actually the moment matters turned the corner for Jon Bon Jovi and, ultimately, for the band. For in the wake of that decisive action, Jon shook himself out of the pit he had wallowed in for too long. He cut out the brooding and the drinking sessions, and seized greater control of his destiny. As soon as it became public that Jon and Doc McGhee had parted company, rock managers began circling. Over the remaining months of the year Jon did consult with several potential candidates. But deep down, he probably always knew that he would form his own management company. In the event, unable to see anyone else suiting his band, he created Bon Jovi Management (BJM).

Bon Jovi was a multi-million-dollar-earning outfit, and Jon felt that he had become too much like the chairman of the board. He wanted to effect changes, to restructure matters so that he was better able to see how fast the road was rising up to meet him and the band. He envisaged a different way of handling affairs. He opted for a scaled-down business team which included ex-tour manager Paul Korzilius and former McGhee Entertainment Inc employee, Margaret Sterlacci.

Now steps also had to be taken to combat the malaise within the band. Almost two years had elapsed since the end of the New Jersey tour. It was time to grasp the nettle. They had to see if they had a future or not; this would entail facing up to what had gone so badly wrong in the past. Jon was so serious about sorting out the mess that, having managed to get the whole band to agree to gather together to tackle this task (itself no mean feat), he also got them eventually to agree to the presence of an independent, professional mediator; not so much a peace broker, as a sounding board for all individual complaints.

At first, any idea of talking to a mediator was met with deep suspicion. But the band eventually agreed to go with it. Jon called it a blessing, because in the presence of this neutral party everyone gradually overcame the strangeness of it all and opened up, revealing their true feelings. It couldn't always have made for a comfortable experience, and some home truths about each other might have hurt, but it was necessary.

Among the feelings exposed was how overworked the band had been by the end of the last tour. Jon learned from Alec that he had felt so worn out that he believed he literally couldn't take the killing pace any more, but that he had to continue because Jon was so determined to keep going. Richie backed up that complaint, revealing, 'I was begging Jon near the end of the tour to go home, but he's a workaholic.' Jon's desire to work all the time, Richie has declared, was practically making him ill. Sambora said, 'I was drinking far too much. I was ready for the funny farm.'

Jon could only plead guilty as charged to being a workaholic. He would not deny that he had been a tough taskmaster. There was, though, another problem bothering the lead guitarist. Richie had once stated that he knew he did not have Jon's rare 'it' factor. 'I know when I'm beat,' he'd declared. But that said, he had been finding it increasingly difficult to play second fiddle to Jon all the time. This was entirely understandable. Sambora is a handsome, charismatic man in his own right, a superb musician and an accomplished songwriter. Yet he felt undervalued by the record company, largely overlooked, certainly overshadowed by Jon's public dominance of the band. He had harboured these insidious feelings for some time and only now let his friend in on them.

Taking all these revelations and complaints on board, Jon had some feelings of his own to express plainly. Among them was surely the notion that the others had perhaps failed to appreciate fully just what a heavy burden he had shouldered all these years. His hands were full *all* the time. Nothing in any area of the band's existence was done without his knowledge and involvement. True, it was his wish to be totally hands-on, but it had taken its toll on him.

After the successful session with the mediator, Jon took the band away for a week to the Caribbean island of St Thomas, where they stayed together in one house, to carry on this clear-out and to see where they were going from there. Once all the grievances, real or imaginary, had been aired, each one was better apprised of how the others felt, and it felt good. Overall, they realised that though they had been burned out on each other, there was no hate. If the rancid, directionless animosity had not been addressed and dealt with, it would have killed the band off needlessly. Instead, as 1992 got underway, they collectively reaffirmed their belief in, and commitment to the band, and were at last raring and ready to revive Bon Jovi.

CHAPTER 7

Survival of the Fittest

THE SECOND CHAPTER OF BON JOVI began in spring 1992, when the reunited band got down to working on material for a new album. They knew they had come together again for the right reasons, but that did not prevent a certain degree of desperation initially. Too anxious to recapture how it all originally began, they tried to break themselves in by creating an atmospheric basement environment at Jon's house in which to jam like the good old days. It was an exercise that was doomed to fail.

Instead of peaky electric light, very little heating and torn lagging hanging from rattling overhead pipes, this time the place was comfortable, bathed in the mellow glow of dozens of candles and dreamy lava lamps. They were also famous, wealthy young stars, not gimlet-eyed, lean wannabes, hungry for a break. In the event, the artificial stimulus was short-lived. After a couple of hours playing music, Jon noted a distinct lack of sustained concentration around him. Miserable at the thought that maybe they *had* lost the vital spark, the problem then dawned on him. As he later explained, 'The truth was, that all the oxygen was being sucked out of the air by these fucking candles! Honest to God, they were putting us to sleep.'

But they didn't need to plunder their past to find their future, and when they realised that, they began a six-month period of intensive work that took them back to Little Mountain Sound Studios in Vancouver; this time under the auspices of Bob Rock as producer. No one underestimated the challenge facing them. It was over four years since they had been together in a recording studio. Against a backdrop of media rumours of band disunity, a lot was at stake to make this new album a success. Once again, Bon Jovi seemed to have to prove itself.

It was also a time of much change in the world. Socially, America was a tinderbox of civil unrest, which ignited in late April with three days and nights of race riots in Los Angeles. Four white policemen had just been acquitted of criminal wrongdoing in the case of black motorist Rodney King, whose beating by the officers the year before had been captured on videotape. Politically, the map was about to be redrawn. Republican President George Bush was coming to the end of his run in office as grim recession gripped the US. And William J. Clinton, on the promise of creating a new era of renewal and hope, would sweep to power near the end of the year, installing the first Democrat President in the White House for 12 years. Clinton's running mate and subsequent Vice President, Al Gore, is a politician to whom Jon Bon Jovi later gave great support.

In this social climate the music world had also altered. The Aids issue had been shoved to the fore by Freddie Mercury's death in November 1991. The hedonistic, reckless rock world which had thus far preferred to ignore 'the Aids thing' had suddenly been forced to confront its glitzy but thoughtless way of life. And as it fell back on its heels a while, through the centre had emerged a new low-key, scruffy, alternative rock movement dubbed 'grunge'.

A blend of pop metal and a resurrected '90s version of drab punk rock, its first exponents were Seattle bands, notably Nirvana fronted by Kurt Cobain. The high critical acclaim afforded to Nirvana's late 1991 hit album, *Nevermind*, and its spin-off single, 'Smells Like Teen Spirit', lit the way for the likes of Soundgarden and Pearl Jam. Bon Jovi, then, had chosen to regroup in 1992 at the height of the grunge rock wave, when critics would salivate at nothing that stood outside of this current trend

While conscious of this future obstacle, neither Jon nor the rest of the band allowed it to affect their own work. Years ago, Bon Jovi had recognised the folly of chasing the latest fad, and continued to prefer standing its own ground. This did not mean that they stubbornly stagnated. Four years is a long, sometimes professionally suicidal, gap between albums. But in contrast to the situation when the time between *Slippery When Wet* and *New Jersey* was too short to allow for proper growth, in the extended period between *New Jersey* and their fifth studio album, the uneven path of life had changed all five men substantially, and these experiences had an impact on the songwriting.

By summer 1992 their new collection had panache. It also had a stripped-down, no-frills rock sound, and showed an unmistakable maturity. Jon warned their fans not to look for *Slippery When Wet III*. That would make no sense. Jon also had no intention of scurrying after the coat-tails of the much-favoured Seattle grunge heroes. On the other hand, as a citizen of a country scarred by frightening race riots, in deep economic crisis with rising unemployment, and where crack cocaine sold on street corners was a deadly scourge, he was not going to write about how sunny life was. Besides, tapping into the bare essentials of the struggles faced at street level had been part of the Bon Jovi pedigree from the start.

That said, it is true that a higher than normal percentage of the song lyrics on this album were personal to Jon himself. In these, he wasn't talking anymore of a Tommy or Gina. He was consciously exposing elements of his own life experiences. He also wrote in the first person far more than usual. It follows then that this Bon Jovi album contained the highest number of solely penned Jon Bon Jovi compositions – six in all; half the record's full complement. There was a sporadic strain of disillusionment throughout, but the dozen tracks collectively were released as *Keep The Faith*.

The cover pictured a hand of each band member piled one on top of the other as if taking a joint oath – an unashamed visual reaffirmation of their brotherhood. And the album title was easily interpreted as a rallying call between the band members, as well as from the band out to their worldwide legion of fans to ignore the rumours of dissent in the ranks and stay faithful. The title track was one of only two three-way collaborations this time around between Jon, Richie and Desmond Child. A strong, moody, sometimes plaintive song, its intro was very reminiscent of the prelude to the Rolling Stones' 1968 number, 'Sympathy For The Devil', and it flirted with being a socio/political song. The other co-composition was a good old sexy rocker called 'I'll Sleep When I'm Dead'.

The material was interestingly diverse throughout the album, and over the months working with producer Bob Rock the band had at one stage operated out of five separate studios in the search for different, distinct sounds compatible with individual songs. Jon had also spread himself thin, chasing from one facility to another, rewriting right up to the wire. This intensive effort had its reward, but Jon soon singled out two numbers that he personally regretted on the final record. One was his own solo composition, 'Woman In Love', a loud, flat-out ode to love. The other was the R&B number, 'Little Bit of Soul', which he co-wrote with Richie.

Keep The Faith only contained three such two-way collaborations. Jon and Richie teamed up with keyboardist David Bryan to create the romantic ballad, 'In These Arms'. The album included two unusual numbers. One was 'If I Was Your Mother', whose chugging, raucous musical style tends to deflect attention from lyrics with potentially complex hidden meaning. The other was 'Dry County'; at nine minutes 53 seconds this is by far the longest track on *Keep*

The Faith. Written by Jon alone, it shows traces of a Neil Young influence. It queries what role religious faith can possibly play in tough, tormented times, and its religious connotations and social comment are captivating. Usually an optimistic songwriter, a renowned advocate of battling through in life, Jon in 'Dry County' allows an interesting insight into his more cynical frame of mind at this time.

To go with the updated sound of the upcoming release, Bon Jovi rethought their whole image. In terms of stage wear, they were happy to opt for a more natural, dressed-down look – jeans, jacket and T-shirt. But it was one particular departure from the past which grabbed the attention – Jon's hairstyle. It frequently riled him that so much attention was paid to this feature. But the fact remained that when he had his famous long mane of scrunched hair shorn to a blow-dried, collar-length straight style, it caused a great deal of fuss; it was even an item on CNN. To Jon, the sharp contrast in his personal style was part and parcel of discarding excess baggage from a defunct decade and moving on. But crazy rumours circulated that he had been forced to cut his hair after it had got badly singed at a barbecue. Keeping a rein on his impatience at such daft speculation was sometimes testing, especially when he still faced questions over it several years later.

Concentrating on what mattered, Bon Jovi put a toe back into the water when their first single in nearly three years, 'Keep The Faith', was released in October 1992. Its accompanying video, filmed on the streets of midtown Manhattan, showcased the band's new look and gutsier sound, and the single quickly claimed the number five slot in Britain. In America, however, the record ran dry at number 29, Bon Jovi's poorest position in the US singles chart for seven years. Jon knew that stepping back into the limelight after a lull would have its risks. Musically and lyrically, the song, combined with the video and capped with the new look, was a package Jon considered rather left field for Bon Jovi, but he believed it would work for the fans the way it had for the band. When it obviously hadn't, he waited for reaction to the album's release.

Conscious of the continuing downturn in the US economy, which hit the purchase of all non-essential items, Richie Sambora admitted, 'Frankly, I was scared it wouldn't do well.' Years later, Jon maintained that he had taken the philosophical attitude that if the album had bombed with the fans, then he would have viewed Bon Jovi as having had a pretty good innings. It would be surprising if this untypically sanguine stance lasted five minutes. The band had not regrouped merely in order to sink. They'd fought before and, if necessary, would do so again. As it happened, when *Keep The Faith* was released in early November it topped the UK chart and dropped anchor at number five in the States. True, they had been used to better in the home market, but it proved that the fans had not deserted them.

Worldwide, *Keep The Faith* went multi-platinum, notching up more than seven million sales – seven million reasons to discount critics' calls that Bon Jovi was passé, irrelevant to the 1990s and ought to fade away gracefully. Far from complying, the band laid plans for an extensive world tour to commence officially the following year, preceded by some warm-up gigs.

They had already played a bar show at the Fastlane in Asbury Park, New Jersey, in mid-October, and had taken part in the popular MTV 'Unplugged' series, which Jon and Richie were credited with inspiring. 'Bon Jovi Unplugged' had been taped at the Kaufman Astoria in New York City on 25 October 1992 and broadcast four nights later. They also played some so-called 'secret' shows, one of which was at the After The Gold Rush club in Tempe, Arizona, where they performed before an ecstatic capacity crowd of just under 1,000, prior to travelling to Britain and Europe on a quick promo excursion.

In early November they appeared at the intimate Astoria Theatre in London, while in the UK capital for a blitz of media interviews. Then they returned home to rest up over the holidays before the major onslaught of the world tour began. At the end of 1992, after all the upheaval and unhappiness of the last two years, Jon's life was back on track. Despite the swipes from the critics, the second phase of Bon Jovi had been launched, and he was looking forward to consolidating this start the best way he knew how – face-to-face out on the road.

On a personal front, feeling revitalised and having passed his 30th birthday, he faced a major change at home – Dorothea was expecting their first child, the baby being due in late May. It was a planned pregnancy, both parents-to-be were thrilled, and it signified a further strengthening of Jon's fulfilment as a married man. He would become a devoted father.

In the new year his contentment continued. Mid-January 1993 saw the release of 'Bed Of Roses', the first of four more singles from the album. The ballad peaked first in Britain at 13, weeks later reaching number 10 in America, a welcome improvement at home with the North American/Canadian leg of the Keep The Faith tour looming.

Bill Clinton had been inaugurated as America's 42nd president, and the nation's spirits had lifted. Erasing the depressing effects of recession would take a bit longer. Viewing the statistics to hand, Jon could see how the economic slowdown was impacting on his business. As yet, their tour was not sold out. It had been a long time since Bon Jovi had been unable to take filling the house for granted wherever they went. The prospect of finding out if their fans were still as committed must have been both exhilarating and slightly daunting. Even as experienced professionals, with all the past discord between them, being Bon Jovi live on stage before expectant audiences might feel different too.

Before the end of January, Jon reportedly came very close to making a dauntingly unscheduled live appearance on his own, before one of the world's biggest viewing audiences of all. With just days to go before the tour kicked off proper, Jon took time out to attend the Superbowl XXVII at the Rose Bowl in Pasadena, California, when the Buffalo Bills played the Dallas Cowboys. Slumped inconspicuously in his seat in the audience, enjoying the varied programme of events surrounding the actual football match, Jon was suddenly buttonholed by NBC-TV producers and asked would he be prepared, if needed, to step on to the podium to sing the US national anthem. A last-minute hitch had occurred, which the officials were worried might prevent country star Garth Brooks from making his scheduled appearance to perform the anthem. The annual Superbowl's global live TV audience ran into several millions, so the agitated television executives were hugely relieved when Jon calmly agreed. In the event, it proved unnecessary to shanghai Jon from the audience, as Brooks was able to take centre stage, after all.

The Keep The Faith world tour began on 8 February 1993 at the Colisée de Quebec in Quebec City, and over the next six and a half weeks the band crossed regularly back and forth between Canada and North America. As anticipated, there were occasional nights when they performed to patchy crowds, but they refused to let this demoralise them, despite the fact that evidence of empty seats played straight into their critics' hands. Their sold-out shows far outweighed the others. What Jon could see from the audiences as the tour swung out through Europe during April and into May, was that it was largely an older crowd out there, proof that their core fans were growing up with them. The only knock-back to that was the performance in America of their next single, 'In These Arms'. Released in mid-May, it secured number nine in the UK, where Bon Jovi were gigging at the time, but ducked out weeks later in the States at 27.

Chart positions, however, took second place for Jon as time grew closer to Dorothea giving birth. He had been the lusty fantasy of millions of female fans for years, but the heart-throb star had made clear that his priorities lay as very much a married man, when he revealed that while on tour he and his wife spoke by telephone every day, and that the most important thing in the world for them was the safe delivery of their child. As the days counted down he was waiting for the call to come. He vowed that even if he had to abandon a gig mid-flow to catch the fastest flight home, he would. 'The rest of the band can carry on without me,' he stated. No dramatic evacuation from the stage was necessary, however. Jon was able to be back with Dorothea when, on 31 May 1993, the couple's daughter, Stephanie Rose, was born.

Overjoyed as he was, professional commitments meant that Jon had to leave his wife and newborn babe to get back in harness as the world tour whisked in and out of Japan, before returning to America where, on 24 June, they kicked off proceedings at the Open Air Theater in San Diego. The metal band Extreme, fronted by Gary Cherone, played support to Bon Jovi throughout this latest leg until it ended on 8 August at the Merriweather Post Pavilion in Columbia, Maryland. By this stage the band had long ago settled in and had allayed any initial internal anxieties that a world tour, thrusting them all together again, might renew past tensions. It helped that they paced things out better. They even had a week's break now before heading back to Europe, and Jon had made sure to benefit from the assistance of a voice coach.

He was also excited to have time with his new daughter, and while the band could cool their heels at home, Jon had the guys over to his house to hang out a couple of times. Richie Sambora lived nearby and Jon enjoyed going sailing with his friend on the guitarist's boat.

The sense of place and perspective provided by this short holiday at home did not let Jon miss the blip on the register which concerned the latest single release. The cheeky rock song, 'I'll Sleep When I'm Dead', was released in July, and by August had gained a Top 20 position in Britain. But its 97th best in America was now Bon Jovi's worst chart showing ever. Jon knew they were still cutting it live, which made this recent US singles chart failure all the more puzzling. It could be that they were in danger of wearing out the album during particularly lean times; there were yet another two cuts from *Keep The Faith* planned for release in the next seven months. At any rate, Bon Jovi barely scraping into Billboard's Top 100 had the critics keen to crow 'I told you so!'

After flying from New Jersey to Berlin, to commence their second European stint this trip, Jon replied to taunts from some sections of the rock press about the shaky beginnings of the tour saying, 'Rumours of my death were greatly exaggerated. A lot of bands have died this year, but our tour did better than anyone else's during our second US leg.' The band was clearly imbued with a new confidence. For one thing, when speaking publicly, all five felt able to touch on the once-raw topic of the stress-filled first years of the decade. They were now determined to box up the trouble as nothing more than 'family squabbles'. As to toughing out these recessionary times, David Bryan crystallised their strategy as going out each night to 'kick ass'.

Collectively, they were agreed that this tour was their most enjoyable yet. They had been so firmly in the eye of the storm before, then so burnt out, that it had robbed them of the real pleasure from their rocketing success. This calmer, more ordered road life made it suitable for Dorothea and three-month-old Stephanie to accompany Jon to Europe. Over the years, Dorothea's usual practice on tour has been to stay at the band's hotel while Jon is working. On this occasion she remained at the Berlin hotel base when the band headed off on 18 August to perform the 126th gig of the Keep The Faith tour at the Waldbuhne, an impressive stone amphitheatre situated in a forest; with the way to the stage area via a tunnel bored through a hillside.

They played a different venue practically every night for their nine days in Germany, looked in on Switzerland before hitting Poland, Hungary, Austria and Czechoslovakia, then rolled through European stopovers such as Italy, Greece,

Turkey and France. Two special dates on Bon Jovi's busy calendar were 18 and 19 September, when they returned to the National Bowl in England's Milton Keynes. Jon still cherished glowing memories of their 1989 appearance there. The band was thrilled when the first show this time around had sold out so fast that a second had to be hastily scheduled. The support acts for both nights were Billy Idol, Little Angels and Manic Street Preachers.

These memorable gigs constituted the curtain drop on the European tour. A fortnight later, Bon Jovi's 'I Believe' bowed in in Britain at number 11, but was traceless back home. The band's concentration, however, was turned to breaking into the Asian market for the first time, performing in Taiwan and Hong Kong before arriving in Thailand for a gig at the Army Stadium in Bangkok. Thousands of overwrought fans mobbed the band on arrival, bringing mayhem to the capital's bustling airport. This kind of euphoric reception became a feature of Bon Jovi's journey through the Philippines and Singapore before the band returned to familiar territory in Australia in early October, where they spent a fortnight playing at major sports arenas.

Two ten-day breaks book-ended an eight-country South American incursion. Then the band flew into Vancouver, Canada, to start the end game to the tour, along the way revisiting the Colisée de Quebec where this return to the limelight had begun. The tour concluded a week before Christmas 1993, in time for Bon Jovi, on 20 December, to honour what had become an annual commitment to play a festive benefit gig at the Count Basie Theater in Red Bank, New Jersey.

Perhaps it is true that they had had to circle the globe to sustain the familiar levels of fan hysteria and substantial album sales. But despite being in competition with a rising breed of alternative bands, and being virtually friendless in music critic circles, ten years on from their formation Bon Jovi had done enough to prove that they were still a major star in rock music's firmament. This was something Jon was determined to maintain, though not at the cost any more of being sucked into the frenetic back-to-back album-tour-album cycles of old. That said, he welcomed the stimulus that the recent roadwork had given him. And although the family took off for a Caribbean holiday, early in the new year Jon invited Richie to join him there so that they could get down to some songwriting sessions for a new album.

There was still a remnant single release from *Keep The Faith* to come; the evocative 'Dry County' raised not a glimmer in America, yet in late March 1994 reached number nine in Britain. Jon had found the six-month period spent on creating *Keep The Faith* an unusually long time to concentrate on one work. He had no idea that this next album would take much longer, just to write the songs. It wasn't uninterrupted time, of course. On St. Valentine's Day 1994 Jon and Richie flew to London to appear at the annual Brit Awards ceremony held at Alexandra Palace, performing 'I'll Sleep When I'm Dead' and backing British-born soul/dance singer Dina Carroll. In late May, the pair also travelled to Nara City in Japan to perform at a music festival designed to showcase musical talent from all over the globe.

All the while plans were in place to release a greatest hits album, partly to bridge the gap that they now realised there was going to be between 1992's *Keep The Faith* and its studio successor, and partly because they had a genuine wealth of hits with every right to appear on such a collection. The process of selection was enjoyable and democratic, but time-consuming. Bon Jovi's first greatest hits album was slated for release in the autumn and would be called *Crossroad: The Best of Bon Jovi* – a highly appropriate title since, by then, the band would have just passed a crossroads in their existence.

In an entirely unlooked-for development to the band's global army of followers, summer 1994 saw the famously close-knit five-piece outfit pared down to four, with the departure of Alec John Such. It was a painful period, which for some time gave rise to confusing signals.

The fact that all was not entirely well in the Bon Jovi camp once more, first became public in July when Alec spoke candidly about his feelings to *Raw* magazine. In the published interview the bass player maintained that he would be touring the following year with Bon Jovi but that, by his own choice, he was not playing bass on the new album. Asked why not, Such stated, 'Jon tells me I [i.e. his bass playing] suck all the time.' Such had no wish, he said, to be involved in a tension-filled situation anymore. He felt that he played better live than in a recording studio. But that was not a view always shared by Jon or Richie.

Alec's other revelations included a claim that he had not been permitted to do any full-blown media interviews. He stated, 'I was told that nobody wanted to talk to me, and that came right from Jon's mouth.' He started to believe that that was true, he added. The idea that some kind of embargo had been placed on the musician giving interviews during their last outing was faintly puzzling. Less than a year earlier, in the midst of the *Keep The Faith* promo, Alec admitted to the press to being something of the mystery guy in the band, prepared to remain in the background. He declared in 1993, 'I could dig it because it meant I didn't get hassled. Hey, I was lazy. But I feel now that I want to contribute more.'

In the same interview Jon had chimed in that the bass player had clearly always valued his anonymity. He revealed lightheartedly that his attempts over the years to encourage Alec to do promotional work had been like pulling teeth. Speaking to *Raw* in 1994, Alec admitted that he had preferred to restrict his exposure to the limelight. Alec's *Raw* interview covered other, positive ground. It gave an insight into the bass player's wide range of private interests, and revealed his ambition to get into band management some day. But in a three-page feature flagged up as 'Metal Stars At War!' it was the negative remarks about Jon that grabbed the attention.

It had never been Bon Jovi's way to wash dirty linen in public, and for a while Jon was reluctant to respond to these remarks. When asked point-blank soon after to clarify what was going on, he confessed, 'I don't know how to answer that.' It was clearly not Jon's wish to give the oxygen of more publicity to speculation on what he regarded as an unresolved internal matter. But now that it had been put into the public arena, answers were looked for.

Jon confirmed that Alec would not be playing on the new studio album. Pressed for an explanation, he restricted himself to a sketchy remark along the lines that what Alec and the rest of the band wanted right then, were two different things. Jon stressed that they all wished Alec well. It was too bland to satisfy the hungry speculation, but it was all the press got for now. Yet the phrasing of one of the frontman's remarks seemed to be significant. When Jon was pressed to explain the bassist's contention that, while he would not be contributing to the album, he *would* still be appearing live with the band, he responded, 'He [Alec] would like to tour.'

Wishing and being allowed to could be construed as two different things. But it would be years before Jon and Richie revealed their personal take on the matter of Alec appearing live with them towards the end of the Keep The Faith tour. At that time their descriptions of some of his performances painted a picture that in their eyes, Alec had become a liability live. Richie spoke openly of mistakes being made to the extent that he felt it could become bad for the band when playing live before millions of people. Jon concurred that although they could perhaps compensate for any perceived temporary deficiencies in the studio, in his opinion it became unacceptable to sacrifice their live sound.

Jon talked of the need for everyone in a band to be able to carry their own weight, otherwise it becomes unfair to the others; 'We couldn't take care of it anymore,' he added. In the end, Jon said, he asked Alec to his house one night in summer 1994 and told him that he was out of the band. After more than ten years together, dropping Alec from Bon Jovi was not something Jon relished, but he later stated sadly, 'I had to do it.' However Alec viewed the situation, the fact was he was no longer in the band.

Ironically, after a slump in chart positions for their singles in America, around the time that Alec John Such left the brotherhood, the band hit big time with a song called 'Always', which dripped words of love and loyalty. Released in September 1994, this strikingly emotive romantic ballad had originally been written for the 1993 film *Romeo Is Bleeding*, a blood-soaked black comedy involving cops, the Mob and a female hired assassin. It was directed by Peter Medak and starred Gary Oldman, Lena Olin and Annabella Sciorra.

After the success of 'Blaze of Glory', Jon Bon Jovi was regularly head-hunted to write songs for movies, and he had agreed on this occasion because he liked the script. It had also been a distinct plus for Jon that Gary Oldman was to be the male lead. Approaching the task as a solo effort, Jon had come up with 'Always'. When he was allowed to preview the finished film though, he was so disappointed that he exercised his right to pull his song from the soundtrack. Describing the film as 'fucking awful', Jon would not be alone in finding fault with it; some critics dubbing it, 'slow, doomy and full of unnecessary excesses.' The same could not be said of 'Always'. Re-recorded as a Bon Jovi number and not on the back of a movie, it hit number two in Britain, making it Bon Jovi's biggest single so far in the UK. In America it lodged at number four and remained in the US Top 10 for a staggering six months.

Soon after, the 14-track greatest hits album, *Crossroad: The Best of Bon Jovi* (which included 'Always) was released. In October it went straight in at the top spot in Britain and stayed there for weeks, becoming the biggest UK seller of 1994. It would make number eight in America. In support of the new single, and in advance of the album's release in

Britain, Jon and Richie travelled to the UK for a promotional drive. One of the highlights turned out to be the day in early September when the two stars 'busked' in London. It happened one lunchtime at the piazza in Covent Garden. As word of their presence spread like wildfire, an estimated 3,000 people turned up, along with the media. Their playlist included old favourites 'Livin' On A Prayer' and 'Wanted Dead Or Alive', the rocker 'I'll Sleep When I'm Dead' and 'Someday I'll Be Saturday Night' (the other new number on *Cross Road* besides 'Always') with, to cap it all, the Paul Simon classic, 'Bridge Over Troubled Water'.

Cross Road: The Best of Bon Jovi became an international multi-platinum triumph, allaying Richie Sambora's earlier unease over releasing a greatest hits compilation. He had worried that this kind of album often pinpoints the end of a band's career. Indeed, the guitarist's suggested title for the collection had been *Elvis Is Dead But We're Not*.

By late October 1994 Jon and Richie had almost completed their marathon work on the material, and were about to start studio sessions for the next album, whose working title was being mooted as *Open All Night*.

There was one final record release of the year when, in December, they took out a cover version of the Charles Brown blues standard 'Please Come Home For Christmas'. The Eagles had last made the charts with this seasonal chestnut, securing a Top 30 hit in Britain in 1978. Bon Jovi's version made number seven but didn't register in America, despite Jon cavorting with supermodel Cindy Crawford on the song's video. Repeated shooting for the kissing sequences apparently spread over a week, which was 'hell', joked Jon. The profits from this single were to go to the Special Olympics, a charity for disabled athletes, which the singer had supported since the 1980s.

With their sixth studio album in the works there was word already of a summer 1995 stadium tour. Bon Jovi was now firmly a four-man band and Jon had decided that Alec John

Such would never be officially replaced. Hugh McDonald from New York City, an experienced musician who 12 years earlier had played on Jon's first hit, 'Runaway', would play bass on Bon Jovi records from here on in, and would appear with them live on stage. Album covers and all promotional material from now on though featured only Jon, Richie, David and Tico. Apart from the fact that the band were still getting used to this sea change in their line-up after all these years, Jon was wary of auditioning bass players, then introducing someone into the limelight as the new fifth member, only for things to perhaps not work out. Bon Jovi had newly come through a bumpy time; the last thing anyone needed was more public upheaval.

Even at the end of 1994, although Hugh McDonald had integrated very well with Bon Jovi working on the new studio album, it was not yet a given that he would be appearing live with them on the next tour. The year just drawing to a close had been a time of change in more ways than one. Having learnt from past mistakes, the individual band members had found a better way of balancing their professional and personal lives. There was no financial pressure to strain themselves with killer tour schedules. They didn't have to continue unless they really wanted to – a far healthier position to be in. They were also each in more settled relationships.

Drummer Tico Torres, not long turned 41, was now dating the Czechoslovakian-born model Eva Herzigova, 20 years his junior. In 1994 Miss Herzigova had been a literal traffic stopper when, as the stunning model for Wonderbra, posters of her pouting provocatively in the said garment had popped up at roadsides all over, with the slogan, 'Hello boys!'

Richie Sambora, too, had recently added yet more glamour to his world with the new woman in his life. He already had a tendency for romancing high-profile beauties. Apart from his relationship with Cher, he had also been linked for a time with actress Ally Sheedy. Back in spring, however, it was revealed that he had become involved with Hollywood actress Heather Locklear, once the wife of the controversial Mötley Crüe drummer, Tommy Lee. The beautiful blonde, popular for her roles in TV soaps *Dynasty* and *Melrose Place*, among others, and the tall, dark-haired lead guitarist made a handsome couple when, on 15 December 1994, they married in Red Bank, New Jersey. Two days later, they went through a formal wedding at the American Cathedral Episcopal Church in Paris.

David Bryan, who leads a very low-key private life, was already married; he and his wife, April, had started their family with the birth of twins in summer. Jon and Dorothea were now expecting the arrival of their second child, early in the new year.

With a growing young family, Jon realised he had to be more security conscious. He had never forgotten how it felt to be a passionate fan. And he appreciated that some Bon Jovi supporters took their deep devotion to the band so seriously that they were prepared to track down the individual members just to be able to hang around outside their houses. But Jon drew the line at people actually coming to his front door at all hours. 'I feel that my home should be off-limits,' he stated. While it was to be hoped that all Bon Jovi fans were harmless, in an age when John Lennon had been cold-bloodedly gunned down in the street, and several celebrities had been made the victims of obsessed stalkers, it was impossible to forget that fame carries its dark side. Jon kept their home security arrangements under constant review.

The anticipated arrival of his second child and his stable domestic contentment did not noticeably slow Jon down. He still worked a 16-hour day, seven days a week and had more than one project on the go at any given time. The new philosophy, shared by all the band, also recognised the need for each member to explore solo outlets, without this causing any ructions. In this respect, Jon was now poised to open up a particularly interesting parallel path professionally. For becoming an actor had infiltrated his personal ambitions.

Unknown to anyone beyond a handful of people (not even including the band), for the past two years Jon had been taking one-to-one private acting lessons in New York City with respected tutor to the stars, Harold Guskin. Applying his native dedication to this plan, Jon had also been reading a lot, poring over books about stagecraft, studying the classic plays and boning up on various playwrights. He was determined not to let the glamour side of the movie world he had glimpsed in *Young Guns II* allow him to run away with the notion that stepping from one profession into another would be a cakewalk.

Jon had not confided in the rest of the band about this new private pursuit because he needed to be certain first that trying to become an actor was something he was definitely going to go through with. He had also embarked on these acting lessons at a time when Bon Jovi's future had hung in the balance. He felt it could only have destabilised the situation further, if the others had discovered their frontman had set his sights on another kind of stage altogether. Music would always be Jon's first love, but, excitingly, his first film role was just around the corner.

CHAPTER 8

The Lure of
Pastures New

JON BON JOVI'S ACTING DEBUT was in the romantic drama *Moonlight and Valentino*, one of the many 'women's films' to flood the cinemas in 1995. Scripted by Ellen Simon and directed by David Anspaugh, this major movie's core cast comprised Elizabeth Perkins, Gwyneth Paltrow, Kathleen Turner and Whoopi Goldberg. Jon's role in the weepy was small but pivotal and he had been both surprised and pleased to have landed it. After years of private lessons with the plain-speaking New York acting coach Harold Guskin, Jon had felt ready to enter the fray. He was under no illusion that it would be easy; from the start, he wanted to be an actor who believably portrays a character in a film, not a famous rock star playing at being an actor.

He acquired an acting agent and, in addition to meeting a variety of people in the movie world, he had for some time been reading scripts passed on to him, before he spotted one role he really fancied – in a complicated cops-and-robbers thriller set in Los Angeles called *Heat*. Written and directed by Michael Mann, the movie already had on board veteran actors Robert de Niro, Al Pacino and Jon Voigt. Jon had put himself forward for the part of the youngest of the four central characters. But although he was seriously in the running for selection and was confident that he could have held his own in such experienced company, he ultimately lost out to Val Kilmer.

'Rejection is routine,' he declared. As he would quickly discover, however, he had entered an arena where lessons in humility are dished out remorselessly. A confident star in his own right, Jon still found his first experience of waiting in line to be auditioned so overwhelmingly nerve-racking that he had quietly backed out even before the read-through. It took another year before he felt ready to put himself into that situation again, when he was determined not to falter a second time. There was, however, an added hurdle – his own fame. In these early days when Jon would meet with film executives, while they were complete strangers to him, to them Jon Bon Jovi was very familiar. 'They think they know you.' said Jon, quickly conscious that this seemed to be something of a drawback.

Jon's involvement with *Moonlight and Valentino* began way back in its development stage, when he had liked an early treatment for the film enough to sustain his interest as the script went through months of structuring. The film was very much a vehicle for the female leads. But the role of the house painter who becomes the focus of sexual fantasy for the individual women, and whose primary function is to restore some romance into the life of a young, desolate, recently widowed academic, was interesting enough to want. As with *Heat*, for *Moonlight and Valentino* Jon had to go through the protracted selection procedure, aware this time that he wasn't exactly the film-makers' first choice. He revealed, 'I was the last guy they wanted in the role, so I went through the audition and call-back process until I got it.'

Jon flew to Toronto, Canada, in the last quarter of 1994 for roughly four weeks' work filming his scenes, only for churning nerves to assail him again, this time en route to the set on his first day. Momentarily, he wildly contemplated baling out. It was better, he figured, to be condemned as an eccentric celebrity than be proved a failure. Quashing these fleeting negative impulses, he carried on, but even then believed he had botched his opening scene in which, as the decorator, he shows up in his works van to unload his materials.

If Jon was clanking on his opening lines, these first-time jitters evaporated fast. As his screen tests had already clearly demonstrated, the camera loved him. Even in paint-spattered jeans and with a battered cap pulled over his long hair, his dazzling smile lit up his expressive eyes. His body language had an attractive ease that came with being a natural performer. Jon acknowledges that the role of the uncomplicated tradesman was not exactly demanding. Nonetheless, ultimately he enjoyed his first filming experience very much. Even though he was the magnet for the ladies, he was not required to tackle the tricky test of his first screen love scene. Jon recalled, 'I have a romantic interlude with Elizabeth Perkins's character, but it's just kissing, which means I keep my pants on!'

Jon started smoking while making the movie, but not through nerves. His whole approach, after day one, had been steadily focused. Elizabeth Perkins recalled that he coped with the difficult and foreign situation 'on an educational level'. Meaning that Jon showed an open appetite to learn from the experienced company of players around him. On set, the film's feel was amiable and lightweight. Off set, Jon noticed no thespian tantrums from the movie's fêted stars. It was also not a hard process, and no one made life difficult. Indeed, it struck the singer forcibly how unusual it was to feel so little pressure in a working environment. His only responsibility was to show up before the cameras, play his part to the best of his ability and go. All else lay in the hands of others.

In advance of the public seeing his big screen debut, Jon chose to define acting as just another creative outlet for him.

But he knew already that this was a second string to his bow which was going to be worth cultivating.

Moonlight and Valentino would hit the silver screens in America in October 1995, followed by general release in Britain the following summer. *Film Review* called it 'so slow at times, it is almost stationary'. And Tom Charity for *Time Out* ended his critique, 'In his first acting role, Jon Bon Jovi is relegated to the status of a sex object and he's every bit as anaemic as the rest.' That, though, proved a minority view. Jon's performance in this small supporting role won him acclaim across the board, and would help land him the lead role in a very different film, shooting for which was a year away.

In the meantime, from sensual screen romancer, Jon returned home to heavily pregnant Dorothea and 20-month-old Stephanie. He had found it a life-changing experience being at his daughter's birth, and was determined to be there again this second time around. Not every aspect of fatherhood had initially come naturally to Jon. Like most new dads, when his baby had cried in the first few months of life he had sometimes been at a loss to know what to do with her. As he once fondly quipped, she hadn't come with an instruction manual. But he had grown to know.

Parenting had changed him. He was a calmer person who worked at cultivating more patience. The introduction of children into a world which had pretty much revolved around him till now, had been something of a wake-up call. There were some obvious things, such as no longer playing music at home at any old hour. And since, when not on tour, he rose around 7.00 a.m., hunching over the guitar or piano writing songs till dawn was now largely out of the question. This time he planned other changes too, including acknowledging a need every day to strengthen his bond with his child. Young as she was, Stephanie already associated seeing an airplane in the sky with 'there goes daddy'. This was something that Jon intended to rectify, both for his daughter and for his first son, Jesse James Louis, who was born on 19 February 1995.

That said, music remained vitally important to Jon. The night before Jesse's birth, Bon Jovi had appeared on the top-rated US TV network show *Saturday Night Live*, a week in advance of the release in Britain of 'Someday I'll Be Saturday Night'. This track from *Crossroad: The Best of Bon Jovi* would notch up a number seven hit in the UK singles chart, at a time when the finishing touches were being put to their new studio album.

It had been a long haul. After Jon had wrapped up filming his scenes for *Moonlight and Valentino*, he had regrouped with the band and bass player Hugh McDonald in November 1994 to start recording the album now to be called *These Days*. First sessions had taken place in Nashville, Tennessee, but during playback certain aspects of the sound had jarred with Jon. They had virtually started again from scratch in upstate New York at Bearsville Sound Studios, Woodstock, with Peter Collins as co-producer alongside Jon and Richie. In the end, three studios in California would also be utilised for this work, as well as – for the first time – Jon's own specially built, state-of-the-art, 24-track home studio facility. The plan was not to overdo rehearsals or pre-production. Having benefited from the enthusiastic reaction to their greatest hits album, they wanted to feel fresh and spontaneous. They had rapidly whittled down a pool of over 40 songs to just 14, those which would make it on to the long-awaited sixth Bon Jovi studio album.

As had become clear over the turn of the year, *These Days* was lyrically deeper, more introspective than any of their albums to date. In some songs the spotlight was aimed squarely at the inequality that was rife in American society. Since the mid-1980s homelessness had become a very serious social problem across the US, and in New York City shelters called welfare hotels had sprung up. One such place, the Martinique Hotel in midtown Manhattan on Broadway and 32nd Street, housed a thousand homeless families in conditions of squalor, deprivation and danger. There were a hundred shelters like this around the city. They were basically warehouses for very impoverished people. Already inclined towards more socially-conscious songwriting, both Jon and Richie had become acutely attuned to the desperate plight faced by many. The album's opener, 'Hey God', was all about social inequality, and had been emotionally inspired.

Richie had been sitting at traffic lights in Manhattan one day, idly glancing out of one of the limousine's rear windows at the wintry scene, when he had made sudden eye contact with a derelict huddling in a cardboard box on the pavement. The sense of guilt that had swept over the musician at their starkly contrasted fortunes was immense. 'I thought "What the fuck can that guy be thinking of me?"' said Richie later. Discussing this incident with Jon, the two of them had pulled together a song to reflect this grim reality. It went even further, querying the lack of intervention in such bleak existences by any so-called higher being. Jon said that he had no intention of sugar-coating such observations anymore, but the cynicism of 'Hey God' still constituted a surprise introduction to the album.

'Hey God' was one of only a handful of hard rock numbers on an album top-heavy with ballads. Of the others in this bracket, two in particular drew attention before and after the album's release. 'Something For The Pain' stood out as the most difficult song of the 14 to get right. The powerful upbeat number began life as a soft metal throwback to the early 1970s, but underwent so many rewrites that it ended up like nothing they had imagined. It took six months before they were finally satisfied with it. The other was 'Damned'. Strong musically, its potency lies in the lyrics, which voice the mental torment and the human consequences of having an adulterous affair that will send one's soul to perdition. Nothing on Bon Jovi's playlist to date was quite like it.

These Days was undoubtedly their darkest and most accomplished album yet. It was late-night listening material, with several sorrowful songs of regret which made an immediate and lasting impression. 'Diamond Ring' was another stark departure from traditional Bon Jovi punchy, soaring ballads. Jon described it as slinky and spooky, likening it to Peggy Lee's 1958 moody classic 'Fever'. Characterising the commitment represented by an engagement ring, in its quiet, sultry way 'Diamond Ring' was a little further out in left field than where Jon had felt they had gone three years earlier with 'Keep The Faith'. By contrast, the title track was in familiar territory, urging as it does an attitude to stand up and help oneself – not to sit back and expect anyone to do it for you. Jon saw 'Lie To Me' as depicting his fictional characters Tommy and Gina moved on a pace, but still struggling in different ways. Jon had been improving vocally with every album, and with the timbre of his voice deepening in his early thirties he had never sounded better.

The first single from the new album, the melodic ballad of lost love, 'This Ain't A Love Song', lodged in June 1995 at number six in Britain, peaking at 14 in America, by which time the band's world tour was well underway and had already proved eventful. Kicking off in Asia in late April, Bon Jovi opened at a sports stadium in Bombay, moving swiftly from India to Taiwan and the Philippines before reaching Thailand at the start of May.

The routine of tour life was well ingrained in them all. And now, in terms of travel, accommodation and spare time, they had designed it much more as a family affair. On stage, however, the projection was still the same – that of available rock gods. For that, the lead-up couple of hours to a gig were as vital as ever. The ritual of going through a set sequence of activities remained important to Jon, particularly in the one-hour period immediately prior to taking the spotlight. In that 60-minute warm-up the process of working through the song set for the night and figuring out which changes to make to ensure that no two shows were the same, was a very regimented business, as was readying himself mentally to perform. In psyching himself up, however, Jon is not trying to become someone else. Of the moment when the house lights go out and it's show time, he said 'I've never felt that I go out there and become *him*.'

Jon disagreed with those bands who, by the mid-1990s, were claiming that stadium gigs were too impersonal, bluntly stating that huge arena concerts were, 'a fucking blast'. With his own loyal congregation, he still worked at retaining the personal touch. Sometimes he would pull a girl from the crowd up to dance with briefly, and was known to pick out and acknowledge a specific individual from the sea of flushed faces stretching out before him. It continued to be a two-way street. The level of adulation remained constantly high. Jon's drastically different hairstyle from the *Keep The Faith* period had vanished, and his legions of female admirers had him back with long, thick, though not curled, hair. They seemed not to care a jot that their idol was a happily married father of two. They hurled their affection at him just as unambiguously as ever.

Temptation still abounded, but Jon knew where the line lay between the tantalising promise he projected on stage, and the reality once the gig was over. Dorothea knew it too. Being married to a sex symbol rock star must be far from easy. Dorothea prefers not to be interviewed. In a very rare moment recently though, she spoke publicly of how she has experienced being physically climbed over by female fans in their single-minded determination to get to Jon on stage. She doesn't know if it's confidence or complacency, she stated, but she takes the pragmatic view that no matter how many women lust after her husband, at the end of the day he is coming home to her. Jon is proud of his wife's self-confidence in this and other regards. Talking of those occasions when he is away without her, he has declared, 'She never calls my hotel room in the middle of the night to see if I'm there, and that's part of the attraction.'

The frenetic lather generated inside the stadiums during the These Days tour had been preceded by an overspill of fervour outside some venues. When the band returned to play the Army Stadium in Bangkok, almost twice as many people turned up as the place could hold, and several thousand disappointed, ticketless fans had to be barred from entering the packed arena. Just four nights later, on 6 May 1995, in the Indonesian capital Jakarta, a riot broke out when thousands of ticketless fans tried to force their way into the Ancol Stadium. It took several hundred police officers to contain the trouble, and dozens of Bon Jovi fans were injured in the fracas.

Calmer waters were restored for the remainder of their Asian leg, and order was maintained throughout Japan. Heading west, after visiting nine other European countries, they landed in Britain for a series of dates, including three consecutive nights at London's Wembley Stadium, commencing on 23 June. It was just past the 10th anniversary of the historic Live Aid concert, which was being marked in various ways in the media. Fittingly, during the encore on the final night at Wembley, Bon Jovi's special surprise guest proved to be Live Aid's most prominent organiser, Bob Geldof; they joined together on a rendition of the Boomtown Rats' 1979 hit, 'I Don't Like Mondays'.

Less than a week later, *These Days* was released. This first Bon Jovi studio album for nearly three years, with its adult, contemporary feel, got to number nine in the States and went swiftly platinum. But it slotted straight in at number one in the UK album charts.

Simultaneously, as the band enjoyed this show of strength, Bon Jovi briefly stepped back from their headliner status to play two support gigs in France, when they opened for the Rolling Stones. Months earlier, as a long-standing fan of these now wrinkly rockers, Jon had written to Mick Jagger asking if his band could play support to the veteran performers, since they were both on the tour circuit at the same time.

The Stones' Voodoo Lounge tour and Bon Jovi's These Days tour crossed paths in Paris, where these two gigs took place at Longchamps on 30 June and 1 July. Jon is said to have told

Jagger in a fax that even to carry his luggage would be an honour. Definitely a man for heroes, Jon was perhaps carrying humility a tad too far. As far as the gigs themselves went, it's quite possible that, apart from hard-core Stones' fans, there must have been those in the audience who were unable to miss the fact that Bon Jovi were a far superior live band to the Rolling Stones of the mid-1990s.

Whatever, reclaiming their top line status, Bon Jovi worked their way through Europe for another week. They had a concert originally planned for the giant Luzhniki Stadium in Moscow, but it was cancelled due to an escalation of trouble between Russia and Chechnya. This meant being able to enjoy a slightly longer break before the North American leg of the tour kicked off in two weeks' time on 21 July, with the first of three dates at the Jones Beach Theater, Long Island, New York.

Weaving back and forth between America and Canada throughout August, they played practically every night, steamrollering successfully and with high visibility from one state or province to another. So it was surprising that when the second single from *These Days*, 'Something For The Pain', saw the light of day towards the end of September, its US peak was a lowly 76. Britain's love affair with the band continued, bringing them another Top 10 hit there.

The month had particular highlights, such as a performance on 2 September at the inaugural concert for the Rock and Roll Hall of Fame at the Municipal Center in Cleveland, Ohio. And days later in New York City, they appeared live at the MTV Music Awards held at Radio City Music Hall.

After venturing through South America and Australia again, another of the major music channel's events stood out for Bon Jovi when on 23 November 1995 they dropped in on Paris to perform at the second annual MTV Europe Music Awards at Le Zenith. In the French capital, Bon Jovi collected the Best Rock Act trophy. But it was an unexpected sideshow moment that made this event remarkable. Jon's heightened concern with socio-political and environmental issues had not only seeped through into some of his lyrics on *These Days*, he was also more frequently lending his services to events such as the Rainforest Foundation Benefit Concert held, back in spring, at New York's Carnegie Hall. And before that, Bon Jovi had helped raise over $50,000 for the Greater Boston Food Bank and a cancer research fund.

The state of the planet's future stability had come into sharper focus for Jon, so he did not hesitate to range himself alongside the stance taken by U2's frontman Bono. The renowned anti-war humanitarian used the globally televised award ceremony as a platform to add his voice bluntly to the already widespread international condemnation of nuclear bomb tests being carried out by France in the South Pacific. Bono's scathing verbal attack on French President Jacques Chirac segued startlingly from a speech that began innocuously enough. In an abruptly phrased outburst that would be widely reported, the Irish star rapped out, 'What a city! What a night! What a crowd! What a bomb! What a mistake! What a wanker you have for President! What are you gonna do about it?'

Before November ended, 'Lie To Me' replicated the previous single's widely varying transatlantic chart performances by making the UK Top 10 while barely registering in *Billboard*'s Top 100. The band also played the first of two South African gigs; the second, in Johannesburg on 1 December, sealed their debut appearance in this troubled corner of the world.

In keeping with their new policy of having built-in breaks, Bon Jovi now reached a five-and-a-half-month hiatus in live performances. Jon had made it clear that he was no longer prepared to flog himself or the band to the point of exhaustion. It was more important that they enjoy the nights they did take the stage, and so the tour was suspended. Everyone welcomed the breathing space. Richie Sambora was able to enjoy married life with Heather Locklear. David Bryan had time to write music for stage musicals, and he teamed up with veteran musicians on personal projects. Tico Torres, who has painted and created clay sculptures all his life, often producing particularly thought-provoking pieces, had the chance to realise a second ambition by mounting his own one-man art exhibition.

For Jon, the other reason for this break in the tour was to allow him to fulfil his commitment to his next acting role. By the time *Moonlight and Valentino* had brought him critical praise in America back in October, he already knew that he had secured the lead role in his second film. Called *The Leading Man*, it was written by Virginia Duigan and would be directed by John Duigan; principal photography was due to start in London in January 1996.

America's *People* magazine had just named Jon Bon Jovi as one of the 50 Most Beautiful People In The World. While this was flattering, it had not prevented Jon from having to shape up seriously for the role of Robin Grange, a hot Hollywood actor come to take up his part in a prestigious London West End stage production of *The Hitman*, a play about politics and morality. As part of Jon's strict regime, he had further reduced his already more limited alcohol consumption. In his spare time prior to the three-month shooting schedule, he had virtually lived in the gym to produce an amazingly slender and well-toned body for the screen.

Though excited by the challenge before him, Jon had two personal sacrifices to make. First, the role required him to cut his hair drastically. 'Short hair does make me feel different,' he said, vowing to grow it long again just as soon as filming was over. The second sacrifice was something he pledged he would never repeat. He had to have his chest hot-waxed to remove its famously thick mat of hair; it was not only an extremely painful process, but his chest had bled. He'd yelled like mad while having it done, he admitted, but conceded that on screen his bronzed bare torso did enhance his sex appeal.

Jon's co-stars in *The Leading Man* were Lambert Wilson, Anna Galiena and Thandie Newton, with whom he had most of his scenes, as well as Barry Humphries, David Warner, Patricia Hodge and Diana Quick, among others. It was the prospective diversity of roles which had made acting appealing in the first place to Jon and here he had a role within a role. As the character Robin Grange, Jon portrays a mysterious, seductive and fascinating figure who leaves the viewer never quite sure, every step of the way, what he is up to. In the stage play, Grange is cast as the ruthless assassin who deviously cloaks his intentions, and gains access to his target by romancing a Jewish scholar's daughter.

As the American actor in London for work, Grange early on makes an off-stage pact with *The Hitman*'s playwright to seduce the writer's wife in order to alleviate the devastating pressure she is feeling over her husband's affair with the play's young actress, Robin's co-star. This arrangement, fraught from the start, develops and shifts course until the playwright loses whatever control he originally had over matters. The more compromised he becomes by the plan, the more power Robin Grange acquires and exerts over him.

Interestingly, Jon did not consider Robin Grange to be devious, when he is clearly a Machiavellian type. The role required depth, subtlety and a particular cunning. And with engrossing authority and style, Jon deftly portrayed a man cutely capable of playing one person off against another. Although this was only his second experience of film-making, he felt more comfortable in this environment, more confident with a role he could get his teeth into, and was able to experiment more on screen. It was now also that he had to handle his first screen love scene. As Robin Grange, Jon has tender kissing scenes with the playwright's wife, portrayed by Anna Galiena. But the actual acted out seduction sequence takes place between Jon and Thandie Newton, who plays the playwright's actress lover.

Robin Grange's reputation as a lady-killer is established when it transpires that he had to quit Hollywood after being caught in bed with the wife of the film studio boss for whom he was last working, and he is really in Britain to let the temperature back home cool down. Jon conveyed this dangerously exciting, sensual predator flawlessly, carrying off the intimate scene in which he tempts his screen quarry down to and almost out of her lacy underwear with a combination of sizzling screen presence, natural roguishness and panache.

Sometimes a source of panic for an experienced actor, the prospect of coping with this close-up love scene on a bed surrounded by a camera crew held no fear for Jon. Sex scenes, he maintained, were something which, in his own way, he'd already been doing for a living for years. 'Trying to seduce an audience is the basis of rock and roll,' he said. 'And if I may say so, I'm pretty good at it. Plus, being married and monogamous, it's the closest thing I can do to having sex without getting into trouble for it.'

For the length of the film's shoot, Jon's base every day was a trailer in Borough Market in south London. Despite being the lead character, he still had loads of spare time on his hands. He quipped that first thing every day, it took him less than five minutes to be rigged out as Robin Grange, while his two female co-stars were an hour and a half being readied.

It was a three-month period in which Jon settled into a contented daily routine. Dorothea had accompanied him to London along with Stephanie, not yet three, and 11-month-old Jesse, and they rented a house close to Wandsworth Common. Stephanie was temporarily enrolled at a nearby nursery school and Jon would walk her to the crèche each weekday morning, before driving to the studio. Socially, Jon and his family found an exhilarating rare freedom simply in being able to walk wherever they wanted to, and being within easy reach of a cinema or a restaurant. To maintain his physique for the three months, Jon also visited a gym where his fame didn't prove to be a hindrance, and all in all he loved living in London.

He also relished being able to live a kind of regular working existence – if starring in a movie could be described as such. It meant that he had plenty of quality time, in one spot, with his wife and young family at a time when changes happen so fast. Stephanie could already keep Jon on his toes, advising him to cover up against the sun or telling him when he needed to shave. And his dad didn't miss it when Jesse celebrated his first birthday.

As an American rock star, ('just off the bus' in terms of having turned actor) in London to star in a film alongside a largely British cast, Jon Bon Jovi might have come up against some degree of prejudice. But that didn't happen.

Stalwart screen actor David Warner, who played Tod, the target of the play's assassin Robin Grange, recalls of Jon, 'He's a very pleasant young person, gentle, who was always polite, always on time and he was surrounded, of course, by real professional actors who were certainly very impressed by him.

'Sometimes, people can be a bit sceptical of someone who is in music, who wants to be an actor. But it all depends what reputation they come in with. Jon Bon Jovi came in with a reputation of being a committed person, who took wanting to be an actor very seriously.

'Nowadays, in theatre, we have all sorts of people coming in just for the sensation value. Like, Madonna will do a play and it'll be sold out whether she's good or not.

'I don't think its difficult at all for anybody from outside to be an actor. Acting is acting. It's not brain surgery. Although, I think a lot of people imagine that anybody can do it.

'I've personally worked with quite a few people in the music business who have come into films – Bob Dylan, Roger Daltrey and Debbie Harry, for instance. And it's very interesting, because they come out of their element and they're kind of in awe because it's the one thing people around them know how to do. Yet, I don't think that necessarily happened with Jon Bon Jovi.

'Socially? We were all very much aware that he's a family man, which is very refreshing. Nobody was invited to his house or spent evenings with him. It was just a question of doing the job and that was it.' Filming for *The Leading Man* went so smoothly that it wrapped up a fortnight ahead of schedule and was destined for release at the turn of the year.

Throughout Jon's happy sojourn in the UK capital, Bon Jovi business had continued to unfold. February saw the release of the title track 'These Days', which quickly claimed a number seven hit in Britain, as well as a satisfying four in America. And that month Bon Jovi won the Best International Group prize at the celebrated Brit Awards, held at London's Earls Court Exhibition Centre.

The band also featured during late February/early March as guests on a variety of pre-recorded TV shows in the UK and abroad. Richie, David and Hugh McDonald came to London to appear with Jon on *TFI Friday*, presented by colourful media tycoon, Chris Evans. Jon was also interviewed by Evans for his popular BBC Radio One show, when an original plan for Jon to be a guest DJ on the programme was scuppered. When the rock star's upcoming one-off stint as a disc jockey was trailered over the airwaves, a worker in the Government's immigration department contacted the BBC to say that Jon Bon Jovi did not have a work permit allowing him to play records as a radio DJ presenter.

By early April 1996, six weeks before the These Days tour resumed, Jon and his family returned home. In America, Jon still owned a property in Malibu, but home was a comfortable house in Rumson, New Jersey.

Jon has stated more than once that he does not pursue an extravagant lifestyle, and he continued to have no time for the ridiculous retinue of minders and flunkeys favoured by some celebrities. But he did have a lingering weakness for fancy cars and motorbikes. In the mid-1990s he possessed enough vehicles to open his own luxury showroom. His huge collection included a vintage Lincoln Premier and a Mustang Shelby, and his energetic personality was mirrored in a penchant for slinky sports cars, Porsche and Ferrari being among his favourite makes.

His biggest buzz, however, came from balancing his family life with looking after his and the band's professional future. For the period until he went back on the road, Jon rose at near dawn with a daughter who was eager to have dad cook her breakfast and watch TV cartoons with her. Once Dorothea was attending to Jesse, Jon would take off for a seven-mile run, followed by a workout in his home gym, before dealing with all the necessary details relating to both strands of his career; he was kept busy reading more film scripts.

That's not to say that the balance was always perfect. Performing had been in Jon's blood for so long, and his body clock was so used to a routine, that there were times when, happy though he was to be home with his family, he still could not help prowling the house, his adrenalin levels telling him it was show time. It wasn't always easy, either, to stick to regular sensible sleep patterns, accustomed as he was to be still winding down from a show at 3.00 a.m.

By early May 1996, the band reassembled to rehearse at a theatre attached to Pepperdine, a private university on the Californian coast, before flying to Japan, where in mid-month at the Fukyoka Dome they began the last section of their 1995/1996 world tour.

Over the next nine weeks, Bon Jovi were committed to 30 concerts spread through 13 countries, and they were determined to be relaxed and have a ball. Jon knew from the speed with which tickets were being snapped up, that they could have successfully doubled the number of shows. This time he resisted the temptation. In interviews he dubbed himself a 'lunatic workaholic'. But although being eternally occupied was his daily bread, there was nothing now that would make him risk fragmenting the health and well-being of what he had worked so hard to achieve. Just prior to plunging back into the fray, he also seemed to be in sentimental, reflective mood. 'When I think about all the things we've accomplished, the things I've seen, it's incredible,' he mused.

To show their gratitude to the growing contingent of new devotees and the army of staunchly loyal long-time supporters of the band, Bon Jovi wanted this summer to give back what they could, to make each gig a memorable experience in terms of playing precisely what the fans yearned to hear, and by creating a visual stage spectacle such as they had never yet been treated to.

The bandwagon rolled out of Japan into Europe. A variety of opening acts loosened up each night's audience. But the masses came armed with a sea of banners and placards proclaiming their devotion to the headliners. Times hadn't changed, in that Jon still drew the most hero-worship. At the Canstatter Wasen in Stuttgart, Germany in June, referring to a particular song on *These Days*, one placard frantically thrust aloft to catch the eye ended with the words, 'Damned 2 Love You, Jon'. But it was Richie Sambora who couldn't take his eyes off it. In fact, he became so frustrated at being unable to decipher the mixture of words and drawn symbols on this placard pledging love for the singer, that he suddenly stopped playing guitar, marched up to his frontman and stabbing a finger out towards the notice demanded, 'What the fuck does that say?' The fact that he had just pitched the entire band into chaos and stopped the show hadn't seemed to register with him.

A fortnight later, the band were heading towards Britain just as Jon Bon Jovi could simultaneously be seen live on stage and on the silver screen, as a well-publicised *Moonlight and Valentino*, in which he was being given third billing, opened in UK cinemas at the end of June 1996. Days later, 'Hey God' was released, halting at number 13 in Britain when Bon Jovi returned to one of their favourite haunts, the

National Bowl in Milton Keynes, for two nights on 6 and 7 July. Around the same time, as they went on to pack out football stadiums in Manchester and Glasgow, the band's popularity across Europe was highlighted in an unusual way as the car manufacturer Volkswagen launched the 'Bon Jovi Golf' model.

When the tour finished in mid-July and the band headed home, they had one very special moment on their social calendar, when Tico Torres married fiancée Eva Herzigova in Seabright, New Jersey on 7 September 1996, with Jon and Richie as proud ushers.

The year climaxed with Bon Jovi playing their seventh annual Christmas benefit gig on 19 December at Red Bank's Count Basie Theater. This year the stage boasted the flash and glitter of pinball machines, a Wurlitzer jukebox and a drinks bar presided over by a guy in a Santa suit. To an exhilarated audience, the band played a mix of their own material through the years and some cover versions. And it was while cushioned by the affectionate warmth of the evening's atmosphere that they more or less signalled that they were bidding the fans another temporary farewell. Solo projects would hold sway in the new year for some considerable time.

David Bryan had showcased 'Texas Rain,' a new composition from his forthcoming solo album. Richie announced that his second solo album was due for release, and Tico had news of an art gallery he was opening in Florida. Jon, too, had a solo work in the making. And on the eve of this Count Basie Theater gig, he had allowed a group of fan club members a special showing of his new film, *The Leading Man*. Having recently opened in Europe, it was due for release in Britain in early 1997.

Film work, in fact, occupied the start of Jon's new year when he went to San Francisco to join the cast of the romantic comedy, *Little City*. The ensemble piece, written and directed by Roberto Benabib, revolved around the intermeshed lives of a group of thirty-somethings, all attempting to work out the meaning of their individual existences and complex relationships. Playing the role of a bartender, Jon co-starred alongside Penelope Ann Miller, Josh Charles, Annabella Sciorra and JoBeth Williams.

Penelope Ann Miller later voiced her appreciation of the 'soft sensitive side' of family man Jon Bon Jovi during that shoot. Primarily, she came away from the experience impressed by the depth of his dedication and his willingness to stretch himself. 'He's willing to put himself out there,' she declared. The Miramax movie, R-rated for its language and sexual content, was scheduled for release in the autumn.

Before that, in March 1997, word came that Jon would soon be seen taking on a cameo role as a drug dealer in a film called *Homegrown*, as well as a fifth role in a new Edward Burns-directed movie – leaving no doubt that he had been truly bitten by the acting bug. Shrewdly, Jon was not trying to run before he could walk in this field. For an otherwise creatively impatient man, when it came to acting Jon preferred to dip into those projects he felt were the most interesting, certainly not the most high-profile or glamorous ones.

In considering the many scripts proffered to him, he was not influenced either by the size of the film company involved. He was just as likely to opt for a low-budget, independent film if the role appealed to him. Even with two movie roles doing the rounds, a couple in the can and more in the pipeline, Jon's concentration by late spring 1997 was directed towards the upcoming release of his solo album. This project was very different to the *Blaze of Glory* soundtrack, and one that was very dear to his heart.

CHAPTER 9

Is Variety Really the Spice of Life?

IT HAD ONLY EVER BEEN a matter of time before Jon Bon Jovi would emerge with what he would class as his first true solo album. Proud as he was of the award-winning *Young Guns II* soundtrack, *Blaze Of Glory*, creating songs to fit a film's plotline naturally had its constraints. In his troubled state of mind back in 1990, working within those parameters had suited his needs just fine. A few years later, he had arrived at a different place in his life and was ripe for another step in the development of his creative talent.

The bulk of the writing and recording for *Destination Anywhere* had been completed during 1996. In the first quarter of that year, while he was in London to film *The Leading Man*, Jon had spent most of his off-camera time ensconced in his trailer in Borough Market, busily penning material. He had been in experimental mood, both in terms of his lyric writing, and especially when it came to the sounds he wanted to achieve. In order to explore this new musical direction, Jon had drafted in five separate producers to help bring a fresh interpretation to his original thinking.

Quickly hitting a rich seam, he had come up with ten songs, six of which he had laid down tracks for in a London studio during February and March. When the These Days tour had reconvened for its final leg in late spring that year, Jon had taken the opportunity to duck into various studios in Europe and the US to record another seven tracks. At every level, Jon's approach towards this new work had been different. With 'modern and spontaneous' as his watchwords, he had opened up his mind more than ever before to the inclusion of all sorts of elements, such as studio effects – even the odd imaginative stunt, like miking up a child's jack-in-the-box toy. 'We'd mess around with all kinds of weird things. Nothing was considered too out there,' he later admitted.

At the instigation of producer Steve Lironi, who in the mid-1990s was most associated with working alongside the British band, Black Grape, Jon had experimented with different drum loops and was keen to create a lighter than usual feel to this album. Jon and Lironi had called upon the production and songwriting skills of Desmond Child, David Foster, Eric Bazilian and former Eurythmics multi-instrumentalist Dave Stewart. Both Stewart and Child also contributed as guest musicians on the album, as did bassist Hugh McDonald

Jon later referred to those solitary hours scribbling away in his trailer, as a bittersweet time. For although he joined Dorothea, Stephanie and Jesse each night in their rented London house next to Wandsworth Common, he had never before spent so many elongated spells alone in his life, and he had found it an evocative experience.

In addition to his determination to be strikingly different this time, his songwriting thought processes had undoubtedly been subject to a variety of external influences. Being in a happy domestic state, enjoying the company of his wife and growing young family, had not softened Jon up around the edges. He pledged in advance that there would be no 'tucking the kids in bed songs'. But the rest of his surroundings did impinge upon him, the London scene in general and, of course, his day job.

Jon certainly makes no claim to being anything remotely like a method actor. But elements of his absorbing, deviously intriguing role in *The Leading Man* as a manipulative, duplicitous character in a film about deceit, tangled emotions, hurt and unexpected outcome could not help but wash back from the film set with him into his trailer, and find direct expression in at least three of the 13 songs he eventually created. The title track, 'Destination Anywhere', spoke of a risky, illicit love affair. The husky ballad, 'Staring At Your Window With A Suitcase In My Hand', dealt with the emotional baggage that comes with kicking clear of a marriage. And of these three poignant songs, 'Every Word Was A Piece Of My Heart' eloquently underscored the fine line between a devoted love and a pernicious hate.

Jon solely composed nine tracks; of the remaining four, three were co-written by Jon with one or other of his record producers. Eric Bazilian collaborated with the frontman on the album's shortest track, called 'Ugly', oddly enough about beauty being in the eye of the beholder. Two of the strongest numbers, and subsequent single releases, 'Queen of New Orleans' and 'Midnight In Chelsea', were the work of Jon with Dave Stewart. The two men had originally met at a party and had clicked immediately. Finding a smooth writing collaboration therefore had not been difficult. 'Midnight In Chelsea' was a mellow musical vignette of what Jon witnessed going on around him as an American in the British capital. Unusually for a Jon Bon Jovi record, it featured girl backing singers.

Melodic female backing vocals also infiltrated the otherwise heavy electric rock number, 'Queen of New Orleans', a sultry song that made for a shimmering, stylish opener to *Destination Anywhere*. 'Janie, Don't Take Your Love To Town', with its sawing strings introduction, projected a British flavour with Jon's familiar vocal slightly altered to hold more than a hint of a John Lennon-style intonation. The reverberating moodiness of 'It's Just Me' is classic Jon Bon Jovi, hitting the spot with a romantic love song about one man's steadfast devotion to one woman, and is one of the album's highlights.

'Learning How To Fall', though, was the song Jon said he personally derived most satisfaction from writing. With slashing harmonica accents, this number really represents an overview of Jon's own journey to the top, his mindset along the way, the obstacles he faced and the will to win out. He admitted, 'It's very me.'

The edgy 'Naked', reflecting a need for society to lose its facade, was followed by the contrasting smoothness of 'Little City', a sympathetic window on the pressures of a lonely existence. 'Cold Hard Heart', with extremely low register vocals from Jon, made for a solid, depressing anchor track, again perhaps a fallout of debilitating emotions from the making of The Leading Man. The penultimate track, 'August 7, 4:15', was the saddest of all because it was a personal tribute to a dead child, the six-year-old daughter of a close friend of Jon's, who died on August 7, 1996.

As was patently clear from the degree of vocal emotion Jon expressed in the songs on this album, he had invested much in its creation. Although he refused to obsess on it, he hoped that when Destination Anywhere was released in mid-June 1997, his strengths as a lyricist would be acknowledged. He had already made a strong impression on his record producers, particularly those with whom he had worked for the first time. Steve Lironi later vouched about Jon, 'He's definitely a rock star in the older sense of the word. He does his thing and it's impressive when you're standing right next to it.'

The British public were also sufficiently impressed for Destination Anywhere to slot in at number two in the album charts in its week of release. And the same month, Jon notched up a number four success with the first single from it, 'Midnight In Chelsea.' In America, *Destination Anywhere* stopped just outside the Top 30 in early July, despite the album being bolstered not by the usual promo video, but by an accompanying short film of the same name featuring Jon and three Hollywood stars; this short film debuted on MTV to coincide with the album's UK release in June 1997.

With a $2 million budget, the 45-minute film had been shot earlier in the year and had reunited Jon with two former screen co-stars – Annabella Sciorra, with whom he had worked on *Little City*, and from *Moonlight and Valentino*, Hollywood favourite Whoopi Goldberg. Demi Moore also starred, as did the fine, versatile actor Kevin Bacon. Directed by Mark Pellington, the contemporary film noir was set in downtown Manhattan. With a script shaped around the album's songs, it features Jon as a man on the run who has to sort out the mess his life has become. The short film contained three of his new numbers, including 'Midnight In Chelsea'.

By the time the album and film were released, Jon had already embarked on a promotional blitz for *Destination Anywhere*. Starting in early June, it took him to Britain, Europe, America and Canada with a blend of TV and radio appearances, plus some live gigs. Then he stepped off his solo tour to take part in the 'Songs & Visions' concert held at Wembley Stadium in London on 16 August 1997. This all-star event had been mounted to showcase 40 years of popular music. Jon joined a mixed line-up which included Rod Stewart, k.d. lang and the American soul singer Toni Braxton. Jon's set incorporated a rousing rendition of Elvis Presley's 'Heartbreak Hotel' and the Bob Dylan classic, 'Like A Rolling Stone'.

On his return to the States, his solo tour was immediately brought to an abrupt halt by an announcement on 18 August that live performances planned for the next few weeks had been cancelled or postponed. When Mercury Records confirmed that ticket sales for pending dates had suddenly been suspended, at first no reason was given as to why. But before speculation could take legs, it soon emerged that Jon had had to make an opening in his work schedule in order to meet his increasing movie commitments.

Before swapping the rock stage for a film set, though, Jon was still occupied with music business in the last week of August. In Britain, the second cut from *Destination Anywhere*, 'Queen of New Orleans', had been released; it debuted at number ten in the singles chart. Back home, in America, less welcome affairs prevailed. This concerned Tony Bongiovi, who had been the co-owner of Power Station recording studio in New York City. The studio had been sold in 1996. But in summer 1997, despite Jon's attempts through the courts to prevent it, Tony Bongiovi had succeeded in releasing an album titled *John Bongiovi: The Power Station Years 1980–1983*, made up of some of Jon's earliest recordings at that famous facility when he was still a struggling wannabe.

The unfortunate and long-running dispute between the cousins was back in the public eye because, as MTV news reported, 'Each is suing the other for ownership of material on the recently released album'. Tony Bongiovi clearly believed that he was within his rights. Jon took the view, 'I am absolutely grateful to the guy, but he doesn't own the rights to my early kid stuff.' The dispute wrangled on.

As these embers from his musical past continued to glow, Jon turned his sights on to the other side of his fast-growing twin-track career. Towards the end of 1996, Jon had already filmed a cameo role in a black comedy called *Homegrown*. Shot on location in Los Angeles, the film centred on a group of Californian marijuana growers who, when their boss is murdered, go into the lucrative dope-dealing trade for themselves.

Written by Nicholas Kazan with Stephen Gyllenhaal, who also directed, the movie's cast included John Lithgow, Hank Azaria, Billy Bob Thornton and Kelly Lynch. Jon Bon Jovi played the part of a drug dealer named Danny. *Homegrown* was described by *Halliwell's Film Guide* as a 'Laidback thriller with a comic tone, interesting for its depiction of the drug business away from its usual urban setting.' It would open in America in autumn 1997. That September, *Little City* was also due for US release.

At the height of summer 1997, while Jon appeared omnipresent on the large and small screen, and with his hitherto heavily publicised new solo album in the charts, he had cut into his tour to make a smallish appearance in a new movie which had started life as *Long Time, Nothing New*, but which would be released as *No Looking Back*. Written and directed by Edward Burns, it also saw Burns playing one of the three central figures, alongside Lauren Holly and Jon Bon Jovi. The romantic drama revolved around Holly's character's dissatisfaction with her humdrum small town existence, working as a waitress and living with her safe, dependable boyfriend. Everything alters when an old flame returns to town and tempts the heroine into breaking loose.

Jon's role as Michael was that of the ultimately cuckolded steady boyfriend, and just as his scenes in the film were limited in number, so the scope was too restricted for much expression. Although, his confrontation with his screen girlfriend when she returns home after an all-night stop-out did have just the required balance of mixed emotions and depth to engender real empathy with his character.

Conveniently, the shoot was entirely on location in New Jersey, so Jon was able to be close to home. It was not a prolonged commitment on his part, which allowed him to re-schedule some solo tour dates. *No Looking Back* was slated for release in autumn 1998.

For a long time now, the number of film roles coming Jon's way had been building steadily. There were occasional industry rumours of his being set to star in a movie which has yet to materialise. And Jon still auditioned for parts he had singled out as being right for him, only to lose out to another actor. One such coveted role that got away had been the lead in the 1996 film *The Crow: City of Angels*. Directed by Tim Pope, it was the sequel two years on to the original *The Crow*, starring the late Brandon Lee. The chance to play a guy who returns from the dead, hellbent on vengeance, had appealed strongly to Jon, but he had eventually been elbowed out of the running by French actor Vincent Perez.

As autumn approached, Jon was able to switch hats and pick up the *Destination Anywhere* PR trail again. In Britain, the last single release from the solo album, 'Janie, Don't Take Your Love To Town', claimed a number 13 hit just a week after Jon had been named as Best Male Act at the MTV Europe Music Awards held at the Ahoy in Rotterdam, Holland, on 6 November 1997.

Hard on the heels of this accolade, Jon called another, longer, hiatus in his solo album world promotion. In fact, he stepped back for almost six months, mainly in order to fulfil yet more movie obligations. But he also became involved in a very poignant musical tribute. It wasn't a high-profile world media event – it was an evening organised to honour a New Jersey police officer.

Long Branch, New Jersey, is situated north of Asbury Park on America's east coastline, and Police Sergeant Patrick King was the town's most decorated officer when on 20 November 1997, in a restaurant in nearby Red Bank, he was murdered in the line of duty by a fugitive, who shot Sergeant King in the head with the police officer's own gun. The killer then stole the police vehicle and became embroiled in a high-speed car chase before committing suicide rather than allow himself to be captured. Sergeant Patrick King was survived by a widow and two young sons. The Long Branch Police Department, aiming to stage a benefit gig for the family, contacted a major concert organiser to help, and the promoters promptly put feelers out to their various clients. Jerry Bakal for FPI Concerts said, 'Jon Bon Jovi responded right away.'

Other artistes were swift to offer their services, and the 'Jon Bon Jovi And Friends Benefit Concert' was planned for 31 January 1998, at the Count Basie Theater in Red Bank. Tickets costing $125 went on sale in the middle of the month, and all 1,435 sold out in roughly one hour, sparking hopes of raising at least $100,000 for the bereaved family. The line-up for the benefit concert was a combination of heavy-hitters and New Jersey popular performers. Jon was joined by Richie Sambora and Bruce Springsteen; Southside Johnny and Little Steven also took part. Because these musicians all lived in the area, they had been acutely sensitive to the whole community's deep shock at the senseless, brutal murder of a well-respected local police officer.

Jon had been proud to play his part in honouring Sergeant Patrick King. In the coming weeks, he himself was honoured with two more solo awards. The first was on 9 February at the Brit Awards at the London Arena, when he snared the prize for Best International Male Artiste; the second was a triumph in the same category on 5 March at the Echo Awards hosted at the Congress Centrum in Hamburg, Germany.

By spring 1998, despite the recent on-stage collaboration of Jon and Richie Sambora, each member of Bon Jovi was still content to pursue his own individual interests a while longer yet. Jon plunged back into acting. *Row Your Boat* was an independent film written and directed by Sollace Mitchell. This time the small cast lined up alongside Jon comprised Bai Ling, William Forsythe, Jill Hennessy and John Ventimiglia. This was Jon's sixth film role, and his second in the lead part. In complete contrast to the confident character striding through *The Leading Man*, in the role of Jamey Meadows Jon swaps confidence and irresistible guile for a less showy, but effectively gentle vulnerability.

Jon's acting range was being road-tested in the varying roles he had undertaken over the past three years, as sunny tradesman, sexual predator, barman, drug dealer and cuckolded boyfriend. But this role of a young man fresh from an 18-month prison stretch for a crime his brother committed, and living by his wits on the streets until he lands a job as an enumerator for the US Government Census, was one that required Jon's deepest performance yet. With a perpetually frayed appearance, his task was to invite the audience to empathise with his character's plight, his efforts to resist his brother's constant attempts to lure him into a life of crime, and to support him in his frankly dishonest wooing of an unhappily married young Chinese woman played by Bai Ling.

For many, Jon succeeded on every level in banishing Jon Bon Jovi, confident rock star, from the mind, substituting him instead with a fairly desperate, sensitive, not always strong individual who tries to please everyone. There was more nuance in this performance, varied layers which Jon exposed or conveyed with a light touch. And although nowhere near as high-profile as one of his future roles, Jamey Meadows seemed to speak loudly of the subtlety with which Jon Bon Jovi was quietly learning his acting craft.

Row Your Boat (named from the children's nursery rhyme) would have its premiere the following year, on 21 July 1999, at the Stony Brook Film Festival held on Long Island, New York. On completion of his filming commitments, Jon once again turned rock star and headed to Europe in late April 1998, visiting Germany, Austria and Switzerland before returning to America in late June, his responsibilities to *Destination Anywhere* finally fulfilled.

Another responsibility Jon takes very seriously is his commitment to various charities, a particular favourite being the Special Olympics. So he was happy to participate, days before Christmas 1998, in a benefit concert called 'A Very Special Christmas From Washington DC – A Celebration of Special Olympics'. Joining an all-star bill featuring Eric Clapton and Sheryl Crow, and in the presence of President Bill Clinton and the First Lady, Jon, dapper in black tie evening dress, sang, 'Please Come Home For Christmas'.

Having been US President for two consecutive terms, Bill Clinton was approaching the beginning of the end of his tenure in the White House. His vice-president, Al Gore, would carry on the torch for the Democrats when it came to fighting the next presidential election in the new millennium. Jon would become an ardent campaigner for the cause.

In the meantime, as the last year of the decade began, Jon touched base briefly with Bon Jovi in January 1999, when the band regrouped to record a number called 'Real Life' along with producer Bruce Fairbairn. This first recording since *These Days* was included on the movie soundtrack to *EdTV*, a satirical comedy directed by Ron Howard and starring Matthew McConaughey, Martin Landau and Rob Reiner. The soundtrack was released in March and its first spin-off single, 'Real Life', lodged at number 21 in Britain.

When the band got together in a wintry New York City for the recording session, it was a good chance to catch up with one another. In the last year, Richie Sambora had been closely concerned with promoting his second solo album, *Undiscovered Soul*. Tico Torres was now staging art exhibitions throughout America. David Bryan had had an accident at home with a power saw, injuring one of his fingers so seriously that he was still recovering and was not able to play keyboards for lengthy stretches.

For his part, Jon was able to share his experiences of working in films. He was far from done with acting yet. In mid-January he parted from his band-mates and headed to Italy to work in his biggest film to date – a wartime action movie called *U-571*. The Hollywood film had been co-written by Jonathan Mostow, Sam Montgomery and David Ayer and was to be directed by Mostow. Shooting took roughly four months, mainly on location in Malta and Rome; Jon's role in the World War II submarine drama was a major one, though not the lead. That post fell to *EdTV* star Matthew McConaughey, who was joined by established screen stars Bill Paxton and Harvey Keitel.

Jon played Chief Engineer, Lieutenant Pete Emmett and as the lead character's close friend he commanded a sizeable share of screen time as one of the four main players. In his first military role, as a naval officer, Jon had to have a drastic crew cut. Almost from the start it was a thrills-and-spills movie, shot mainly in the dark, full of suspense involving men in peril on and under the sea. The water scenes were shot in a massive tank on the film studio's back lot. It was Jon's first experience of the joys of being lashed for hours on end by pumped-through salt water. The director's quest for authenticity left the actors' eyes and mouths stinging. 'It's not easy,' said a drenched Jon during a break in filming, 'but it's a helluva lot of fun.'

Off-duty, fun was tightly rationed for Jon this trip. By dint of his huge popularity in Italy, it was impractical for him to join other cast members on nights out to the cinema or a restaurant. If he did, he invariably had to make a strategic early exit to avoid causing a riot. Yet he did try to wind down socially, blending in in crowded pubs for an unobtrusive quiet drink. One night he sabotaged his own efforts when, clearly missing live performance, he was unable to resist an invitation from a local band to come up and sing. *U-571* actor Erik Palladino was there, and described how the whole place just 'freaked out' when Jon Bon Jovi suddenly appeared on the little stage.

Film production ran to plan and only a little over time. Jon absorbed everything that was going on around him. The movie's plot-line and the frantic action scarcely allowed for a great deal of character association or development within his particular role. Yet director Jonathan Mostow believed that he had identified a rising, engaging acting talent in Jon Bon Jovi. He predicted stoutly, 'Mark my words, Jon will be a major movie star in the next few years.' Jon has said all along that he still has much to learn as an actor. While he gathers screen experience, he is also catching the eye of seasoned professionals. After filming wrapped in Rome in May, Jon was thrilled to receive a gift from co-star Harvey Keitel, a book on acting technique inscribed by Keitel with the affectionately encouraging words, 'To the son of a Marine. You're not half bad.'

U-571 would open in American cinemas in April 2000, becoming a US number one blockbuster smash hit. In Britain, however, the movie would cause something of a furore. *U-571* was all about a group of US submariners sent out on a special operation to capture a specific German U-boat, intent upon obtaining from its arrested crew the famous Enigma code machine.

In real life, breaking the Germans' coded messages played a pivotal role in turning the tide of the Second World War in the Allies' favour. The problem was, the Nazis' ingenious Enigma code machine was seized by the British before America had even entered the war. This was a fictional film, designed to do no more than entertain. But it dealt with an extremely important real-life event, and this rewriting of a crucial piece of history enraged enough people in the UK for one Member of Parliament, Paul Truswell, to table a motion in the House of Commons making a strong protest about what Truswell termed 'a gross distortion of history.' It was unusual for a film to produce quite this level of heat. But unaware of this looming furore in Britain, Jon returned home in spring 1999, proud of his participation in his biggest film.

That summer he resumed his charity work. In early June, he was among several celebrities who took part in a Donatella Versace London fashion event labelled 'Diamonds Are Forever: The Millennium Celebration', which was in aid of a variety of causes. A week later Jon and Dorothea hosted a fundraiser at their New Jersey family home for sufferers of autism. The invitation-only bash offered good food, good drink, live music, and the chance to take part in a charity auction when the well-heeled guests from the whole spectrum of the entertainment world were encouraged to dig deep.

Although Jon had left film sets and locations behind him for the present, acting remained in his system. Earlier in the year came news that a film project in which Jon had first registered his interest two years ago, was still in development. With the working title of *Love Hurts*, the proposed movie was said to be about a fictional rock band, and was in the busy hands of producer Jerry Bruckheimer, more recently noted for his high-octane thrillers. While this venture lay in the unspecified future, Jon took on a small, one-off cameo role in the popular, raunchy US TV comedy series *Sex And The City*.

Starring Sarah Jessica Parker, Kim Cattrall, Kristin Davis and Cynthia Nixon, each fast-paced episode revolves around the individual sex lives of four beautiful New Yorkers cutting it as liberated '90s women. Jon had accepted the offer to appear in an episode titled 'Games People Play' as a photographer named Seth, who hits it off with Sarah Jessica Parker's character after they encounter each other in a shrink's waiting room. Jon filmed his scenes in New York City towards the end of June at a centrally situated restaurant, as well as at Silvercup Studios in Queens. 'Games People Play' first aired on 29 August 1999.

Between heavily promoting his solo album, *Destination Anywhere*, and appearing in four films since 1997, Jon had managed to maintain a high enough public profile during the band's long hiatus to please his fans. They also eagerly awaited seeing him in a main role in a major Hollywood movie the following year. But in summer 1999 the really big news for the worldwide Bon Jovi faithful was that the band members had at last decided that, two and a half years on from the end of their last tour, they had now exhausted their individual need to pursue solo projects. The time was ripe to get back together and begin preliminary work on a new studio album for release in 2000.

Jon and Richie soon began writing new material and making demos of their initial batch of songs. From the outset they were determined to work to a relaxed timetable. But that in no way signalled any form of apathy towards the new project. On the contrary, their enthusiasm for the new album was sky-high. Like the others, Jon was fully aware that times had changed again in the music industry, but that only spiced up the challenge.

CHAPTER 10

Storming Back with a Vengeance

NOT FOR THE FIRST TIME Bon Jovi was destined to feel like the comeback kid in rock music. Although Jon and Richie had achieved prolific songwriting output throughout the latter half of 1999, by the time they would launch their seventh studio album in summer 2000, five years would have elapsed since the release of *These Days*. By then, the industry was geared strongly towards the early-to-mid teenage market. Depressingly for real music lovers, the rise of the heavily promoted manufactured pop idols was well underway. Bands rarely grew up together any more, slogging it out on the gig circuit, earning their stripes, writing their own songs and playing their instruments.

Auditions had become the norm, to assemble a group of strangers, barely out of school, who were deemed to look well together. Bleakly, choreographers had become more important than record producers. And, massive media hype propelled a mediocre performer, singing a cast-iron popular cover version to the top, and called it talent. Certainly, the individual shelf life of these manufactured pop stars is extremely limited. But where this change counted for established acts like Bon Jovi was that a new generation of music journalists and DJs had come in who tended to be deaf to anything not in vogue. This made it tough for real bands to get widespread exposure and airplay.

Tico Torres admitted, 'We were very worried at that point. We didn't know if we'd fit in.' And David Bryan said it all about the task before Bon Jovi at that time when he declared 'We'd always been the underdog.' The keyboard player flatly acknowledged a sense in certain circles that Bon Jovi's new offering would not do well. And although Mercury Records retained full confidence in the band, some record company executives were aware of a question mark hovering out there as to whether the New Jersey guys had more hits in them. Jon naturally had no desire for the new album to bomb, but neither did he intend to become neurotic about its chart performance.

Recording work took place entirely at Jon's state-of-the-art home studio. When it was completed in February 2000, he made it abundantly clear that his sole motivation for making this album had been to get back into the collective groove and to derive enjoyment from its creation. As to the current problems in getting one's record on to major radio playlists, the frontman stated bluntly, 'I couldn't care less about kissin' some programme director's ass to play my record.' That self-contained, assured attitude was also reflected in the theme of the new work. Called *Crush*, in part it consciously went way back to the band's roots. In tone, it unashamedly adopted the big, happy rock and roll sound. Most important, the content flagrantly telegraphed the truth that Jon Bon Jovi was comfortable in his skin.

That confident serenity found infectious expression in the number 'Just Older' – the very title indicating an absence of anxiety about critics pouncing on him. Not that the chance of having laid himself open to attack had escaped Jon. The seeds of this song were sown a couple of years earlier while he was working on *Destination Anywhere.* He had occasionally slipped in an early version of it when playing live gigs to promote the solo album. But he had always been conscious of the title. He later joked, 'I thought, "Oh Jesus! I can see it now. Jon's old. He's 38!"' In 'Just Older' he openly refers to more lines appearing on his face. But the heart of the song was that achieving anything worthwhile in life involves being ready to take risks. Jon touched a chord with many of his own age group, and older, too when in a dozen words he made clear how long hair can be a state of mind. That's to say, that although appearance may alter with age, the rebel can still exist within.

The strong 'Two Story Town' punched home a defiant determination not to be stifled by a small-town mentality. 'Thank You For Loving Me' was a straightforwardly sentimental love song with multi-generational appeal. 'Say It Isn't So' again resurrected a faintly Beatlesque tone as one half of a relationship prefers to hide ostrich-like from the truth. But the *tour de force* of the 13-track album was undoubtedly its opening salvo, the power-filled anthemic rocker, 'It's My Life'.

Arguably Bon Jovi's best number to date, it is, self-confessedly, Jon's most self-indulgent song. He explained, 'Here was a guy saying, "I want to do movies. I want to make music. I want to make solo records when I feel like making them."' This was true in spirit, but the song's lyrics are all about how we pass this way just once and need, therefore, to seize control of our own life. Its pounding potency and stirring passion made it Jon's own signature tune, as well as the standout track in the album.

'It's My Life' makes an instant impact on most people. It did on video director Wayne Isham when Jon asked him to come to the recording studio and listen to *Crush.* Isham recalled how Jon and Richie played him the songs then, 'like excited kids' the songwriting duo urgently probed, 'So! What do you think?' Despite their years of experience Richie Sambora admitted, 'Every time you come out with a new record, it's like throwing a hand grenade and waiting to see what happens.' Wayne Isham's reaction to this particular song pleased the pair. 'I was weepy,' he said. 'I just enjoyed the message so much!'

'It's My Life' would quickly become a firm favourite with the fans too. Fittingly, in mid-March 2000, Bon Jovi invited a thousand of them at short notice to participate in the making of the video to accompany the number, which would be released as the first single from the forthcoming new album. Jon had already invited actor Will Estes, with whom he had worked on the movie *U-571*, to appear in the video. The fans were needed to form the audience for the 'in performance' sequences, which would be spliced along with Estes's scenes to make the overall video. A hotline telephone number was set up, and there was a strictly over-18 age stipulation placed on those interested in taking part. Otherwise, selection was made simply on a first-ring, first-in basis.

Directed by Wayne Isham, the video shoot for the concert scenes took place in Los Angeles in the tunnel between Second Avenue and Hill Street on a Sunday night, starting early evening and stretching towards midnight as numerous retakes were filmed. The band played other numbers to keep the good-natured crowd from becoming restless between shots, and were rewarded with a genuinely ecstatic reception to 'It's My Life' caught on camera.

'It's My Life' was released in early June 2000, grabbing the number three slot in the UK singles charts, though stopping at 33 in America. However, when *Crush*, co-produced by Jon, Richie and Luke Ebbin, followed less than a fortnight later, the album made number nine in *Billboard*'s Top 100 and catapulted to the top in Britain. In fact, *Crush* gave Bon Jovi their fifth consecutive number one UK album; it remained in the charts for 29 weeks.

By now there was a tangible buzz of anticipation for the band's Crush world tour. It was due to commence in July, and a string of warm-up gigs had been taking place for weeks. For Jon, being back in harness with Bon Jovi was something special all over again. When he performed live to promote *Destination Anywhere* he was accompanied by proficient musicians whom he much respected and who were perfect on a nightly basis when it came to replicating exactly the solo songs for audiences all over the world. However, when Jon included Bon Jovi material in those sets, he felt the difference of not having his 'real band' around him.

Jon had first retrieved that special sensation when he and Richie had knuckled down to compose the songs for *Crush*. He revealed, 'When he and I started singing together, it was that magical combination again.' Jon had also yearned to recapture the feeling of intimacy between himself and the Bon Jovi audience. The warm-up gigs brought that back to him, starting on 27 April with the band's appearance at Tradewinds, a club near to the beach in Seabright, New Jersey, and repeated a week later with a gig at Chicago's House of Blues. Asked about these low-key yet throbbing performances, Jon replied descriptively, 'I could smell the people and they could smell me.' Whenever these warm-up dates were announced, sometimes with scant warning, the stampede for tickets ensured that they sold out in a matter of minutes. And these promo appearances were not confined to US shores.

In the second half of May, Bon Jovi decamped to Britain to play on *Top Of The Pops* and to guest on the irreverent *TFI Friday* television show, before heading to Monaco to perform at the Laureus Sports Awards ceremony held in Monte Carlo. With swift stopovers in Italy and Germany, the band returned to America in early June in anticipation of the release of *Crush*. At this point in time, *U-571* was packing them in at the US box offices, and Jon was attracting critical praise for his supporting role in the wartime movie. He had by now shot some scenes for a small role in a new feature film to be premiered in the autumn, and his third lead role was already in the pipeline. But his fans were happiest having him back in his rock star persona, getting ready to take to the road.

Remaining a while longer on the slip road towards the start of their tour, Bon Jovi appeared on the syndicated *The Late Show with David Letterman* on 13 June, the day of *Crush*'s release in the States. Three days later, still in New York City, they performed at the Rockefeller Center as part of the Outdoor Summer Concert Series, which was open to the public and aired live in the morning during *The Today Show*. Towards the end of the month, at the Convention Hall in Asbury Park, New Jersey, they fitted in a benefit concert, whose proceeds were shared by three charities coping with blood disorders, cancer victims and the Food Bank program.

With rehearsals over, the Crush world tour officially kicked off on 12 July 2000 with five dates in Japan. Jon flew out with the band to the Far East bolstered by the fact that the album was already a success, and secure in the knowledge that their tour tickets were selling like hot cakes in every territory. When Bon Jovi had returned to the limelight in the early 1990s after a four-year recording hiatus, prophecies that they had become redundant and would be buried by the grunge movement had been proved wrong. Now, with their album a hit, in live performance they would again put to flight any suggestion that Bon Jovi was struggling to be a viable band.

Times and trends had changed in the new millennium, but Bon Jovi would prove beyond doubt their right to write their own ticket. Jon was clear in his mind about what people looked for. It wasn't complicated. He stated, 'People want somebody to entertain them. They want a showman who writes songs they can relate to. They don't want to be so miserable all the time. They want to have their rock stars back!'

Bon Jovi fans got that in spades as the spectacular Crush tour ignited with two dates at the Tokyo Dome. In the capital, then in Nagoya, Fukuoka and Osaka, the band went out on stage blisteringly determined to take no prisoners. Jon engaged with each audience on an emotional level, and the trade-off was magnetic. Putting heart and soul into his scintillating performance, he would glisten with sweat as he hammered home their beloved up-tempo anthems. The new songs already felt familiar to the delirious fans, and 'It's My Life' proved to be dynamite as a live number.

Playing two and three encores, some nights the sheer adrenalin rush made it hard to leave the stage. The correspondingly wired audiences were likewise reluctant to vacate the auditorium. The reception was the same when the band arrived in Finland to commence the European leg on 5 August before a capacity 10,000 crowd at the Elysee Arena in Turku. Jon's energy levels only seemed to soar when, having played next in Helsinki, the band showed up in Sweden for a two-hour set at The Globe in Stockholm. Even before the band arrived on stage the intensity in the arena had built to fever pitch.

When Jon greeted the audience with the alluring threat that they were in for a long night and would go home sweaty at the end of it, those eager girls whose vivid imagination went into overdrive were already a fair way to fainting. Heaving with emotion, the place exploded when Jon later leapt off stage and ran along the front row, tantalisingly almost within arm's reach of the screaming fans.

Their ninth gig of the Crush tour, at the Scandinavium in Gothenburg, was the last indoor concert in Europe. And the barnstorming success of their first outdoor gig this trip at the Georg-Melches Stadium in Essen, Germany, on 12 August, was bluntly summed up by Jon himself when, with a bold if affectionate grin, he announced at the end of the performance, 'We are Bon Jovi and we've kicked your ass!' With gigantic screens providing the backdrop to a towering stage set, a jaw-dropping light show came into its own as darkness fell, and the colourful fireworks finale sent the faithful off into the night feeling thoroughly entertained.

During this European leg, Bon Jovi were supported by Toploader, a British band who also filled that post when, having blazed a trail through Germany and Austria, the Crush bandwagon rolled into the UK. Dates were scheduled for the Britannia Stadium in Stoke-on-Trent, the Gateshead Stadium in Newcastle and, over the water, at the RDS in Dublin, with two nights, on 19/20 August, at London's Wembley Stadium. Before 72,000-capacity crowds these were historic gigs, in that Bon Jovi was the last rock band to play at this venue before demolition work was scheduled to start.

In early September, the single, 'Say It Isn't So', was released in Britain where it charted at number ten. By this time the tour had gone on to take in Belgium, Switzerland and the Netherlands before returning to Germany, where the European leg ended on 8 September at the Zeppelinfeld in Nuremburg.

With a seven-week break sewn into the tour schedule between the European and American legs, the band headed home. In Jon's case that meant returning to the mansion in which he and his family had been living since the previous year. Situated in 16 acres on the waterfront in Middletown, New Jersey, not many miles southeast of where he grew up in Sayreville, the neoclassical mansion had been designed by architect Robert Stern and had taken two years to build. The interior decor is 17th-century French; in some rooms the antique furniture is so delicate and valuable that Jon swears he's scared to sit on certain pieces.

The beautiful home also incorporates a home cinema system, a gym and a high-tech recording studio. In the grounds stands another of Jon's pride and joys – a replica of a typical English pub he calls The Shoe Inn, complete with dartboard, pool table and pinball machine. Jon's way of winding down at home traditionally involves a Friday night family get-together, usually watching a movie. On Saturdays he likes having friends over to shoot pool or to play darts in his very own pub, where he enjoys nipping behind the counter and becoming barman for his guests.

Needless to say, the seven-week break was not all spent kicking his heels at home. 2000 was the year of the US Presidential campaign. Democratic Vice-president Al Gore and his running mate Senator Joseph Lieberman were up against the Republican ticket of Texas Governor George W. Bush, son of former President George Bush, and ex-Secretary of Defense Dick Cheney.

Jon's political allegiance lies with the Democrats. He firmly believed that Al Gore was the right man to succeed Bill Clinton in the White House, and so he became passionately involved in the strung-out election campaign. Less than a week after returning home from Europe, Jon joined a host of like-minded celebrities for a fundraising event on 14 September held at Radio City Music Hall in New York.

Called 'The Concert For Al Gore', it featured the legendary Paul Simon, Sheryl Crow, Lenny Kravitz, k.d. lang, Bette Midler and the Eagles' Don Henley. Jon performed 'Wanted Dead Or Alive' solo, and joined in on collective renditions of such classics as the Beatles' 1968 number, 'Revolution'. The event was compered by Hollywood star Michael Douglas, and raked in $6.5 million to the Democrat campaign coffers. For Jon, it was a night of hope and aspiration. When Al Gore came along amid a sea of waving US flags, shaking hands with a string of his main high-profile supporters, Jon's urgent thumbs-up gesture had a 'lets hope we can do it' look.

In his spare time Jon hit the campaign trail, often travelling with Al Gore. He performed at more fundraisers along the way and, on the hustings, he addressed the outdoor crowds, strongly urging the local populace everywhere to see Gore as the next President of the United States. Bill Clinton's apparently less charismatic deputy was delighted to have Jon Bon Jovi's support, and not just because it pays politicians to court the youth vote through the celebrity world. The Vice-president admired Jon's unaffected attitude, his having genuinely stayed true to his roots and the fact that Jon was a man devoted to his family and his community. Gore later declared, 'We only asked Jon to campaign in the real tough battleground states,' adding candidly that if there was a next time, he would want Jon Bon Jovi to be campaigning at his side in *every* state.

As late summer 2000 unfolded, Jon continued to make room in his Bon Jovi business schedule for avid electioneering. On 4 October he further flagged up his support for Al Gore by hosting a fundraising event at his own mansion estate in Middletown. Guests forked out up to $25,000 for the privilege of being there, and part of the evening's proceedings included Jon and Richie Sambora performing acoustic versions of some of their best loved hits. At the end of his address the Presidential hopeful suggested to his attentive audience and host, 'This may be the single most fun event of this entire campaign.' It certainly proved to be hugely lucrative, raising nearly $1 million.

Not everyone in the neighbourhood was impressed though when, to facilitate Al Gore's 26-car motorcade making its way to Jon's estate, local law enforcement officials had to close off two busy New Jersey highways temporarily during the rush hour, prompting a deluge of calls to local radio stations from frustrated commuters complaining about the disruption.

Meanwhile, Bon Jovi fans were counting down the weeks to the start of the band's first US tour since 1995. Their recent radio station appearances had proved popular, particularly two performances on 20 September at the China Club in New York City. And two days later, when Bon Jovi took part in the VH1 'Storytellers' TV series, it was a ratings winner.

Jon's personal profile around this time was already high when, on top of his musical and political activities, he showed up on the big screen once again, this time in the movie *Pay it Forward*. This unusual film about a schoolboy's plan to come up with a goodwill scheme that would spread nationwide and ultimately make the world a nicer place in which to live, had been scripted by Leslie Dixon from the bestselling book by Catherine Ryan Hyde and was directed by Mimi Leder.

The movie's main players were Kevin Spacey, Helen Hunt and Haley Joel Osment. Jon's task was to portray the estranged, no-good husband of Helen Hunt's character, who briefly reappears in his wife's and son's lives, having supposedly dried out. Living sober, he is determined to make a fresh start. His good intentions last roughly two minutes, and the violent, abusive man he still is reveals himself.

Jon had shot his short scenes for this role in the early part of 2000. As Ricki McKinney he does not have much to do except arrive one night contrite, then turn threatening. Jon described his volcanic character as 'rather evil', and he is mainly a fleeting counterbalance to the film's otherwise overall sweet sentiment. Such a brief appearance, following his prominent role in *U-571*, might have seemed a backward step. It was, nevertheless, another notch in his burgeoning film experience. *Pay It Forward* opened in US cinemas on 20 October 2000.

By now, the North American dates of the Crush tour had been officially announced and, with the album already certified platinum, such was the clamour for tickets that the gig to be held on 16 November at the Continental Airlines Arena in East Rutherford, New Jersey, sold out in just ten minutes. One of the support acts due to join this month-long stint was the punk band Less Than Jake. Drummer Vinnie Balzano, talking about how, growing up in New Jersey, he had come to regard Bon Jovi as part of rock royalty, confessed to MTV news, 'I'm speechless that we have the opportunity to go out on tour with them.'

Commencing on 3 November at the Independence Arena in Charlotte, North Carolina, in four weeks Bon Jovi would play 15 major venues in 11 states, plus a swift two-date incursion into Canada. Along the way, Jon occasionally still swapped his rock star mantle for more political flag waving. Despite the economic prosperity the American people had enjoyed under Bill Clinton's eight-year watch, the US had fallen victim to the same malaise which would afflict British politics in the new millennium – serious voter apathy.

The 2000 US Presidential race ought never to have become such a close-run affair. But the fact was, inciting widespread interest in the election was proving very difficult. So, days after the Crush tour resumed, on 6 November Jon and Richie joined other music stars to perform on Ocean Drive in South Beach, Miami, at a 'Get Out The Vote' public rally for Al Gore and Joseph Lieberman.

The eve of polling day gig proved to be a last hurrah. The election produced extraordinary developments in Florida when it came down to the wire. Amid a deal of confusion, George W. Bush, a man with virtually nil political experience, somehow claimed the most powerful political post in the world by the skin of his teeth. Politically minded people around the world could scarcely comprehend what had happened, or how it *could* have happened. Jon Bon Jovi, like millions of American Democrats, was gutted at the result.

However, he concentrated on his tour and on energising the fans flocking to see the band in state after state. If proof were needed that his personal pulling power had not diminished, despite his private domesticity and his interest in politics, it was provided in November 2000, when *People* magazine readers voted 38-year-old Jon Bon Jovi the Sexiest Rock Star on the planet. After two nights in Toronto and Montreal at the end of the month, on 2 December the tour once again came to a halt, this time with a gig at the Great Western Forum in Los Angeles, California.

Crush promotion continued to occupy Jon's time, mainly in Europe. In early December the single 'Thank You For Loving Me' lodged at number 12 in Britain. A week later, Bon Jovi took pride in performing in the Norwegian capital at the Nobel Peace Prize Awards ceremony. Three days later, back in America, Jon got involved once again in the festive fundraiser on behalf of the Special Olympics, held in Washington DC at the White House. In the next two days there were two other charity show appearances in San Diego and Los Angeles, over on the west coast.

Anthony and Matt Bongiovi have both spoken of there never being a five-minute downtime period in their eldest brother's day. All these years on, Jon's band-mates are still struck by his perennial need to punch the clock, to get stuck into something and make it happen. When the cameras caught a tuxedo-clad Jon Bon Jovi smiling, serenading and hand-shaking his way through the night of the White House charity gig, it belied the high level of behind-the-scenes commitment he gives in supporting this cause and others like it. Executive producer of the Special Olympics Christmas event, Bobby Shriver, commented in heartfelt accents afterwards, 'That guy works like a dog!'

That didn't mean that there were no sacrosanct times. There had been years when the festive break had been spent on the road in transit between gigs, or in characterless hotel rooms. But for a long time now, the December holiday period was virtually cordoned off for Jon to be with his family. And to give him the chance to enjoy following the fortunes of his beloved New York Giants.

In the new year, Jon was able to mix a fleeting return to work with his love of football when, on 28 January 2001, Bon Jovi joined in in the pre-game Super Bowl XXXV festivities at Raymond James Stadium in Tampa, Florida. Around the same time, Bon Jovi reached a pinnacle of their own when they secured their first two Grammy Award nominations – Best Rock Performance by a Duo or Group for 'It's My Life', and Best Rock Album for *Crush*.

This news made the fans lust all the harder for the band to get back on the road. But for a good part of the first quarter of the year Jon had something entirely different to get his teeth into – making a new film called *Vampires: Los Muertos*, the follow-up to John Carpenter's 1998 low budget horror film, *Vampires*, starring James Woods and Daniel Baldwin. Written by Tommy Lee Wallace, who would also direct, this new movie centred on a modern-day vampire hunter on a mission to destroy a colony of the undead. In playing the ruthless slayer, Derek Bliss, Jon was taking on his third leading role in his ninth feature film.

Jon had praised the script as 'pretty hip', and throughout the shoot he relished working with Wallace and producer Jack Lorenz. The movie would be partly filmed at Sony Pictures Studio in Culver City, California, but principal photography took place in Mexico at outdoor locations which Jon considered to be incredible. His supporting cast included Cristian de la Fuente, Natasha Gregson Wagner, Arly Jover and Darius McCrary, and the film's shockingly violent opening sequences warned of a gruesome contemporary treatment of a familiar plotline.

Derek Bliss, paid by the Van Helsing Group, travels about with a surf board concealing a wide arsenal of vampire killing equipment on the roof rack of his car. He is a strangely kind and compassionate character, as well as being an extraordinarily efficient vampire hunter, and although it seemed an odd role to have attracted Jon, he looked quite comfortable in the part.

Jon's highly photogenic looks, thoroughly utilised by director of photography Henner Hofmann, illuminated the screen and probably for many viewers were solely responsible for keeping them watching, despite all the stomach-churning gouging, slashing and decapitation going on.

Presumably, Jon had envisaged that this role would again broaden his experience, but he ended up unhappy with the film. All that had been promised to him prior to accepting the part had been fulfilled by the film-makers. On a daily basis, he had keenly showed up to work with the cast and crew. To Jon, the problem with the final product lay in the cut.

Showing the kind of bluntness with which he can condemn something he himself has been a part of, Jon later declared the movie 'embarrassing' and the first 15 minutes as 'atrocious'. It improves, he stressed, but stated, 'You don't realise what is bad, until you see it cut together.' That *Vampires: Los Muertos* simply wasn't a very good movie meant it was not given a cinema release. It would go out in America on cable TV and was released on video in Britain in November 2002.

Jon's film career was taking a route whereby his individual performances were attracting steadily growing respect, especially within the industry. But, *U-571* apart (in which he had fourth billing), the kind of success he was looking for had thus far eluded him. He had never felt like rushing his fences when it came to cultivating his acting career, and his desire to hang in there was not in doubt. So, shrugging off disappointment along with the sands of north Mexico, he closed that door for now and headed back to the US, where band rehearsals would soon get under way for the resumption of Bon Jovi's world tour. It would now go under a new name.

In March 2001 news started leaking out that Bon Jovi were to bring out their first live album later in spring. Details were initially sketchy and song selection had yet to be finalised, but it ended up a 15-track album of rock songs titled *One Wild Night Live 1985–2001*. Thirteen of the numbers were Bon Jovi classics harvested from the band's best live performances from the previous 16 years, with two live cover versions – the Boomtown Rats' hit, 'I Don't Like Mondays' and Neil Young's 'Rockin' In The Free World'.

In the album liner notes Jon described the collection of songs as being 'about pure appreciation for who and what got us here.' Richie Sambora told journalists, 'Our fans have been asking us for this record for a long time. We're very proud of it. It's a great snapshot of our career.' The upcoming live album also explained the Crush tour renaming itself the One Wild Night tour. It kicked off Down Under on 24 March 2001 at the Colonial Stadium in Melbourne. It was a relief concert, proceeds from which were directed to the state emergency services to help cope with the fallout from a series of natural disasters which had afflicted rural Australia.

A five-date tour of Japan followed, before the US/Canadian leg commenced on 18 April at the Desert Sky Pavilion in Phoenix, Arizona. For this particular trek Bon Jovi were supported by the Baltimore band SR-71, a young four-man outfit who, with their penchant for power-pop songs, must in some ways have reminded Bon Jovi of themselves at the outset of their touring career. SR-71's recently released debut album, *Now You See The Inside*, had gone gold, but they were conscious of being at the bottom of the greasy pole.

At that stage in their own career, Bon Jovi had had to battle some backstage animosity into the bargain. But SR-71 already knew that that would not be a problem for them. Vocalist Mitch Allan made no secret of his huge excitement at joining Bon Jovi to play to mass audiences, and at the sort of warm reception they anticipated getting from these experienced rockers. Jon himself was singled out for a spot of hero-worship as Allan declared, 'It's a trip, man. In junior high school, we looked up to him. It doesn't get any bigger than actually having the chance to support him on the road.'

The trek took in California and Nevada before making a quick raid into Mexico City to perform at the Furosol, then returning to US soil for a one night stand in Salt Lake City in Utah, and seeing April out in Denver, Colorado. The month of May embraced near-nightly appearances in long familiar major arena and amphitheatres until, after a performance on the 15th at the Bi-Lo Center in Greenville, South Carolina, Jon had to dart home to Middletown in order to carry out an unusual duty and to receive a singular honour

Jon's complete disinterest throughout his school years meant that he had no fancy diplomas or qualifications to his name; he had never had that safety net of academic achievement to fall back on if his all-or-nothing, headlong pursuit of a musical career had failed. But as he had grown in stature, he had used his fame to plough back into society a commitment to helping others in a variety of ways. It was in recognition of these endeavours, as well as his success in music, that Monmouth University in West Long Branch, New Jersey, not far from where Jon lived, had decided to award him an honorary Doctor of Humanities degree. They had also invited the rock star to give the commencement address to that year's clutch of graduating students.

By his own admission, although appreciative of the honour, Jon had initial reservations about accepting the invitation. His primary thought was to query if he really had anything of value to impart to these graduates. He also became aware of a raised eyebrow element in certain – as Jon put it, 'old blue blood' – quarters locally, that he had been asked at all. John Bongiovi once put his eldest son's nature in a nutshell by saying that the moment someone suggests that he's unable to pull something off, he will go all out to prove that he can. No one among the blue blood brigade was going so far as to say that, precisely, but a mere whiff of a sniffy attitude would probably have spurred to Jon to take to the lectern.

And so he did, on 16 May 2001. Before over a thousand students seated in serried ranks on chairs set out on the lawn at the rear of Monmouth University's Woodrow Wilson Hall, Jon Bon Jovi received his honorary degree. Standing in a long black graduation gown on this breezy day, he then delivered a commencement speech which resonated with his audience. There was more than a fond trace of appealing to the local psyche in his address. He talked of the huge number of students across America that day, simultaneously receiving their degrees from world-renowned academic institutions, who probably figured that because of that their diploma was somehow more valuable. 'But remember,' Jon declared. 'We're from Jersey. We've been underdogs all of our lives.'

Prior to coming to Monmouth University, Jon decided that his best line was to illuminate the pressures he had faced and overcome in order to succeed. As an inspirational figure, it followed that he would tap into the vein which said, don't let prejudicial attitudes from others hold you back. He revealed to the students that while carving his niche in rock music, he had encountered put-downs from critics simply on the basis that he had not hailed from New York or Los Angeles. Touching on that brief phase in the early days when he had tried to emulate some of the popular stars of the day, thinking that way held the key, he said, 'We tried to keep up with the Joneses until I realised that even if you win the rat race, you're still a rat.'

Throughout his address he received spontaneous cheers. But when he was finished and gave a small wave, which held more than a hint of self-consciousness, he was rewarded with a great collective roar and thunderous applause. For roughly two hours after that, Jon shook hands or slapped palms with the stream of graduating seniors who filed by, collecting their certificates. When all the degrees had been dished out, he left, a police escort clearing the way for his limousine out of the campus and out of Long Branch itself.

In fact, Jon was leaving the country, flying to Ontario to rejoin the tour for a gig next day at the Corel Centre in Ottawa. The other Canadian concert saw Bon Jovi bring the house down at the Colisée de Pepsi in Quebec City, Quebec. And it was at another Pepsi Arena, this time in Albany, New York, where the US/Canadian leg ended on 20 May.

Two days later, *One Wild Night Live 1985–2001* was released. In America it locked on to the number 20 slot, while in Britain it sailed to number two. In the UK this same month, the single, 'One Wild Night', also secured the band a Top 10 hit. This success in Europe mirrored the enthusiasm Bon Jovi found when the live show arrived at the Olympic Stadium in Stockholm, Sweden, at the end of the month, and was repeated throughout Belgium and the Netherlands, before the band pitched up on 8 June in Glasgow's Hampden Park. Scotland's national football stadium is famous for resounding to the 'Hampden Roar', hugely intimidating to opposing teams. That night, Scots Bon Jovi fans proved that they could be just as astoundingly vocal in staunch appreciation of their US idols.

Other stadium gigs in Britain included the McAlpine Stadium in Huddersfield, the National Bowl in Milton Keynes and Cardiff's grand Millennium Stadium. And once again, before the band returned to Europe, Jon strayed into the hallowed halls of academe.

Responding to requests from students' representatives at Oxford University, on 15 June he addressed the Oxford Union, the world-famous debating society. Celebrity guest speakers before Jon had included Michael Jackson, even Kermit the Frog. Jon, though, took the task seriously. He began to see addressing academic audiences as another challenge. 'It's not vanity,' he stressed, when accepting the invitation. 'It was more, okay – this is a new curve. Let's do it.' Asked if he didn't feel intimidated at the prospect, Jon replied, 'I'm not frightened of failure. I'm frightened of standing still.'

Jon addressed Oxford Union members at the Frewin Court for 20 minutes; his theme this time was promoting a need in life to be passionate about one's pursuits and to have the perseverance to work to realise the dream. He also paid public tribute to the vital support he had received from his parents in his early days, stating, 'My folks saw my desires and never discouraged me. With people like that in your life, you cannot fail.' Citing his own experience, Jon made no bones about his tunnel vision to becoming a rock star, and the total self-belief which propelled him through the many lean times. However, he also sounded a cautionary note when he said, 'Make your plans in pencil, because they're gonna change!' Before leaving, Jon stopped off for a pint of lager in the Oxford Union bar and patiently posed for snapshots with students. Then he shot off once again to rejoin his band.

Having hit five countries throughout Europe, the One Wild Night tour went home to America where, on 8 July, they opened at the Marcus Amphitheater in Milwaukee,

Wisconsin. As the year-long excursion entered its final stretch it was already acknowledged as an all-round colossal triumph, even before it wound up with two massive sold-out shows at Giants Stadium in East Rutherford, New Jersey, on 27 and 28 July 2001.

To those who, 12 months earlier, had been ready, if not itching in some cases, to write Bon Jovi off as a major force in music, the huge success of the elongated tour, as well as of the now multi-platinum *Crush* and the live album was a metaphorical poke in the eye with a sharp stick. Aiming directly at their critics, David Bryan took delight in declaring, 'Our victory lap was Giants Stadium!'

And indeed it didn't come any bigger for band and fans alike than these consecutive gigs – marking Bon Jovi's first performances in this massive famous venue in the Jersey swampland since summer 1989. Visually, both were spectacular events. The huge stage set was an inflatable futuristic city which constantly changed colour. There were three giant video wall screens. Punctuating certain songs, as well as providing a noisy grand finale, there were showers of flashy fireworks. And the sound system was excellent – all designed to pamper a hometown crowd, which reciprocated by giving their heroes a fanatical reception.

Starting on the Friday night, Jon arrived on stage with so much pent-up energy looking for an outlet that he was initially as frisky as a spring lamb. But settling in, he and the band proceeded to rattle the stadium's girders with rousing renditions of so many audience favourites that the tens of thousands of adoring fans were swept along on a tide of delirium. An electric charge crackled in the air, and Bon Jovi were very much experienced men at work. Their commitment, energy and sheer passion could not be faulted, whether Jon was oozing emotion as he crooned the lyrics to 'Bed of Roses', or power-driving himself and the band through an extraordinarily riveting rendition of 'Keep The Faith', which he performed theatrically as well as sang. During the long instrumental ending, Richie Sambora's lead guitar work became so fast and intricate that the man and the instrument seemingly merged into one.

Other magnetic moments came when, changing into a blue New York Giants shirt numbered '01' over his leather trousers, Jon on six-string acoustic guitar accompanied Richie, initially on the 12-string part of a double-necked acoustic for the opening sequences of 'Wanted Dead Or Alive'. Jon jokingly requested the audience beforehand to 'All rise for the playing of our national anthem.' The audience promptly took over and sang the opening verse themselves. It made for a breathtakingly powerful show, and Jon's sudden clenched fist gesture of inner satisfaction at one point clearly articulated how he felt, as his blue eyes raked over the massed ranks before him.

The band had sensibly paced themselves over the course of the tour. But in actual performance, the adrenalin rush had flowed as fast as ever. And that couldn't just halt with the end of the tour. Fired up and invigorated by their experiences, Jon already had song ideas ricocheting around in his head. Richie, too, had the general framework of some numbers sketched out.

It was quickly clear that this time there would be no great delay before they knuckled down to creating the next album. On the contrary, Jon was keen to envisage an album for release the following summer. They took some weeks off, then Jon arranged for Richie to come stay at his home in Middletown so that they could exchange ideas and start developing new material. They planned to start writing songs on Tuesday 11 September 2001 – a date that was destined to become branded in the brain of every living soul on the planet.

CHAPTER 11

A Native
Resilience

THAT SEPTEMBER MORNING, ordinary, innocent citizens in the US had been unsuspectingly going about their normal business. In the Bon Jovi house, daily routine reigned too. By 8.40 a.m. eight-year-old Stephanie and six-year-old Jesse had been taken to school. In advance of getting down to some songwriting with house guest Richie Sambora, Jon was midway through a robust exercise workout in his home gym. Minutes after Dorothea walked into the room, all scheduled television and radio programmes ceased, and the news channels locked on to the fact that a plane had slammed into one of New York's famous World Trade Center twin towers.

The death toll was already obviously running into thousands. It was a surreal nightmare. Jon was frantically wondering if he ought to hare over to the school to get his children; at the same time he was having to contemplate waking up his friend to news of this mind-blowing crisis. The problem here was that Richie's main home right then was on America's west coast, which meant that his Hollywood actress wife Heather Locklear and their little daughter, Ava, were 3,000 miles away. Said Jon later, 'The phone lines were dead. If this was Armageddon then I was going to shelter my kids in my house, but how to do that without alarming my friend who couldn't get to his family?'

It transpired that the rest of the band had personal panic on their hands, too. David Bryan's sister was arriving for work at one of the World Trade Center buildings, and had emerged from the escalator leading up from the underground commuter station directly beneath the towers just when the first plane rammed its target. A policeman yelled at her to run for her life, which she did.

Tico Torres, meantime, had the horror of knowing that his wife, Eva Herzigova, was in the air on a flight from Miami to New York. In the mêlée, initial news reports suggested that there could be as many as another three hijacked planes which had yet to hit their preordained targets. In fact there were no others, but the drummer could not know that then, and it was agonisingly long before he learned that her flight had been diverted to Atlanta.

Jon revealed, 'The smoke [from the twin towers attack] literally wafted over my house.' According to the frontman his community, Monmouth County, New Jersey, suffered more fatalities as a result of that terrorist attack than had been inflicted upon it during the Second World War and the Vietnam conflict put together.

With the devastation all-pervading, Tuesday was spent in a weird limbo. After the initial emotional reaction, a kind of numbness took over as, once Richie was able to make long-distance contact with his family, like billions of people around the world everyone in Jon's house sat glued to the TV news channels.

For sanity's sake, if nothing else, it was vital next day to attempt some semblance of getting back on track. And so, difficult as it was, 24 hours later than planned, Jon sat down with Richie to start writing songs for the new album. 'Such a trivial thing,' Jon called what they were doing, when measured against the enormity of events beyond the perimeter of his luxury estate. It was impossible not to be scarred by events and, by the same token, not to let this influence their work now. The terrorist atrocity and its repercussions, which everyone knew would be vast and far-reaching, infiltrated their thinking. But Jon was acutely aware of a need to guard against allowing the album to turn into a 9/11 record.

Of course, he wanted to avoid the inevitable bandwagon risk. But it was more than that. The emotions swamping the entire nation right then were naturally raw and profoundly negative, and Jon was wary of being sucked under by them. He did not want to freeze-frame an entire body of work so that, while immensely poignant immediately post September 2001, its relevance would diminish with time.

Progress at this early stage could not expect to be fast in the circumstances. But then the phone calls began stacking up. To help launch the long healing process faced by the victims' families, a variety of ideas for fundraising events quickly sprouted, and requests for Jon or Bon Jovi to take part in many of these soon flooded in.

The first high-profile event was a hastily arranged telethon called *America: A Tribute To Heroes*, which was broadcast live from New York, Los Angeles and London by satellite on 21 September. Jon and Richie were among a host of music, film and television stars who took part in one capacity or another. The two-hour uninterrupted telecast was aired on all major US TV networks, and was ultimately shown in 156 countries. It took the form of a mixture of musical performances and celebrity appeals for public donations. It raised over $150 million for the United Way Relief Fund.

To encourage maximum generosity, the phones were manned by Hollywood heavyweights such as Tom Hanks, Whoopi Goldberg, Jack Nicholson and Robin Williams. The musical performances came from, among others, Billy Joel, Alicia Keys, Sting and Neil Young. It was a sombre occasion. Ten days on from the atrocity, America's cauldron of seething emotions included a rising rage. Not surprisingly, this kaleidoscope of feelings was reflected by the evident state of mind of many of the performers through their telling, individual choice of song.

Belligerence uncompromisingly shone out when Tom Petty opted to perform his band's 1989 hit, 'I Won't Back Down'. A more subtle strength in the face of adversity was represented by U2, who appeared via satellite to contribute their more recent 'Walk On'. And Paul Simon gave what for many was the show's anchor performance when he turned in a soul-searching, moving rendition of his all-time classic, 'Bridge Over Troubled Water'.

The difficult choice of which song to perform had bothered Jon from the moment he had taken the phone call asking him to take part. On the night, he and Richie decided on their acoustic version of 'Livin' On A Prayer'. Very different from the high-voltage, pounding electric band version of the song, this introspective acoustic duet in crucial ways changes the whole tenor and subtly re-shapes the meaning of the lyrics, which invariably makes a memorable impact.

The whole experience of driving into New York for this appearance left a lasting impression on Jon. He has described the city at that time as feeling like it was under martial law, with a plethora of police officers on maximum alert, checking people out, dictating and even restricting the flow of traffic.

Although everyone involved with *America: A Tribute To Heroes* felt the occasion deeply, the performers taking part in the east coast leg took probably the starkest approach to proceedings. There was absolutely no appetite for the usual backstage green room hospitality. After Jon and Richie had played their part, Jon declined an invitation from one of the other stars to go out to dinner; instead, he slipped off home quietly. His need to be with his family was all that mattered. In fact, he was back in Middletown before the telethon itself was over.

Taking part in this tribute was only the start of Jon's intense involvement in supporting 9/11 causes. Two days later, he and Richie again performed at New York Fire Department's Battalion 8 Firehouse as part of an *NFL Performance TV* programme. At the Firehouse, he spent time with some of the firefighters' widows, and afterwards was vocal in his admiration for the bravery of these men who had unflinchingly risked and given their lives on that monstrous day. He declared, 'As everyone was coming down the stairwells, they were running up them. For me to have done the telethon and then to sing "America The Beautiful" for the NFL – those were the most difficult and rewarding things I've ever done in my career.'

Five nights later, on 28 September, Jon was back on the stump, solo this time, headlining a 'Twin Towers Relief Benefit' gig at the Stone Pony in Asbury Park; the night's activities raised $7,000 for the charity coffers. And in early October Jon and Richie recorded a special version of 'America The Beautiful' which could be downloaded on the internet. In his personal introduction to the track, Jon asked those who did download it to make a donation to libertyunites.org.

That these charity events and more like them should have such a pull on Jon's attention was no surprise. At every turn locally it was impossible not to be confronted with suffering, when around 160 people from Monmouth County had been killed in the World Trade Center towers. Some friends and neighbours were having to attend so many heart-rending funerals in quick succession that it was in danger of temporarily turning their minds. Money in itself was not the answer, and could never fill the aching void left by a lost loved one, but raising as much cash as possible for these shattered relatives was the most effective thing stars like Jon Bon Jovi could do.

On 18 and 19 October then, Bon Jovi became involved in concerts designed to help the local community. Called the Alliance of Neighbours benefit gigs, they took place at the Count Basie Theater in Red Bank. Other participants in these two, four-hour concerts included Bruce Springsteen, some

E Street Band members, singer Phoebe Snow, as well as guitarist Scotty Moore, drummer D. J. Fontana and bass player Jerry Sheff, all three of whom had once been sidemen to Elvis Presley.

The latter concert was televised and broadcast across New Jersey, Maryland, Delaware and Pennsylvania with bottom-of-screen details of how to donate. Ultimately, they raised so much money that the Monmouth County relatives of those murdered each received tens of thousands of dollars swiftly, efficiently and without being entangled in streams of red tape. Referring to Bon Jovi, Red Bank's Mayor Edward McKenna Jr told the media, 'These guys all remember where they came from, and they take care of people who need to be taken care of.'

Although pressure of work would soon start squeezing out time for many more such benefits, hard on the heels of the Count Basie Theater concerts came another high-profile appearance on 20 October 2001 at VH1's *Concert For New York City* at Madison Square Garden. This stellar event also featured Paul McCartney, the Who, James Taylor and Macy Gray, among others. John Sykes, then president of VH1, had rung Jon to invite him and his band to perform at the extravaganza; Jon had accepted on the spot. Sykes appreciated that kind of unequivocal commitment. He said later, 'It was probably one of the biggest nights in music since Live Aid.' Taking part in it certainly meant a lot to Bon Jovi. Richie Sambora considered it a great honour, albeit one that stemmed from a great tragedy. And Tico Torres later described the event as resembling an elegy.

Some in the audience were wearing a white T-shirt on which was imprinted the photographed face of their respective dead relative. Mingled with the bereaved was a swathe of emergency services workers taking a well-earned shift break from the gruesome work going on among the rubble of the still-smouldering ground zero. Sporting a straw stetson and a shirt half of which was designed as the

American flag, Jon played a six-string acoustic guitar; once again their set featured the alternative version of 'Livin' On A Prayer'. The heightened sensitivity redolent in this rendition touched countless hearts and minds that night.

There was a sense on stage that the mood out in the audience, although fragile, was receptive to encouragement towards taking – a month on – the first of many steps to recovery. And one New York firefighter, Marc Dore, later went on record as stating that, without doubt, 'Livin' On A Prayer' delivered acoustically was adopted as a healing anthem, and proved instrumental in raising the emotional spirit of New York City. In Madison Square Garden that night, he had personally drawn from it a comforting reassurance that life would be alright again because everyone would stick together.

Although Jon willingly allowed these benefit gig appearances to trespass on his time, work still continued at other times on material for the new album, and by now about a dozen songs had been demoed. Despite seeing up close and personal the appalling human cost of terrorism, Jon still remained adamant that its negative influence would not weigh down the tone of the record. He felt that he had been sharpened creatively to a point where he needed to stay lean and focused in his lyrics. He was determined, too, that the never-say-die optimism with which Bon Jovi's most popular songs had always been associated should prevail.

As usual, he was soon to spread himself even thinner as the time arrived to fulfil his next acting obligation – making his television debut in an extended guest role in the new season of the quirky legal series *Ally McBeal*. Shooting was originally slated to commence at the beginning of October 2001, but Jon approached the series creator and executive producer, David E. Kelley, to request a month's delay in view of his involvement in the 9/11 benefit concerts; Kelley agreed.

Jon had been written in to appear in nine episodes of *Ally McBeal*, and when casting was announced it emerged that

Kelley had had the rock star/actor in his sights for some time to take a role in one of his high-ratings prime time shows. Jon had not been particularly attracted to working in television, and had resisted all lures for a good six months. But now, as David E. Kelley declared himself delighted to have finally drafted Jon into *Ally McBeal*, the singer expressed his gratitude that the talent behind so many hit US TV series had faith in him making a worthwhile contribution to this latest season of the comedy/drama series.

Replacing the troubled Robert Downey Junior in the show, as the character Victor Morrison Jon portrayed a building contractor who starts off doing work for Ally McBeal, only to become the love interest of the neurotic lawyer, played by Calista Flockhart.

Shooting for this extended guest role as the sexy tradesman with whom the lawyer swithers about becoming involved would span roughly five months and when Jon headed to Los Angeles in November to join Flockhart and the rest of the regular cast, he left behind a wife once again pregnant, by some four months.

Jon said at the outset, 'I know a little about acting and a lot about love. This is an exciting challenge for me.' The high degree of dedication with which he approached the part was immediately obvious to everyone on the set. Calista Flockhart described Jon as immensely disciplined from day one, and she praised his artistic honesty as an organic actor. 'I think that's one of his strengths,' she said.

Although Jon must already have been aware of the off-the-wall elements to *Ally McBeal*, one of his earliest scenes was still disconcerting. As Victor, Jon is bent over a task at a building site when Ally McBeal rounds the street corner. One glance at his neat, tightly clad backside has her behaving like a dog in heat and, acting on a sudden animal impulse, she cannot resist taking a quick sniff. The brief scene was embarrassing enough for a viewer to watch, let alone to act out. But as Jon later put it, it was harder on Calista than it was on him. Especially as Victor then gets to tell Ally right off for seeing him and his strapping co-workers as nothing but sex objects, further humiliating the already red-faced legal eagle.

Despite his initial reservation about taking on a TV series role, portraying Ally McBeal's boyfriend was a part Jon had envisaged as a good opportunity for him. The day-to-day business too, of working with Calista Flockhart and everyone on the production was in itself not an unhappy experience. However, Victor Morrison's character development over the span of the nine episodes did not, in the end, live up to Jon's original expectations.

Morrison emanated a tangible sensuality and an attractive self-assuredness, but the suspicion that stronger traits lay untapped, grew over the weeks. Frankly, Jon slated the guy as ultimately turning into a 'spineless nonentity'. Which was a pity, considering that he had spent well into the new year concentrating on the role.

It has to be said that the show's executives clearly took a different view because, so far into production, they asked Jon to consider shooting more than the original nine designated shows – they were toying with a plan of marrying Victor Morrison to Ally McBeal.

Jon himself was already less than enamoured of the character's nature. Dorothea was expecting their third child in mid-May. And although Jon had made time while he was shooting *Ally McBeal* in Los Angeles to go along to Henson recording studios with Richie to lay down yet more tracks, Bon Jovi were now champing at the bit to get on with the album. He therefore politely declined the opportunity to prolong his stay on the show.

Ally McBeal had first hit the TV screens in 1997 and for all its oddball content had been a ratings winner over the years. However, this season in which Jon had joined the cast would prove to be the show's last, although while Jon was there no one on the set knew it was closing. It's Jon's belief, in fact, that even David E. Kelley was expecting another series beyond the current one. Nevertheless, when these new shows aired on Fox Network TV starting in spring 2002, it was the final curtain.

Springtime, as it unfolded, had its moments. Besides cramming in recording work on the album, on 24 February Bon Jovi had joined Christina Aguilera, *NSYNC and others to perform during the closing ceremonies at the 2002 Olympic Winter Games in Salt Lake City, Utah. The spectacular event took place at the University of Utah stadium, and to Richie Sambora, being invited by the organisers to take part in these ostentatious proceedings which are watched by billions around the globe, was proof positive that Bon Jovi had consolidated a secure position in the otherwise all too ephemeral world of popular music. 'It's like we are perennial American artistes and that feels really good,' he said.

Like his band-mates, Jon Bon Jovi has today reached elder statesman of rock status, which to the casual observer can seem confusing when the guy has defied the aging process so well that he looks to be in his mid-twenties. In fact, on 2 March 2002 Jon reached the big 4-0. To mark the milestone, Dorothea threw him a surprise 'tarts and vicars' party when guests turned up at the hired church venue in costume as priests or hookers. Jon was thrilled and had a whale of a time.

Come April though, his attention was firmly focused on the development of the new album, which he already knew would be called *Bounce*. Easily read as a reference to the American people's collective resilience and ability to get back up off their knees after the 9/11 assault, the title was also a nod to Bon Jovi's own stamina, tenacity and longevity. With shooting for *Ally McBeal* over, Jon was able to convene intensive band recording sessions at his home studio, and was reaping the rewards. He was also convinced that, along with his co-songwriters, he had pitched the 'voice' he was looking for with this album just right – something Jon was very sensitive to.

He explained later how he had wanted to avoid writing songs in the first person which spoke say, of praying for a loved one to make it home safely from the disaster zones. He said, 'I didn't live that first hand. My community and my friends did, but my own family was safe.' Yet he had an urge to remind people how those terrible events suddenly threw much, if not all, of life into sharp perspective. Jon stated, 'People finally stopped and took notice of the wasted time spent over the last 20 years, doing a whole lot of nothing.'

That precise acknowledgement that the atrocity, dramatically forcing the world off balance, had provoked a cry for people to think about making every moment of the day count from now on, was powered home in the song 'Everyday', written by Jon, Richie and one of the band's co-producers, Andreas Carlsson. This rocker was one of the three tracks on the album directly tied to the events of 11 September.

The second was 'Undivided' – a thumpingly bruising number which made graphic reference to rubble, smoke and dust, and took the defiant stance that those who had sought to destroy the people in America may have inflicted a horrendous death toll on the country, but by their evil acts they had also only generated an even more determined and unified nation. The third was 'Bounce', which bullishly echoed the 'we might be down but we ain't out' attitude.

A less direct approach found expression in 'The Distance' and 'Love Me Back To Life', where the strain centred more on advocating a desire to re-engage with life. But a whole raft of emotions steers its way through *Bounce*, some more turbulent than others. At an early stage, while running a thread of hope through the lyrics, Jon had found it important to tap into the art of storytelling with more precision than he had done in the past. It is an art he believes is fast fading and he missed it. The upshot was the poignant pop ballad, 'Joey', as well as the love song, 'You Had Me From Hello', for which the original inspiration is said to have stemmed from the 1996 Tom Cruise movie, *Jerry Maguire*.

For certain numbers on *Bounce*, Jon and Richie utilised variously the songwriting talents of Jon's long-time friend Billy Falcon, and stalwart cohort Desmond Child, in addition to Andreas Carlsson. Three songs were Bon Jovi/Sambora compositions, but one was Jon's solo effort – 'Right Side Of Wrong'.

In the mid-1990s, bass player Alec John Such once highlighted the frontman's deep-seated penchant for writing 'cowboy' songs. It broke out again in this number, which romanticises outlaw behaviour, telling the tale of a guy breaking the law for apparently excusable reasons. In the fraught climate post 9/11, Jon made sure to balance the moral scales by having the robber pay for his actions by coming to a sticky end.

Exploring the human condition had also produced 'Misunderstood'. The overall dark and light of the album crystallised in the broody yet exultant 'Hook Me Up'; the story behind this, Jon revealed, came from a newspaper report concerning a young boy in the West Bank living smack in the middle of the conflict between Palestine and Israel. 'This kid was on a ham radio, trying to communicate with the outside world.'

The composition of the album was evenly split, with as many hard rock numbers as there were love songs. The tender anchor track, 'Open All Night', would frequently be singled out, once it transpired that Jon wrote it to depict how he had envisaged the development of his *Ally McBeal* character Victor Morrison's relationship with the show's heroine. While shooting for *Ally McBeal*, Jon had discussed the alternative scenario he imagined with Richie, who had long been looking for a reason to use the title 'Open All Night'. The composition had gelled quickly, and Jon was prepared at one point to offer this unreleased song to the producers for inclusion in the show. Instead, he made Calista Flockhart a present of the lyrics when he left *Ally McBeal*.

Bon Jovi albums had always been synonymous with cinemascope-style ballads, but a deeper dimension underpinned 'All About Loving You'. It was a four-way work between Jon, Richie, Andreas Carlsson and Desmond Child. It was hard though, to escape the feeling that this deeply reflective love song, about dedication to a long-time love, was simply Jon 'talking' to Dorothea.

In any event, *Bounce*, produced by Jon, Richie and Luke Ebbin along with co-producers Child and Carlsson, came under 'work in progress' for a little while longer yet. It was easier on Jon that it was being recorded at his home studio, for he could stay close to Dorothea, whose pregnancy was drawing near to full term.

Yet for all his conscientiousness as a father-in-waiting, Jon ended up being caught on the hop miles away when their new addition to the family decided to surprise everyone and come early. Approaching the end of the first week of May 2002, Jon sought the advice of his wife's doctors before agreeing to leave New Jersey for New Orleans, where he was expected to take part in an MTV show. The expert opinion was that the baby wasn't due for another week. So Jon left.

After the show he decided it was so late he would stay overnight and return home the next day. After a few drinks, he went to bed. Jon was sound asleep when suddenly the bedside telephone burst into life, just as fists began pounding on the hotel room door. In his groggy, half-awake state, at first he cursed the ruction thinking that fans had, not for the first time, found out where he was staying the night. However, the attempts to get his attention were so frantic that Jon quickly realised that it was his road manager who was yelling in the corridor and assaulting the woodwork.

The words, 'The baby's on its way,' catapulted Jon into action. Before long, he had shot from the hotel to the airport, where his private Falcon 2000 jet was being made ready. 'We beat the pilots there,' Jon later recalled. It's an indication of his superstar status in America that not only were his pilots granted special permission to fly at 600 mph (100 mph faster than the normally permitted speed) but the Federal Aviation Authority even cleared airspace for Jon's flight over Washington, DC.

The official assistance did not end there. When Jon's jet landed on the tarmac in New Jersey, a state trooper was waiting to pick up the anxious husband in his squad car, which then did twice the highway speed limit along the Jersey Parkway. Jon got to the hospital delivery room just in time to see their third child come into the world on 7 May 2002 – a baby boy they named Jacob Hurley. The dramatic dash will make a great story to tell Jake, as he is already known, when he grows up. But right then, in their respective ways, his overjoyed parents were wiped out by the experience.

Not long after his second son's birth, Jon intended to settle right back into concentrating on the new album, the release date for which was set for October, and for which there was much to be done in terms of making videos and arranging promotion. Dorothea, however, had other ideas, and decided to show her determined husband some steel of her own. She wanted Jon, herself and their three children to take a ten-day family holiday. When Jon, considering his work plans, was about to refuse, she warned him that if he tried to thwart her, she would seriously lose her temper. Jon has a well-deserved reputation for being iron-willed. But, affectionately, he has never hidden the fact that his wife can be an equally strong character. Ruefully he has admitted, 'Like every smart man, I know to pick my fights.' In this instance, Mrs Bongiovi won the day.

Two months later, Jon's battle with Mother Nature proved to be a more hair-raising affair. 'Everyday' was going to be the lead-off single from the forthcoming album, and in July, since the concept for the number's accompanying video involved depicting the band spreading their message to the wide world, Bon Jovi chose to film some footage at VLA, one of the world's largest astronomical radio observatory installations, situated in the vast expanse of San Augustin, in the remote Socorro region of New Mexico.

The band were being filmed standing among, and dwarfed by, the 27 massive satellite dishes when the weather began to turn bad. By the time it came to the final take, which was being filmed from a helicopter, a raging lightning storm had erupted. Those people who could be evacuated, were. But that left the band, the video producer and the aerial camera crew, who were determined to complete the shoot. Surrounded by these massive receiver dishes, Bon Jovi ran a big risk of being electrocuted. However, they all managed to finish the take and bail out to safety.

Within days came the start of magazine layout photo shoots in New York City, followed a month later by rehearsal warm-up gigs. On 21 August one such intimate gathering was held in the Grand Ballroom of The Manhattan Center. Before an audience of family, privately invited friends and record label personnel, Bon Jovi, in a clearing in the middle of the room, performed a set which road-tested half a dozen of the new songs. Between numbers, Jon joked with the attentive audience and introduced the upcoming new album track, 'Misunderstood', by confessing to sometimes being brought into line by his wife. Richie Sambora could scarcely conceal a smile when the singer owned up, 'This butt's been kicked a few times!'

The momentum towards the launch of the album was well plotted, but it hit a particularly high plateau on Thursday 5 September. This was the kick-off date for the 2002 NFL season, and Bon Jovi were leading the national celebrations. Jon's first task on that hectic day was being interviewed by Katie Couric on NBC TV's *Today* breakfast show. On leaving the television studios, he went straight to the New York Stock Exchange. As a multi-millionaire, the shrewd star lives by one reliable motto when it comes to matters financial – never get involved with things you know nothing about. The frenzied complex world of high-stakes share dealing, therefore, holds no great lure for him. But at 9.30 that morning, he still took pride in ringing the opening bell.

A large chunk either side of noon was subsequently spent at the Marriott Marquis in New York City, where the band held court, carrying out a steady stream of media interviews before conducting a 20-minute press conference. It was all leading up to a massive free concert extravaganza in Times Square to launch the NFL season, and which would also double as the beginning of the events planned to celebrate the regeneration of New York City, one year on from the terrorist attack.

The Times Square concert, to be covered live by various television and radio stations, was being trailered by its two on-site TV presenters, as 'the world's largest tailgate party'. It commenced at 4.30 p.m. For two and a half hours acts DJ Skribble, hip hop artiste Eve, Alicia Keys and Enrique Iglesias came and went. But the half million people corralled into Times Square, as well as the many more tuning in via the media, were waiting to see the headliners Bon Jovi, who took to the stage at 7.00 p.m.

The ecstatic greeting they received presaged an hour-long performance, during which the band created an incredible atmosphere. After Jon declared, 'New York is alive and kickin' tonight, baby. Strap in. Here we go!' they barrelled their way through a playlist which blended old favourites with 'Bounce' and 'Everyday', the latter song receiving its world premiere before a live audience.

In a display of patriotism, an American flag floated out from the waistband at Richie Sambora's left hip as he played. And at the end of the evening, while Bon Jovi performed 'America The Beautiful', members of New York's police and fire departments unfurled over the heads of a massive section of the crowd a Stars and Stripes banner which stretched right across Times Square.

During 'Everyday' Jon wore an NYPD football cap given to him by a fan who had struggled through to the long runway protruding from the stage. Now and then he would give the odd smart salute into the crowd. Images of the band were projected on to the giant screens set among the famous neon advertising hoardings. In confident, strong voice, Jon had never looked better in his life. Dressed simply in dark denims and a sleeveless pale blue T-shirt, he energised the crowd, generating a warm rapport with them; he was at one and the same time apparently accessible, and a golden-haired rock god in his prime. And the people adored him.

Broadcasters, struggling to be heard above the clamour of the excited masses, hailed it an amazing atmosphere and event for New York City. Minutes before the end, New York City Mayor Michael Bloomberg addressed the crowd. Then, after the emotional rendition of 'America The Beautiful', as happens in Times Square every 31 December to ring in the New Year, the countdown to the NFL kick-off saw a glittering neon ball steadily drop. Jon and the band promptly dashed from the stage to climb into a squad of cars and, with a full police escort, headed for a nearby heliport. It had been an electrifyingly stimulating experience. But Jon was only really able to take in the hugeness of the event when, once airborne in one of the six helicopters taking the band and others to Giants Stadium, he was given an aerial view. Midtown Manhattan had been shut down since the afternoon. Jon later said, 'That's when it hit me. We caused one helluva traffic jam that day!'

Leaving the west side of Manhattan, the fleet of helicopters headed out noisily across the Hudson River to East Rutherford, New Jersey, soon arriving on the landing pads at Giants Stadium. The NFL 2002 season opening game between the New York Giants and the San Francisco 49ers kicked off at 8.30 that evening; Bon Jovi were due to perform for the half-time show. On arrival at Giants Stadium the band were whisked away to some locker rooms which had been specially set aside for them, and from there they watched the game until at half time they took to the stage erected in the end zone. For the second time that evening they performed 'Everyday' as part of their set.

CBS TV had filmed the Times Square event to create a one-hour special, which aired in a primetime slot the following night. On a high after such a blisteringly successful mass media event, Bon Jovi immediately flew to Britain, where, by contrast, they played a couple of lower-key gigs. On Saturday 7 September they took part in a Capital Radio concert at London's Wembley Arena. And while in the city, they also appeared at the Shepherd's Bush Empire.

At this point, it had been several years since Bon Jovi had played indoors in the UK. And this particular night's performance was made all the more special for many Londoners when, to the crowd's surprise, the highly respected singer/songwriter Ray Davies strolled on stage to join the band. Together they performed a rendition of the Kinks' 1972 single 'Celluloid Heroes'. That night, Bon Jovi ended with two rousing encores, then left the fans baying for more. The gig was carried as a live global webcast to more than 60 countries, and was beamed by satellite to a series of cinemas throughout the UK, as well as to Amsterdam, Berlin and Hamburg, where audience reaction was reportedly wild.

With the level of goodwill flowing around Bon Jovi, the release of their eighth studio album was a source of much anticipation. In September, the worldwide release of the single, 'Everyday', had harvested a number five hit in Britain, and an instant number one triumph in Canada, but a surprising number 31 peak in the States. *Bounce* was expected to far outstrip that, and it did. Released on 8 October, it chalked up the highest-ever US chart debut for a Bon Jovi album by bouncing straight into *Billboard*'s number two position. Likewise, it debuted at number two in the UK album charts.

It was especially rewarding, because competition was particularly stiff then, with music seeing the successful return to the spotlight of several veteran performers, each with loyal legions of their own. *Bounce* beat the Rolling Stones' 'best of' collection, *Forty Licks*, released to mark the band's 40th anniversary year, into third place. But immovable by any artiste or band, at number one on both sides of the Atlantic for a third consecutive week was *Elvis: 30 No. 1 Hits*.

Although thrilled with the performance of *Bounce*, in the very earliest days of its release Richie Sambora had the feeling that Bon Jovi were going to dethrone Elvis Presley. He revealed, 'From what I'm hearing, we're neck and neck with the King right now.' The daily number crunching showed that sales figures were fluctuating, with not a colossal margin between them, shuffling Presley and Bon Jovi just ahead of each other, turn and turn about. But it wasn't to be.

At every turn during the promo for *Bounce*, despite having been alert to this potential pitfall at the outset, Jon still found himself having to deflect blanket media accusations that this was a 9/11 record. He pointed out, with reference to the three directly influenced tracks, that had he *not* included songs relating to what happened that day, he would have been remiss. However, he was adamant that he had not and would not jump on to any 9/11 celebrity bandwagon.

Come November, Bon Jovi took time to play at various charity events in America, despite the growing list of PR obligations scheduled for the run up to the recently announced start of their Bounce world tour. On the 14th the band showed up in Spain to perform 'Everyday' live at the MTV European Music Awards, staged at Barcelona's Palau St. Jordi stadium. The next morning, having jetted straight out of Barcelona after leaving the stadium stage, the band was back around dawn on US soil to perform in Miami, Florida. Televised live on the *Good Morning America* breakfast show, the free concert took place at South Beach on Ocean Drive, and was part of the ABC TV network's '50 States – One Nation, One Year' initiative.

Days later, Jon was front cover material for the first time in *People* magazine. In addition to granting an exclusive interview for the six-page feature, he relaxed his rule about his domestic privacy to allow photographers inside his elegant family home in Middletown, where he and Dorothea posed together.

As Jon's face smiled out from the newsstands all over America on a *People* issue titled 'Jon Bon Jovi Secrets Of A Rock Star Dad', Bon Jovi were once again involved with an event on the NFL calendar. On 28 November the band provided the half-time entertainment at the annual Thanksgiving Day game, which this year took place at Ford Field in Detroit, Michigan, where the Detroit Lions took on defending Super Bowl champions, the New England Patriots.

In the first week of December, Jon and the band hit the west coast to make more media and public appearances. 'Misunderstood' was being geared up as the second cut from *Bounce* to be released in various territories; on its release on 9 December in Britain it would enter the singles chart at number 21. But primarily, Bon Jovi had begun rehearsals in Primm, Nevada, for the Bounce tour.

Before the sales for *Bounce* were factored in, and prior to the upcoming tour, Bon Jovi's career statistics had already gone way beyond impressive. Approaching the end of 2002 they had sold more than 92 million albums worldwide and had played over 2,000 concerts in 47 countries, to more than 31 million people.

Although unwilling to rest on their laurels, as multi-platinum artistes they had finally arrived at the luxury point where, in terms of going on the road, the most important thing was to go out there and enjoy themselves to the hilt while pleasing their fans. The first chance they got to do that came when the Bounce tour kicked off with three major dates in Australia. Bon Jovi headlined the huge Rumba Festivals, first on 8 December at Melbourne's Telstra Dome, three days later at the ANZ Stadium in Brisbane, and again at a Telstra venue, this time in Sydney on the 14th.

Basking in the kind of exuberant welcome the band had become used to receiving over the years in this country, on the day before their last festival appearance Bon Jovi decided to stage a free acoustic performance, playing on board a barge in Sydney's Darling Harbour. Among the excited crowd which had gathered on land to watch, three people got so carried away that they dived into the water and began cleaving their way towards the barge. The two women responded to strident requests from nervous security to turn back to dry land. But the man headed determinedly alone for the band.

Stopping singing, Jon reached down and helped the dripping, delighted fan on to the boat, amused at the guy's unbridled enthusiasm. The local police, however, were less charmed by the incident and later arrested the reveller. When Jon discovered that the authorities were considering pressing charges he let it be known that, in that event, the band would pay any fine slapped on the fan. He told the Australian press, 'We'll deal with it for him.' The police response came back repressively, 'Revellers should not be encouraged by anyone to break the law.' To Jon it didn't come into such realms and was something and nothing. A drama of a more serious nature occurred just three days later during the return journey to the States.

On Monday 16 December, having safely completed the 14-hour flight across the Pacific Ocean from Sydney to Los Angeles, the Qantas 747-100 passenger airliner with almost 200 people on board had taken off again, this time bound for New York. When not long airborne, one of the port side engines failed, forcing the aircraft to make an emergency U-turn back to Los Angeles International Airport. Jittery passengers later reported hearing an enormous bang, then seeing flames licking out from one of the huge turbines. As the investigation into the cause of the engine failure got under way, Jon and the others restarted the last stretch of their flight some four hours later.

At the turn of the year Jon attracted yet another glossy magazine award when he was voted by *Cosmopolitan* readers as the 'Fun, Fearless Male of the Year'. It had certainly taken an intrepidly determined individual to carve out this glittering career. 2003 also marked the milestone of the band's 20th anniversary year, which got off on a fittingly proud footing when, on 7 January, at a press conference held at Madison Square Garden, New York, the annual Grammy Award nominations were announced and Bon Jovi was included in the Best Pop/Rock Performance by a Duo or Group category for 'Everyday'. Rivals for this trophy were Bowling For Soup, the Dave Matthews Band, No Doubt and *NSYNC. The ceremony itself would be held on 23 February.

The day after this announcement, Bon Jovi began the seven-date Japanese leg of the Bounce world tour at the Sapporo Dome, Sapporo, ending on 21 January at the Dome in Nagoya. Five days later, back in America, they took time out to perform at the Super Bowl XXXVII post-game shindig at Qualcomm stadium in San Diego, before commencing the first US leg with a gig on 8 February at the Bryce Jordan Center in State College, Pennsylvania. This was followed closely by a two-night stand at Continental Airlines Arena in East Rutherford, New Jersey. After arena dates stretching out over Atlanta, Nashville, Columbus and Detroit, Bon Jovi then made a quick trip to Canada for dates in Toronto and Montreal.

They had newly returned to the US for a concert at the Boardwalk Hall in New Jersey's Atlantic City when, on Sunday 23 February 2003, the night of the 45th Grammy Awards arrived. For the first time in five years, this prestigious event on music's calendar was held in New York City, and the occasion at Madison Square Garden saw several songs which had been influenced by 9/11 all vying for awards. On the night, though, Bon Jovi's 'Everyday' lost out for the Best Pop/Rock Performance by a Duo or Group when the distinctive trophy went to No Doubt for 'Hey Baby'.

For long-time music lovers, the event had been hallmarked anyway when Paul Simon and Art Garfunkel, there to be honoured with the Lifetime Achievement Award for their musical legacy, lived up to mounting pre-ceremony media speculation and performed together for the first time for several years, treating the audience to a rendition of the hauntingly beautiful classic number 'Sound of Silence'.

As the press hinted that these musical legends were considering the possibility of re-teaming for some live shows, Bon Jovi carried on with the Bounce tour, which took in appearances in 19 states before wrapping up this North American leg with gigs at the Key Arena in Seattle, Washington on 15 April, and two nights later at the Arco Arena in Sacramento, California. On 19 April, the band took part in a benefit concert at the 12,000-seater Mandalay Bay Events Center in Las Vegas, Nevada, in aid of the Tiger Woods Foundation. After this, they dispersed for a five-week break with their respective families.

On 20 May, refreshed and raring to go again, Jon led his band back on stage, this time at Spain's Palau St. Jordi in Barcelona, before hitting Madrid's Estadio La Comunidad. An appearance at the Steigerwaldstadion in Erfurt, Germany, continued a varied European leg which ended three weeks later at the Eintracht in Neumunster. Bon Jovi was vibrant and highly motivated throughout, firing on all cylinders when they arrived in Britain in time for summer.

Crossing over the water to the Republic of Ireland, they turned in a scorching performance at Dublin's Lansdowne Road stadium on 20 June, before travelling to Glasgow in Scotland for a concert two days later at Rangers football club stadium, Ibrox. On 24 June it was at the Wolves football ground, Molineux, in Wolverhampton where they continued to woo the fans. And again with a single day off in between, they promptly headed to Manchester's Old Trafford sporting venue.

Wherever Bon Jovi played, the crowds rewarded them with unstinting loyalty and vocal enthusiasm. But nothing would beat the band's memorable performance on Saturday 28 June at London's Hyde Park, the scene of so many major rock events since the 1960s. The three-hour concert, before an estimated audience of 90,000 people, constituted a truly electrifying climax to this European excursion.

As summer rolled on, buoyed up by the unqualified success of the Bounce tour, Bon Jovi returned home for a second set of US concert dates starting on 11 July at the Tweeter Center in Tinley Park, Illinois, the pinnacle undoubtedly being a double-header on 7 and 8 August at Giants Stadium in East Rutherford, New Jersey. To crown this, they were soon to celebrate the achievement of 100 million albums sold.

To commemorate this feat and the 20th anniversary of forming the band, Jon became involved in plans to release a special box set. He wanted it to be better than simply a collection of remastered past album tracks, and was trawling through a wealth of unreleased Bon Jovi songs. It was a painstaking process, and vital to get right. Richie Sambora told *Billboard*, 'It will consist of the rarities that no one has ever heard before. Mostly songs that we'd written and really liked, but which hadn't belonged on a particular album.' Jon did not rule out penning some fresh songs for inclusion too. The release date for this special box collection had to be set, and beyond that further projects are under consideration which will soon see the light of day.

No one should be in any way surprised by the fact that Jon has big plans for the future. If there is a flaw, though, in being forever forward-looking, it can be forgetting to live in the moment, a charge to which Jon has recently pleaded guilty. But, essentially, he is a man with few regrets.

A working-class guy who became an international superstar, he has remained steadfastly true to his roots, earning himself firm respect along the way. As *U-571* co-star Will Estes said, 'Stardom is a piece of sketch paper to Jon. He knows what's important.' Top of that list of priorities come his family and friends. His wife, high-school sweetheart Dorothea, is his most reliable touchstone; along with their children, she forms the light of his life. And the deep sense of loyalty instilled in him by his eternally supportive parents helps bind together the ultimately unbreakable and special bond he enjoys with his Bon Jovi band-mates.

Having hared off at a sprint in his early teens, in his quest to make it in music, for stretches of his life Jon has undoubtedly pushed himself, and sometimes others, too far. But his very tenaciousness is a vital key to his success. He is an intriguingly driven man, with a diverse, ever-unfolding talent. Being an award-winning singer, songwriter, musician and heart-throb rock star was not enough for him. He has sought another outlet for self-expression by becoming an actor; having appeared in nine movies in seven years, he is steadily gaining in stature.

Whether Jon will ever fulfil director Jonathan Mostow's prediction and become a major movie star in the coming years, he certainly knows he will go on acting for as long as he is creating music. It is a world that fascinates him. Beyond this, he is currently extending his repertoire even further, having written two film screenplays which have already been bought by major studios. In mid-June 2003 news emerged that Jon had been signed up to star in *One Wild Night*, a Universal movie based on Jon's original idea for film in which four wealthy couples engage in wife-swapping with unforeseen and far-reaching consequences.

Often regarded as the embodiment of the American Dream, Jon will modestly declare, 'If I could do it, anyone can.' Unashamedly proud of his achievements to date, his key to the future lies buried in his past. 'If you can go back to what moved you in the first place,' he has maintained, 'there's no reason why you can't go on forever.'

Charismatic and dynamic, he is an inspirational figure to many. But the bottom line is this: beneath the good looks, wealth and glamour, Jon Bon Jovi is a natural-born survivor with the kind of grit which has taken him to where he is today, and which ensures that his future opportunities can be nothing other than interestingly wide open.

DISCOGRAPHY

New York Rocks 1983 (Various artists, includes Bon Jovi's "Runaway"), WAPP, 1983

Bon Jovi, Polygram Records, January 1984

7800 Fahrenheit, Polygram Records, April 1985

Slippery When Wet, Polygram Records, August 1986

New Jersey, Polygram Records, September 1988

Blaze of Glory (Soundtrack of *Young Guns II*, Jon Bon Jovi solo project), Polygram Records, August 1990

Keep the Faith, Polygram Records, November 1992

Cross Road: The Best of Bon Jovi, Polygram Records, October 1994

These Days, Polygram Records, June 1995

Destination Anywhere (Jon Bon Jovi solo project), Polygram Records, June 1997

Crush, Polygram Records, June 2000

One Wild Night: Live 1985–2001, May 2001, Universal Records

The Power Station Years: The Unreleased Recordings (Credited as John Bongiovi), September 2001, Masq Records

Bounce, Def Jam Records, October 2002

Index